72 -

8/08

sk

22 -

WHERE
THE
ASHES
ARE

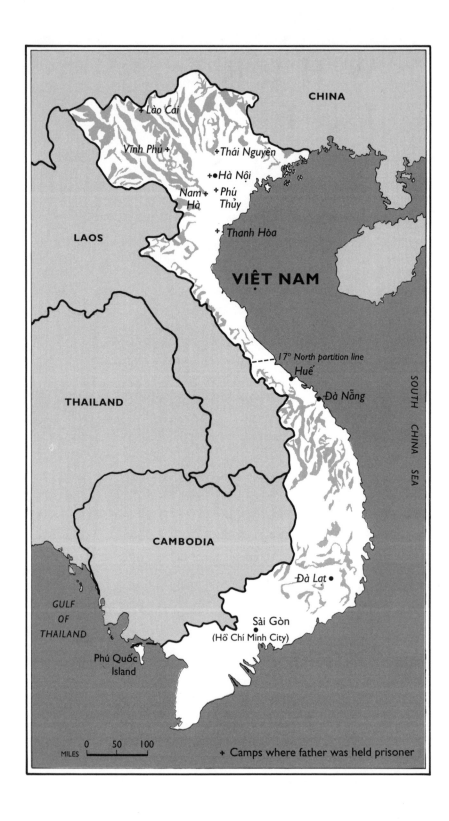

CHINA

+Lào Cai

Vĩnh Phú +

+Thái Nguyên

+•Hà Nội

Nam +
Hà

+ Phú
Thủy

+ Thanh Hóa

LAOS

VIỆT NAM

17° North partition line

Huế

Đà Nẵng

THAILAND

SOUTH
CHINA
SEA

CAMBODIA

Đà Lạt •

GULF
OF
THAILAND

Sài Gòn
(Hồ Chí Minh City)

Phú Quốc
Island

0   50   100

MILES

+ Camps where father was held prisoner

WHERE THE ASHES ARE

The Odyssey of a Vietnamese Family

NGUYỄN QÚI ĐỨC

Addison-Wesley Publishing Company
Reading, Massachusetts   Menlo Park, California   New York
Don Mills, Ontario   Wokingham, England   Amsterdam   Bonn
Sydney   Singapore   Tokyo   Madrid   San Juan
Paris   Seoul   Milan   Mexico City   Taipei

Portions of this book have appeared in different form on National Public Radio's "All Things Considered" and in *The New York Times Magazine* and *City Lights Review.*

Many of the designations used by manufacturers and sellers to distinguish their products are claimed as trademarks. Where those designations appear in this book and Addison-Wesley was aware of a trademark claim, the designations have been printed in initial capital letters (e.g., Dumpster).

Library of Congress Cataloging-in-Publication Data
Nguyễn, Qúi Đức.
    Where the ashes are : the odyssey of a Vietnamese family / Nguyễn
Qúi Đức.
      p.   cm.
    ISBN 0-201-63202-0
    1. Vietnamese Conflict, 1961–1975—Personal narratives,
Vietnamese. 2. Vietnam—History—1975–   3. Refugees, Political—Vietnam.
4. Nguyễn, Qúi Đức. I. Title.
  DS559.5.N587 1994
   959.704'38—dc20
                                              93-25869
                                                    CIP

Poems copyright © 1991 by Hoàng Liên

Poem on page 63 adapted from translation by John C. Shafer and Cao Như Qùynh. Poems on pages 120, 123, 129, 130, and 131 adapted from translations by Nguyễn-Khoa Phồn-Anh. Poems on pages 67 and 112 translated by the author.

Jacket design by Ted Mader and Associates
Text design by Janis Owens
Map by Karen Savary
Set in 13-point Perpetua by DEKR Corporation, Woburn, MA

1 2 3 4 5 6 7 8 9-MA-959493
First printing, December 1993

To the memory of my sister Diệu-Qùynh, and to you

Contents

Acknowledgments

For their help and support, I am grateful to many: Alix and Tom Lockard, Trần Tưởng Như, Hùynh Công Anh, Heather and Alex Hiam, and Robert Sharrard of City Lights Books all gave valuable advice and urged me on; Robert Linsenman, my fabulous and inspired agent, gave me tremendous faith; Karolyn van Putten, Nathan Schafler, Bill Helgeson, and other colleagues at KALW enabled me to be away and encouraged me always, as did David Omori, Wei-Tai Kwok, Iris Hsu, and Greg Chew at DAE Advertising; fellow travelers Mark Hilditch and Sharon Doorbar; and the people of Essaouira, Morocco, who opened their homes and took care of me while I struggled to write, in particular Mounaim Hamani Abdelkader, Rmouti Halima, Attar Kabir, and Lachioualh Abdoullatif.

I have been blessed with a most thorough and patient editor at Addison-Wesley, John Bell. I owe him my profound gratitude. Tiffany Cobb and Rachel Parks were also helpful.

My deepest thanks go to the editors and producers of National Public Radio's "All Things Considered." I am especially indebted to Peter Breslow, a thoughtful producer who taught me how to write, and made it all happen. He has been the kindest friend.

I thank everyone in my family for allowing me to tell my side of their story. They nurtured my hope of completing this book. For details about my father's years in prison I am indebted to his memoirs, *Ánh Sáng và Bóng Tối* (*Light and Darkness*), published by Văn Nghệ, Southern California, in 1990. This book is dedicated to my parents, who, in spite of circumstances, gave me a wonderful childhood and continue to inspire much of what I do as an adult.

My wife Gillian Allison, who has lived with this book and without me for the past two years, gave me her absolute support, her kindness, and her love. I thank her, for everything.

A Note on Vietnamese Names

In Vietnamese convention, a person's family name comes first and given name last. Thus in my name, Nguyễn Qúi Đức, Nguyễn (pronounced "Nwin") is my family's name; my family and friends call me Đức (pronounced "Duke"). This is the reverse of the form used by people of European background, and in America I often use the form Duc Nguyen to avoid confusion. When a title is used, it is with the given name. Thus, General Hoàng Xuân Lãm would be referred to as General Lãm. Lãm is his given name, Hoàng his family name.

My father's full name is Nguyễn Văn Đãi. My mother's maiden name is Nguyễn-Khoa Diệu-Liễu. After my parents married, she was formally addressed as Bà Đãi, that is, "Mrs. Đãi." Close friends might call her Chị Đãi, or "Older Sister Đãi." I called my parents Cha, meaning "Dad", and Mạ, "Mom." My sisters were given hyphenated names, Diệu-Quỳnh and Diệu-Hà, as is customary for girls in Việt Nam. Diệu, pronounced "Yew" (the consonant D, without the bar through the vertical shaft, signals the English sound Y), is a common middle name for Vietnamese women.

Readers will notice the references to my many "uncles" and "aunts." Depending on the forms of address used, Vietnamese distinguishes between uncles by blood and by marriage, uncles who are older than one's parents and those who are younger, and maternal and paternal uncles. The same mutations apply to the forms of address for aunts. When I was small, whenever my mother introduced me to an uncle, from how she referred to him—"Bác" or "Cậu" or "Chú"—I would know immediately what relationship he was to us.

Vietnamese is a monosyllabic language, and I have chosen to write the geographical names as I learned them in school: Việt Nam, Hà Nội, Đà Nẵng, and Sài Gòn, which although officially named Thành Phố Hồ Chí Minh, Hồ Chí Minh City, still is referred to by most people by its original name.

WHERE THE ASHES ARE

ONE

The Year of the Monkey

"Wake up, wake up!" my mother shouted. "We've got to get out of here! How can you sleep through all this?" She pulled the covers off me, handed me my clothes, and rushed out of the room.

"Wait!" I cried out, throwing off my pajamas. One leg in and one out of my dark blue school trousers, I stumbled over to my sister Diệu-Hà's room. My mother was yelling, "Are you deaf? Get out! We're going downstairs!"

It was five in the morning. Explosions and gunfire echoed through the high-ceilinged rooms of the government guest house. Arched corridors surrounded the twenty bedrooms on the second floor of the massive French-style mansion. My parents had taken the master suite at the end of the hall while my two sisters and I had large rooms next to one another. We had arrived at the end of January 1968, two days before the lunar New Year. Our family were the only guests in the building. Rather than having us stay at my grandfather's small house, my father felt we would be safer at the guest house, where extra platoons of local soldiers had been assigned to protect him. He also preferred the guest house because it was built along the bank of the river in Huế, the old imperial city, and away from the town's noisy center. The nearby train station was defunct, since the war had disrupted all but a few railway lines.

For many years my father had been working for the government of South Việt Nam. Assigned to central Việt Nam as a civilian deputy to the military governor, he was based in Đà Nẵng, a coastal town just over an hour's drive from Huế. He sent us to visit his parents there regularly, especially at holidays. He came along on this holiday visit—for the lunar New Year, Tết, in 1968.

Although my father had been warned about a possible escalation in the fighting, he said to my mother: "There's a ceasefire. It's New Year's. We'll be safe." But he abandoned his plan to drive and instead arranged for a flight to Huế. We'd landed at the Phú Bài airport in midafternoon.

The road into town had been taken over by an endless convoy of tanks and army trucks transporting U.S. soldiers, most likely toward Khe Sanh, an American base that had been under siege for several months. Along with a few other civilian cars, small trucks, and innumerable motorcycles, we inched our way toward Huế. I kept looking out the car window, glimpsing rice fields here and there. Mostly, though, the view was blocked by the olive green steel of tanks and trucks.

My mother sought to distract us. "You kids are going to be spoiled this year. I bet your grandparents will have lots of treats for you. But I want you to behave."

Settled in at the guest house, on the second night of our stay my mother and sisters and I fell asleep just after twelve, insulated by its thick walls and heavy curtains. Endless rounds of firecrackers went off as the people of Huế celebrated the arrival of Tết. No one knew that along with the Year of the Monkey, the dreaded Việt Cộng soldiers had also arrived. No one could tell when the firecrackers stopped and the gunfire began.

Diệu-Hà and I followed my mother into my other sister's room. Diệu-Quỳnh had buried herself under a pile of blankets. Mạ shook her. "Come on, we're going downstairs!" As she started to rifle through Diệu-Quỳnh's drawers, grabbing clothes for her to change into, she said to Diệu-Hà and me, "Go see if your father's downstairs, and stay with him!"

We rushed down the corridors toward the double staircase. Its marble steps formed a half-circle framed by an intricately carved banister. A bullet shattered a porthole as we skipped down the steps. Diệu-Hà screamed. Pieces of glass and marble flew by. We raced past the elephant tusks in the huge vestibule and toward the reception hall. A chilly wind blew through the huge room. Someone had opened the drapes and shutters of the dozens of windows rising from knee level to ten feet above my head, each framing a view of the River of Perfume, Sông Hương.

In the somber light I could make out dark foliage swaying by the riverbank as a coat of morning mist rose above the water. Nature paints winter scenes in Huế in shades of gray, but this morning I could see rapid bursts of orange and red fire coming from behind the bushes. A flare shot out from the far distance. Exploding with a thud, it hung from a small parachute and cast a brilliant midday light over a large area of the river as it floated down. Rockets exploded across the burning sky and fell to the ground in rapid succession. Deafened, Diệu-Hà and I dove behind an antique cabinet at the end of the room. My father had been nowhere in sight.

That night he had stayed up late to read a French book that contrasted two warriors: North Việt Nam's famed general Võ Nguyên Giáp and William Westmoreland, commander of the U.S. ground troops in South Việt Nam. Just before four o'clock Cha had left his bed and gone up to the rooftop terrace, where he marveled at the red and green tracers flying across the sky like shooting stars. Despite his interest in the generals, he had little understanding of the role of flares and tracers as tools of warfare. They were simply a beautiful sight as they burst over the night sky.

"Your father's still up there. Been on that roof an hour! He'll get killed!" Mạ wailed as she came down the staircase. Seeing the open windows, she took us into a chamber behind the reception room. "Where's Diệu-Quỳnh?" she exclaimed. "She was just on the stairs with me!"

In the midst of the gunfire and explosions, my sister had gone back to bed—a mad thing to do, since bullets were now flying indoors. By 1968, however, most of what Diệu-Quỳnh did was irrational. For four years she had been showing signs of mental illness. Ordering Diệu-Hà and me to sit still, my mother dashed back upstairs. A bullet came through Diệu-Quỳnh's room, hitting the lamp on her bedstand. Sparks flew in all directions. Mạ grabbed my older sister by the wrist and led her downstairs, calling out to my father all the while.

"We shouldn't worry too much," he said in his usual un-ruffled tone when he entered the room a few minutes later. When he had finally left the roof, he went downstairs to look for the butler, then into an office off the living room. "I called the provincial office; they say the fighting is far away."

"Look out the windows!" my mother shot back.

"I did," Cha replied, still calm and composed. "Our soldiers are still at their posts." From the rooftop he had been able to see men in green surrounding the guest house.

We gathered together, crouching on the floor. No one spoke. My father glanced at the spacious desk and heavy armchairs, hoping to hide behind the furniture until the gunfire died down.

Between explosions came the sound of someone knocking at the front door. My parents put out their arms. We sat still. The pounding grew louder. After a moment of hesitation, Mạ stood up. "It's our soldiers," she declared. "Come on!" My sisters followed her through the reception area to the vestibule. As my father and I reached the door to the reception room, we heard her scream.

My father led me back to the office in the back, locking the door behind him as quietly as possible. We went to the desk, and I held his hand as we lowered ourselves behind it. My father didn't know what else to do. Spotting a steel safe in the corner of the room, he went over to open it, then without a word closed it again. Not even a nine-year-old boy could fit inside.

"I have a young son in the house," my mother was explaining to the intruders in the vestibule, Việt Cộng soldiers in olive green uniforms. They wore no insignia or badges that showed affiliation or rank. Whether because of the darkness or distance, his poor eyesight, or his unfamiliarity with military matters, my father had mistaken them for our own Southern Republican Army troops.

One of the soldiers now threatened to shoot anyone still hiding in the house. "Tell us where everyone is and you'll be safe, Sister," he assured my mother.

"Please, please don't hurt us, please!" she begged. "Just let me go find my son."

Cha groped behind the heavy dark green drapes along the office wall, where a set of double doors opened onto a hallway. We tiptoed through the hall to the doors that led outside. My father motioned me out first, then carefully closed the doors behind him. I ran down the steps and turned toward the hedges that separated the guest house grounds from the riverbank. "Hey, boy!" someone cried. I turned. A Việt Cộng soldier sitting cross-legged pointed his rifle at me. I ran back to my father.

Back in the hallway inside the house, Cha quietly approached each door to the offices surrounding the reception area. A gun muzzle protruded from one, and we backed off. The doorway to yet another office also had a gun muzzle poking out from it. There was no escape.

Out in the courtyard it was still dark. Dozens of people in nightclothes shivered in the early morning dampness. Slowly the soldiers separated families from one another. The guest house was to be used as a temporary holding center. More people were brought into the courtyard. A disheveled Frenchman of about thirty entered the area barefooted, a trench coat thrown on over his pajamas. Hands clasped together, he tried to explain his situation to two Việt Cộng soldiers. "De Gaulle, Hồ Chí Minh, *amis,*" he kept saying. "Friends."

The two Việt Cộng waved him away. One of them shouted, *"Không biết tiếng đâu!"* They did not speak any foreign languages.

"They're regular soldiers," my father whispered to a man next to him, whose crisp white shirt was tucked into pajama trousers. "Such a strong northern accent."

"You're right," the man whispered back. "The way they call everybody 'Sister' and 'Brother' is strange." The men and women before us were not part of the so-called National Liberation Front within South Việt Nam. Hồ Chí Minh was now sending in troops from the North for an outright offensive, a full invasion.

In the confusion our family took refuge in a small temple just off the grounds of the guest house. Searching through his wallet, my father took out all his business cards and hid them under a mat. "Just say you're a teacher," whispered my mother.

He never had the chance. When a Việt Cộng woman found us in the temple a little more than an hour later, she jabbed her index finger into his chest. "You, Brother, I know who you are," she said. "The Party and the Revolution will be generous to all those willing to confess their crimes against the People."

"The Party" could only be the Communist party headquartered in Hà Nội. The enemy's arm had now reached into the heart of Huế. "Don't lie!" the woman continued. Putting her finger up to my father's nose, she said, "Brother, we know— you're the general staying in this house. Such opulence. We'll take care of you."

We lost track of the time as the soldiers sorted out all the people gathered in front of the guest house. At last, however, they accepted my father's protestations that he was not a general but a government functionary. He and the other men were taken inside the mansion. Women and children were sent to a neighboring building, down into a long rectangular basement with extremely thick walls and a single narrow door at one end. The rocket explosions had ceased, but the sound of gunfire continued. We had become accustomed to it and no longer jumped at the bursts from automatic weapons. Ten families followed each other below ground. I ended up leading the way into the darkness.

"Go to the far end. Go!" my mother urged me, and made sure that Diệu-Qùynh stayed with us. She knew that, on capturing a town, the Communists would use residents as workers to support military operations. Women would be sent to look for food, or nurse the wounded. If not required to take up arms themselves, men would have to gather the wounded and the dead. Diệu-Qùynh, a tall girl of eighteen, was at risk of being drafted for such service. Turning to the family behind her, my mother explained, "My daughter is ill. A big girl, but not all that wise." It was an explanation she would feel compelled to repeat often in the next days. I finally settled for a spot below a minuscule window with iron bars. In the damp, cavernous basement, the tiny hole let in a faint ray of the light that signaled the first day of the Year of the Monkey.

Throughout that day and most of the next night the adults carried on a whispered debate, trying to make sense out of what had happened. "They can't win," the guest house chauffeur pronounced. "I bet they'll retreat soon. The Americans will bomb, and our troops will rescue us in a few days." My mother listened dispassionately. She sighed often, and refused to eat any of the food the family next to us offered. Busy with their prisoners in the mansion, the soldiers left us alone.

On our second day of captivity, a female voice shouted into the basement. "Mrs. Đãi! Is there a Mrs. Đãi down there?" My mother picked her way toward the door. "Your husband's up in the house. He wants to see you," the voice announced. My mother went up alone, warning me to keep my sister Diệu-Quỳnh from wandering out. During the night, Diệu-Quỳnh had been difficult, continually demanding hot water. For the last year or so she had been obsessed with matters of hygiene, compulsively washing her hands as well as any household utensils before she would use them. Finally realizing that this was a luxury, she now sat silent and withdrawn. I asked Diệu-Hà to stay with her, then went to sit at the door to wait for my mother.

The guns had gone quiet at some point without anyone noticing. More soldiers had arrived in the compound and were now setting up a crude hospital. A stretched-out army poncho served as an awning, sheltering three bamboo cots that had been shoved together. The soldiers put a mat of woven branches and leaves on top of the cots, enlarging the surface to accommodate five wounded men. Looking like pallbearers carrying a white porcelain coffin, three young men and a woman in civilian clothes brought in an ancient French bathtub. They filled the tub half full of water, warning us not to use it. No one seemed to be in charge, yet a lot of orders were being issued. Sitting by the door of the basement, I watched the men and women from the North. From the way they handled the everyday artifacts of city life, they must have spent years in the jungle. One came with a beer can with a pull tab on its top. He shook it, hearing the sound of sloshing liquid inside. When he pulled the tab and the beer exploded, he threw the can on the ground and ran away. "It's a grenade! A grenade!" he yelled. I dared not laugh.

Later, I watched two men struggle to start a motorized tricycle. They tried to push it, but the gears were engaged. They gave up after a while and walked away. Half an hour later they came back on two bicycles whose frames had been lashed together with branches, with which they were hauling a few bags of New Year's food: cakes of sticky rice stuffed with pork and green beans and wrapped in banana leaves. I was wondering who the food was for when my mother came back. "What are you doing here?" she asked, roughing up my hair. "We're going up to see your father in a while." She did not sound excited. After checking on my sisters, she set about looking for food for my father.

"Mạ, what are they going to do with him?" I asked. I repeated the question again and again, but my mother would only shake her head; finally she responded, "Oh, he'll be all right. They said all he needed was a few days of reeducation. They're taking him somewhere, but he'll be back."

Taken where? Would we be rescued first? Would they let him go? I didn't think she knew the answers to my question. I tugged at her sleeve. "Mạ, what's 'reeducation'?"

She glanced at the wounded Việt Cộng lying beneath the poncho. "It's like school, that's all. Now help me with this pot."

Spoiled since her youth by household servants, my mother had rarely gone near a kitchen. Now she was cooking a big pot of rice she had secured from a woman in the basement. The Việt Cộng had set up a few clay burners and gave us some coal. Other than the rice, there was nothing to cook. We ate it with pickled leeks and cucumber, which normally accompanied fancier foods during Tết. The rice tasted of the river water my mother had used to cook it in. The Việt Cộng had allowed her only a small amount of water from the bathtub to take to my father. She was happy to have cleaner water for him to drink—until she tasted it. It smelled of Mercurochrome, the red disinfectant common in Việt Nam. The soldiers had used the water to wash the wounds of injured men, then poured back unused portions, now laced with Mercurochrome. She found a tiny bit of tea to steep in the water and packed some rice into a big bowl for my father.

I sensed that my father was happy to see us, but his face showed no such emotion. He took the woven basket Mạ handed him, which contained a towel, two T-shirts, and a pair of pants she had found on her previous trip to the guest house to see him. "There's no need—you will be well provided for," a Việt Cộng cadre said. "You'll be in reeducation for just a short time. Now that the region is liberated, you'll be allowed to come back soon."

In the big hall across from the master suite, my father kept caressing my head. I couldn't think of much to say. Some prisoners crouched along the wall, watching us. Others were curled up on the floor like shrimps. My mother gave my father the bowl of rice and the tea. I waited to see if he could taste the Mercurochrome, but I couldn't tell from his expression.

I glanced around my parents' bedroom. It had been turned upside down. The book my father had been reading about Giáp and Westmoreland still lay by his bed. My mother's jewelry and toilet case had had a hole gashed through it with a crude knife.

"Your mother will take you over to your grandparents' in a few days," Cha said. "I'll be back after a time."

Later, sometime past midnight, Communist soldiers took my father and a dozen other men away. Standing on a stool with my mother at my side, I watched through the tiny basement window. A rope was hooked through my father's elbows and tied behind his back, while his wrists were bound together in front of his chest. He was also tied to the man in front of him. It would be sixteen years before I saw him again.

᷈ PLEASE DON'T SHOOT, WE'RE REFUGEES!

My mother's memories of the war against the French served her well. She had written the words in English on two large pieces of paper and hung them on a motorcycle just outside the basement door when the American soldiers came. For two days the Việt Cộng and Northern troops had been withdrawing. By the fifteenth day of the Year of the Monkey they had all left, without saying anything to us. There had been no gunfight, no explosions. Later that afternoon U.S. soldiers took up positions on the grounds before entering the guest house. That was when my mother had thought to put up her sign.

Later she translated for the remnants of families huddled in the basement the American order to immediately evacuate the area. Most families had just a suitcase each. Ours was on the front seat of an army jeep that was now leaving the gate of the guest house and turning into the main boulevard. Although the other refugees were to head south on foot, my mother's help as a translator earned us a ride with the young American soldier at the wheel.

As the vehicle headed along the river, my mother suddenly gasped. I followed her gaze toward the river. Huế's venerable bridge, the Trường Tiền, lay partly in the water. No words can describe the sense of despair we felt at that moment. For decades the bridge had stood as one of the city's most cherished landmarks. Built by the same firm that had constructed the Eiffel Tower, the Trường Tiền, six short spans covered by twelve intricate steel arcs, had been immortalized in many Vietnamese poems and songs. From the riverbanks one could see young girls bicycling across the bridge, their white *ao dài* tunics fluttering in the wind like angels' wings. In recent years the Trường Tiền had remained an elegant but fragile treasure from the prewar period, sharply contrasting with the New Bridge farther down the river. The Americans who built the New Bridge intended it as an expression of friendship with South Việt Nam, but its flat, ugly slabs of concrete made it look as though it were constructed for tanks. Blowing up the sacred Trường Tiền symbolized both the recklessness and the gravity of the war. As the jeep rolled along my mother asked the driver, "Did they do this?"

"Yep, V.C. blew up the darn thing," he replied casually. We turned to stare.

"Have we come to this? How did we come to this?" my mother muttered again and again. Our hearts were pierced with pain and shame; the violated bridge also signaled that my father's imprisonment was a more serious affair than we had thought.

The American took us to the university in Huế, where we found my uncle and his wife safe on the sixth floor of the campus high rise. We had driven past his house after we left the river road. A rocket had torn through the side of the house. My mother had feared for their lives.

The high rise had been appropriated to house thousands of evacuees. Though it had little by way of supplies or equipment, the sixth floor was now a temporary medical clinic. My uncle, who was the chief surgeon and administrator of Hué's hospital, was in charge. It was in a danger area and had no electricity. My uncle took us into a room reserved for doctors, nurses, and their families.

My mother, sisters, and I shared a mat in these quarters. Fenced in by suitcases and the haphazard heaps of people's belongings, I felt trapped. I jumped at the chance to stand watch each day on the front balcony. From there I could see the river and watch for the navy ships the Americans said were coming to take us to Đà Nẵng. The fighting raged on in parts of Hué, particularly in the inner citadel across the river. It no longer made sense to try to reach my grandparents. We worried about them, stuck in an area where there was now house-to-house combat.

An American artillery unit on the riverbank was regularly firing mortars across to the other side. One soldier would drop a small rocket into a cannon about four feet long, his partner would pull a lever, and with an explosion the rocket would fly off. The artillerymen were methodical, working with well-rehearsed movements and rhythmically putting their hands over their ears just as the cannon exploded. It only took a few seconds to blow a Catholic priest in a black robe to pieces. I could see his tattered body thrown up in the air. I watched the Americans prepare each new rocket, and could not scream for the next victim to hide.

Death happened swiftly, and frequently, in those days. The green field behind the university had been turned into a grave-yard. Every day the same men would dig grave after shallow grave. Men, women, children, their bodies wound in pieces of fabric, sheets, or straw mats, were laid to rest with no ceremony. I roamed the balcony ringing the sixth floor for hours. "What do you do out there all day?" Diệu-Hà would ask in the evenings.

"Just wander," I said.

One morning an old man in a faded army shirt and a pair of black shorts was drawing water from a well at the edge of the field. I had watched him for most of the morning. He pulled cans of water from the well to fill up two buckets. Using a pole hoisted across his shoulders, he then carried the buckets back to the high rise. It was exhausting work. From the balcony I could see that his hair was mostly white, his legs thin and dark. Whether the man let out a cry or not as he slipped I did not hear, but I could see the blood turning his hair red. His head had struck the cement wall encircling the well.

Half an hour later he was being readied for burial. A man, perhaps a son, wrapped a mat around the body. Two others comforted a woman thrashing by the side of the hole dug in the ground. Each of them had tied a piece of white cloth like a loose turban around his head in lieu of the elaborate white clothing Vietnamese traditionally wear at funerals. Once the dead man was buried the woman knelt on the ground, but her sons guided her away after just a few perfunctory bows.

I was still watching from the balcony when one of the men rushed out and, with desperate movements, unearthed the body. The two grave diggers leaned on their shovels nearby. Clawing at the corpse, holding it to his chest, the man rocked it back and forth. Although I could not hear, I could see his mouth open in an anguished cry. I wanted to get Diệu-Hà to come see the scene, but by the time I was ready to move away the old man was being buried for the second time.

In the next days I abandoned the balcony and explored other

floors. I didn't tell anyone in my family what I saw in those escapades for fear that I might not be allowed to leave the room again. The ships the Americans had promised had still not come.

The building was full of wounded people. Stretchers and straw mats lined the corridors. My uncle and his colleagues tried hard but were often helpless without professional tools or medicines. The bodies kept multiplying. Small as I was, it was difficult to make my way through the mass of wounded and dying people. Once in a while I would pass an inert body, a candle burning near the covered head. The wounded moaned, the grieving sobbed. The whole place smelled bad.

Once I heard a woman breathing and moaning in gasps on the staircase. Two men held her from behind while a woman on the lower steps supported her legs. I hesitated a moment as the woman began to emit loud cries. When I approached to peer over the men's shoulders, I caught sight of a baby's head between the woman's legs, and soon after came the sound of the newborn infant's first cries. A life was making its difficult beginning, amid the atmosphere of easy deaths.

By now several American ships had come to Huế to evacuate refugees, but we could not fight the crowds that surged to the river in the hope of getting aboard. "It's a helicopter! It's a helicopter!" I shouted as I reached the door to our room toward the end of our second week at the university high rise. My mother and sisters bolted from the floor as my aunt reached for our suitcase. It had stayed packed and ready for this occasion. We rushed down the staircase, out the campus courtyard, and across the street. The artillerymen cleared an area as the helicopter landed. "Stay by the tree!" my mother shouted to us as she plunged into the mob to get to the pilots. She shouted out my father's name—"I'm his wife, I'm his wife!"—to the airmen. They swept her onto the plane, then came for us moments later, one man lifting both Diệu-Hà and me off the ground. Another pushed

Diệu-Quỳnh through the crowd. The aircraft had indeed been sent by the military governor to try to rescue my father.

As we settled into the canvas seats the crew fired warning shots into the air to clear away the crowd, and the helicopter took off. Far below the machine gun mounted at the open doors, the ruined Trường Tiền Bridge, its span broken in half, became smaller and smaller. Inexplicably, it was the cries of the newborn baby I heard in my mind as the craft's blades chopped through the air and carried us over the mountains to Đà Nẵng.

☙ "Diệu-Hà, don't mess up your father's desk, please," Chú Cường said.

"I won't," Diệu-Hà replied.

"But do you have to sit there?"

"Why not? I'm studying," she proclaimed. At twelve, Diệu-Hà was as ever the spoiled child of the family. A captivating girl and now an excellent student, she had always seized everyone's affection. Diệu-Hà's schoolbooks were piled up on either side of her. She looked minuscule behind the desk, which seemed big enough to hide an elephant.

Chú Cường, a house servant, always guarded the desk as though it were a treasure all his own. Made of heavy dark wood and with curving lines, it sat just beyond our living room in an area separated from the rest of the ground floor by a rosewood room divider with panels of deep green fabric. Directly above the desk was a white ceiling fan whose churning blades were reflected in the desk's glass-covered surface. Many days after school I would watch the images of the Asian weeping pine trees outside the large windows behind the desk which were projected onto its glass top, forming mystical dancing figures. Other days, when the windows were closed, the sun would shine through the bits of colored glass in the top panes, casting morsels of red, green, blue, and yellow light on its surface.

Every afternoon Chú Cường would methodically go over the desk with a feather duster, then wipe the telephone and the glass top with a cloth. A bottle of ink and a blotter were arranged on either side of the pen holder, a gift from an American general. Books and magazines were stacked neatly on top of each other, and Chú Cường would place my father's files in a row so that the labels showed. He kept a set of fresh Chinese cloisonné ashtrays handy to replace the one on the desk when it was soiled. Just after dinner each night Chú Cường would check the desk again, making sure nothing had been disturbed. It would be clean and orderly whenever my father came to sit at it to work or to read before bed.

Now my father's books remained, but his secretary had taken the files away.

"Why do you keep cleaning the ashtray?" I asked. But Chú Cường went on cleaning the one that now was never dirtied.

"Mister will be back soon enough," Chú Cường said.

"Mister" was how Chú Cường and the house staff referred to my father. They were all male, except for the cook and one other woman. My parents taught us to call them all Chù, or "Uncle," and their wives Thím or O, "Aunt." In deference to her age we addressed our cook as Bà, or "Mrs." Bà Thành cooked our daily meals; Chú Tuấn, a short, wiry man with a crew cut, prepared the elaborate French dishes my parents served when they had guests. O Vy, who had worked for my mother for many years, accompanied Bà Thành or Chú Tuấn to the market and helped out around the house, mending or ironing clothes. Chú Cường did the laundry and cleaning, while Chú Hiếu, a witty and dedicated man, served the meals and supervised the rest of the staff.

The two drivers we addressed as Bác, which also means "Uncle," but one whose age or wisdom is superior to that of one's father. One of them, Bác Thiều, had been my father's classmate in elementary school. Bác Thiều drove the family car,

Bác Trí the black Peugeot reserved for my father, who often drove himself to work. He never knew that Chú Khử, one of two policemen assigned to protect him at all times, always followed the Peugeot on his motorcycle.

Except for Chú Cường and Chú Hiếu, everyone lived at the back of the house, opposite the driveway and badminton court. With a house full of "aunts" and "uncles," we had what amounted to an extended family. Bác Trí's children became my ready friends, playing war games among the banana trees.

My family had lived in this house in Đà Nẵng for just over a year. In 1966 General Hoàng Xuân Lãm had asked that my father, a government official who was studying at Michigan State University, be transferred to Đà Nẵng as his civilian deputy. My father moved to Đà Nẵng early in the year, bringing with him my older brother Đinh. After a few months Đinh received a scholarship to attend Bowling Green State University and left for Ohio. The rest of our family arrived in Đà Nẵng in 1967.

Even at age eight, I did not like Đà Nẵng. In contrast to my birthplace, Đà Lạt, a mild-temperature resort town dotted with lakes and green hills and traversed by roads that glistened after the rain, Đà Nẵng was full of flat, sandy roads and noisy crowds. There were few trees, and the river was brown and sad as it reached the coast. It was always so terribly humid that I felt suffocated. The dark-skinned residents looked unhealthy and always seemed to be too busy making a living to be congenial. From dawn to late at night, Đà Nẵng was all business. Most distasteful was the atmosphere of war—military vehicles and uniformed men were always around town, loud and violent and dangerous.

The government had assigned my father a tall house with a huge garden that bordered on the unused train station. Its front gates opened directly on a clump of bamboo shading the imposing portico, which had a veranda above it. Gray-blue shutters complemented the aged tile roof with whimsical concrete figures around its edges. The front yard was covered with a blanket of white and gray pebbles and encircled by two rows of pine trees. In the afternoon, arms extended, I would run, along the paths of white sand between the trees, pretending to be an airplane. Or I would fold paper planes and send them sailing out from my bedroom balcony into the branches and bushes of the rear garden, where they occasionally got stuck in the wire mesh of the poultry coop beyond the back porch, which housed my father's Ping-Pong table.

It was quite a house, but it had been vacant for years. No one dared live in it since the two officials who had occupied it before both met untimely deaths. The swimming pool in the back had been filled in after someone had drowned in there as well.

"It's this house," Chú Cường confided to another member of the house staff after my father's capture. "Mister is not superstitious, but he should never have come to live here. Bad, bad spirits."

The staff went about their work in the numbing days after Tết, trying to be of more help to my mother and us children without making it too obvious, and acting as though my father were away on a business trip, or on vacation. Only occasionally would someone let an unfortunate comment slip.

"Mister always liked his rice this way," Chú Hiếu observed one night while serving dinner. It was a bit damp and soft. Immediately he became embarrassed.

"What will they give him to eat in the jungle?" my mother asked, upset at this reminder of my father's whereabouts. "In those mountains, all he'll have to eat is manioc."

꙰ "He's up there. In the Bạch Mã Mountains," said General Lãm. "I'll rescue him."

"Are you sure?" my mother asked.

Indeed, less than a month after Tết, General Lãm had attempted a rescue operation in the mountains above Huế. His commando troops discovered a group of thatched-roofed houses which the Việt Cộng used as a way station. Captives from the Tết offensive in Huế were kept there on the way to the North.

"They knew we were coming," General Lãm said. "Half an hour earlier, and your husband would be here with us now."

The Việt Cộng had rushed out of the area, taking only those prisoners they considered important and leaving behind some policemen and civilians. My father had been held in the way station for several days, but those who were rescued by General Lãm's forces didn't know much about his condition; he was being kept in isolation.

"We chased them, but couldn't find them in the dark. They had escaped by morning. But we'll find him. I'll bring him back. Now we know he's alive."

It would be four years before we had any further news of my father.

Except for a few areas on the outskirts, Đà Nẵng suffered no Việt Cộng attacks during the Tết offensive. People repeated the tidbits they gleaned from radio and newspaper reports. "The way they're going at it, there won't be a house left standing in Huế." "They're even fighting inside the citadel. Temples, thrones—nothing's sacred." "If the Americans bomb, that will be the end." "They won't. How can they destroy the imperial city?" "The Americans don't care!" "I can't believe the army allowed the Việt Cộng to get so close! Right in the middle of Huế!" "I knew they wouldn't stick to the cease-fire! Never trust the Việt Cộng!" "Did you hear? Colonel Khoa, the mayor, went into a hospital and wrapped his face up—covered it completely with gauze!" "How can we ever win the war? Bunch of cowards running cities and towns, the whole war!"

Voices of pessimism increased as people learned more about the damage in Huế, Đà Lạt, and other cities. In Sài Gòn, blocks from the presidential palace, five American servicemen were killed defending the U.S. embassy.

"They'll do it again," my mother said. "They'll do it again, and they'll win."

Somehow, she had gone back to her job as principal of a government school for girls with thousands of students and hundreds of teachers. Diệu-Hà and I went back to the lycée. My teachers and classmates must have heard about my father's capture, but no one said a word. Diệu-Quỳnh was a junior at a Vietnamese school but her attending school at all was a pretense. She could write thoughtful essays and performed well in language classes, but her teachers reported that she simply didn't care about school anymore.

TWO

You're Like Your Father Now

"Mạ, Mạ!" I yelled out from the front balcony of our house. "It's Cậu Vịnh! And Grandfather."

Uncle Vịnh, the husband of my father's sister, Xuân-Liễu, honked the horn as he pulled the white jeep into our driveway. I rushed down the staircase and ran around to the garage. My mother appeared at the doorway and called out to me, "Come greet your grandparents! Thank Heaven you're all safe!"

"*Thưa Ông*," I said. My grandfather didn't seem to hear my greeting. With trembling steps he climbed out of the jeep.

"How come you're not in school?"

"But it's Saturday!"

I reached for his sleeve to guide him and my grandmother into the house. The thinness of his wrist made me shiver.

While we were ensconced at the university in the days following my father's capture, in the inner citadel across the River of Perfume my grandparents and other relatives were having their own ordeal. My uncle was an officer in Sài Gòn's rural development program, which mirrored the Việt Cộng's efforts to gain a foothold in the countryside. Even in calmer times Uncle Vịnh and his colleagues had been targets of nighttime assassination attempts. With the enemy now in control, he was sure he would be killed. At the beginning of the Tết offensive he had crawled into an underground chamber in the garden and stayed there for a week. Aunt Xuân-Liễu had told the Việt Cộng he was on an assignment in Sài Gòn.

"And where is your brother the deputy governor?" a Việt Cộng cadre asked.

"Oh, he's in Đà Nẵng," my aunt lied.

"Then who had dinner here two nights ago? We will find him!"

We had indeed visited my grandparents the day after arriving in Huế by car for the Tết holiday, promising to come back early the next morning. That was the night the Year of the Monkey began, among the firecrackers and gunfire.

"We'd better get out of here," Uncle Vịnh had said to my aunt. Aunt Xuân-Liễu was crouching down next to the piece of roofing which concealed his hiding place.

"What about the house?"

"Do you want me to die? They'll come back. I'm sure they're watching us," Uncle Vịnh said. "What if they search the house? They'll kill me. I can't hide in here forever!"

"But where are we going to go?" my aunt whispered. "Can't you hear the gunfire? What about my parents?"

"We have to get out! We have no choice!"

Avoiding the house-to-house battles, sporadic gunfights, rocket explosions, and troops of Việt Cộng soldiers, my uncle led my aunt and their two children on foot to a relative's house on the outskirts of town. Despite his age, my grandfather also went with them, while another relative carried my grandmother on his back. It took a night and a morning for them to reach safety.

Two months later Uncle Vịnh drove my grandparents to Đà

Nẵng, leaving them with us before going back to his family in Huế. Their arrival destroyed whatever semblance of normality we had managed to reestablish. My grandfather was a stern man in his seventies, still in good health. But our relatives argued that he would not survive the bad news about his only son, so my mother kept it secret.

It was extraordinary that my grandfather didn't know about my father's capture, which had been reported in all the papers. Hungry for news about the war and my father, after my grandparents' arrival Mạ continued to listen to the radio—but only in her bathroom, as though it were an illegal or shameful act. Newspapers and letters were carefully screened, and the mailman's arrival sent us scurrying to make sure nothing fell into Grandfather's hands. Whenever the bell rang Chú Cường or Chú Hiếu would rush to the front gate. All visitors had to be intercepted, for fear they might inadvertently disclose to my grandfather the secret of his son's imprisonment.

For as long as I could remember, my father had always displayed my grandfather's virtues. He cherished education, modesty, and moderation; he was devoted to his work. But whereas my father was disciplined, my grandfather was rigid. Whereas my father invited respect, my grandfather inspired both respect and fear. And whereas my father never lost his temper, his father was known to send everyone running with his shouts, even in the years when only a few strands of silver hair remained under his headband.

My grandfather had had an admirable career as a mandarin. His own grandfather had been a regent through the reigns of three young kings. Forced to sign a peace treaty with the French in 1884, my great-great-grandfather had been cursed by history. The French sent him into exile in Tahiti, where he died a few years later. My grandfather was among the first of his descendants allowed to take the Chinese-style examination for mandarin. But although he passed with a high score, he was not allowed to enter government service until he was in his forties. He worked his way up as an administrator of various regions in central Việt Nam, but later shunned the Western-style government established by the French, remaining loyal to the Vietnamese court in Huế.

At the time he retired he was a *quan Phủ,* a governor of the region stretching from Huế to towns farther north. He was literate in Chinese and had also mastered French. My summer vacations, spent in Huế, were punctuated each morning with lessons in Vietnamese literature, French diction and spelling, and geometry from nine until noon. Hands behind his back, tall and erect in his white traditional clothing, my grandfather would tower over my cousin and me. We sat at a table on the veranda just outside the front door, intent on our lessons despite the heat and humidity of the Huế summer and the singing of the cicadas that clung to the bamboo shade above us. Though we listened to their song and yearned to catch them, we kept our eyes on the pages of exercises my grandfather had assigned. When Grandfather arrived in Đà Nẵng in 1968 the lessons resumed, now in the afternoon, after his nap and my return home from school.

My mother had explained that my father was in Sài Gòn on a business trip, but my grandfather did not stop wondering about his son.

"But why has he not phoned, not written?" he asked during the second week of his visit. "Whatever work he's doing, he has to phone home once in a while! Can't you call him? Don't they have a phone where he is? Or has he taken on another family?" My grandfather's questions grew louder.

He took over my father's desk, and when the phone rang he would often pick it up before my mother or any of us could reach it. Chú Hiếu disconnected the wires; the phone was not working, we told him, and it would take time to get it fixed. Gradually word got out to those who visited our house not to disclose the secret. We regained some measure of comfort.

"Cu Bé! Cu Bé!" Bác Thiều, the chauffeur, beckoned me by

my nickname, "Little Boy," as I stood on the veranda over the front portico, looking out onto the street. My mother was late coming home from work. "Come with me, let's get your mother home," Bác Thiều said when I ran down to meet him.

"Where's Mạ? Is she still at work?"

"No, no—just come with me."

Bác Thiều took me by the hand and led me out the gate. I looked for the family car.

"Your mother's just over here," Bác Thiều explained, tugging me down the block.

I started to cry as soon as I saw her. She was doubled over on the sofa, sobbing. The owner of the house, a woman I didn't recognize, said "Come on, Mrs. Đãi." She patted my mother's back. "Your son is here—he'll take you home."

I wanted to get away from this stranger, back to our house with my mother. Later I learned the woman was a relative of a teacher at my mother's school. We would come to know her well. It was the first time I had seen my mother cry. She reached out for me, but tears kept her from saying anything. When she finally stood up, she attempted a smile at our hostess. "But I can't even go home, to my own home!" She burst into tears again.

Such moments continued to embarrass me in the weeks to come. Sometimes I would come back from the neighbor's house determined to tell my grandfather the truth. The afternoon lessons became unbearable; I was constantly anxious for my mother to come home, constantly fearing that she had had to stop again at the house down the block.

"Đầu óc để vô mô? Cứ lo' lo', đãng đãng hoài—không lo mà học đi!" "What are you doing with your brain? You're constantly drifting off—pay attention to your studies!" Grandfather would shout at me.

"Your son needs more attention. Is he always this distracted when his father's away?" he'd complain to my mother after dinner.

"Yes, I'll talk to him," Mạ would answer softly, then follow

me upstairs. Lying in my bed, I sensed that she too was alone in
her room, crying.

The next day there would be more lies to tell.

"Did he call you today at your office?" my grandfather would
ask as my mother walked in the door.

"Uh, yes—he did, but I was in a meeting. He left a message,
just that he's quite busy, and he's been to Thailand, I think."

"Thailand? What for? Shouldn't he come home first?"

"Or maybe he's going there. It's really difficult to get
through, and nobody can hear anything on the phone."

"Maybe the military has better phone lines. I'll ask General
Lãm, next time he comes around, if we can use them—or you
ask him."

"Yes, I'll ask," my mother would say.

Diệu-Quỳnh often stood near the stairs listening to these
exchanges. Afterward she would simply look at me, expressionless,
and walk back upstairs. Diệu-Hà would play the piano—or if she
didn't, I would pound out violent, dissonant chords until my
mother would come out. "You're too loud!" she would scold,
then retreat upstairs while I continued to bang on the keys.

One day Diệu-Hà and I came home from the lycée to find
the front gate open. The front yard was full of cars.

"Bác Thiều, who's here? Why is everyone here?" I asked
from the backseat.

"I don't know," our driver answered. "I saw your uncle
Phong pulling in when I left to pick you two up."

"The front door is open. Let me go see, please!" Diệu-Hà
jumped out of the car.

"It's Dr. Tùng's car," I said to her, pointing to the black
Volkswagen Beetle.

"Bác Triêm is here too," she said. His motorcycle was leaning
against the wall.

"Everyone's here!" I followed Diệu-Hà through the front
door and stepped into the entrance hall. We held our school

briefcases in front of our chests. There were about ten people in the living room, most crouched down on the floor. No one noticed us. I tiptoed toward the entrance.

My grandfather was on the floor, leaning back against an armchair, legs stretched out in front of him. Someone had pushed the round coffee table to one side. A hand was waving a glass of water in front of his face. His eyes were open, their gaze wide and chilling. He was staring at the water but didn't see it. Chú Hiếu came in from the dining room and handed a face towel into the crowd. An uncle gently pressed the cloth to my grandfather's face. I could see Dr. Tùng, listening as he held a stethoscope to my grandfather's chest.

"He'll be all right," the doctor said, removing the stethoscope from his ears. "Let's move him to bed. He needs rest."

The group moved. I suddenly realized my mother was not there. Chú Hiếu caught my eye and pointed to the area beyond the living room. I pushed Diệu-Hà along the corridor, past the piano, and into the space behind the room divider.

My mother was sitting at my father's desk, cradling her head in her arms, which were folded on its glass surface. Diệu-Quỳnh, an aunt, and Chú Cường stood behind her. As Diệu-Hà and I approached we could hear the sound of weeping.

"Where's your grandfather?" my mother asked when she looked up.

Diệu-Hà pointed to the guest bedroom, beyond the dining area. My mother got up, but Chú Hiếu entered and motioned for her to sit down again. "He's sleeping. You can rest," he said.

Uncle Phong had told my grandfather about my father's capture. He survived the news and went back to Huế a few weeks later.

❧ "Madam, Colonel Hinh is here with his wife," Chú Cường announced.

"Please invite them in, and please prepare some tea."

It was a Sunday morning, a couple of months after we had come back to Đà Nẵng from Huế. Colonel Hinh was General Lãm's chief of staff, a dark man in an ill-fitting uniform. His wife wore an *aó dài* of deep red fabric adorned with black roses; her hair was done up in a chignon, the beehive style popular in Việt Nam in the late 1960s.

"I hope you brought some news," my mother said after she had exchanged greetings with the couple.

"I'm sorry," the colonel said. He had a Northern accent. "We still have troops out looking for him. We'll let you know, of course, if there's any news."

"Oh, here," his wife said. She took a couple of cans of cooking oil from a bag she had with her. "We brought you a little oil."

The oil had come in an American aid package. The cans bore a stenciled logo of red and white stripes above a rendering of two hands in a firm clasp.

"Thank you, that's kind of you," Mạ said. It was not out of the ordinary to bring a gift of oil or other sundry items, but for Colonel Hinh and his wife to make such a show was strange. My mother had only met them once or twice before. Normally a gift like this would be quietly handed to the staff, by a driver or an aide, or perhaps sent over after the visit. Gifts of greater value might be given to the family's children—never to the host or hostess. "Have you just been to the market?" she asked.

"Oh, no, we came to see you. I mean, we set out to see you this morning," the colonel answered.

"The oil came from a special shipment just this week, only for officers," his wife added. "We thought of you right away."

"That's kind. Have the Việt Cộng been pushed back completely?"

"Ah, yes. Don't worry," said the colonel.

There was a slight pause. "Your work must be tiring," the colonel's wife said.

"Oh, not too bad. You should come to visit. You don't have any girls at the school, do you?"

"Oh, no, we have two boys."

It wasn't until after they left that my mother hit on the crucial remark the colonel had made. "What did he mean, 'It must be difficult getting to work from *here*'? It only takes five minutes! They already took the one car away—now does he want the house, too? Where are we going to live? Not even two months, and look at how they're treating me. What will happen when he comes back?"

She dialed General Lãm's office. "General, you're surely not going to allow anyone to kick us out of here?" she asked when he came on the line.

"Oh, no," he assured her. But during the following weeks Colonel Hinh kept visiting with his wife, each time bearing a small gift and dropping further hints. My mother avoided confronting him on the issue but countered with her own subtle hints about General Lãm's assurance.

As my father's absence lengthened, General Lãm provided no comfort regarding our financial situation. My mother could not receive compensation since the government, not knowing his exact location, refused to declare either that my father was a prisoner, or that he was dead. Since he was a civilian, he could not be classified as missing in action. "They said he was on vacation at the time he was captured," my mother said to a relative. "What does it matter? I'm without my husband!" We learned that in their hurried retreat after Tết the Việt Cộng had killed many of their captives just outside of Huế. Some had been buried alive. My mother visited one of the mass graves that had been found. The decomposed bodies and the signs of violent death so horrified her that she hurried back to Đà Nẵng, abandoning any thought that my father could have been among the dead. When I saw a film of the unearthing of the piles of bones which the Ministry of Information showed later on television, I could not sleep for days. The traditional music that was played as a background for these grisly scenes would come back into my head, each note on the zither a shot that chilled my spine.

The South Vietnamese army kept the enemy at bay, though it was helped by the Việt Cộng's need to recover from the effort of mounting the Tết offensive as well as the subsequent losses. Still, the Việt Cộng were active. Troops would hide in the mountains during the day and at night venture out to assemble cannons and send barrages of rockets flying into Đà Nẵng, shocking us awake. We would all jump from our beds in what soon became a reflex, and rush to safety. Scrambling out of bed and downstairs to get to the bunker made of sandbags on the first floor, I was frightened even more by the short, urgent blares of the warning siren. My mother had had the bunker built on the back porch where my father once had his Ping-Pong table. Stacks of sandbags supported iron bars, which were themselves covered with still more sandbags. A cupboard held tinned food and bottles of water. Shortly after the explosions started we would be inside, motionless, a dim light bulb casting large eerie shadows on the walls.

Between barrages of rockets were moments of complete silence. But we knew that though for a brief respite no one was hurt or killed, rockets were relentlessly being loaded in these moments and launched. We sat paralyzed by fear, prisoners in the hands of enemies far away. Hours would pass in that great quietness until one of the house staff or perhaps a visiting relative mumbled what we had each been praying: "It's over—no more shelling." In the morning we would learn where the shells had landed, which parts of the city had been hit, and whether we knew any of the victims. There were dozens every night.

One night, with the rockets exploding at regular intervals,

Diệu-Quỳnh bolted out of the bunker. "I can't stand it anymore!" she screamed.

"Diệu-Quỳnh! Diệu-Quỳnh, please don't! Come back!" my mother shouted, rushing after her.

I ran out behind them. Diệu-Quỳnh was jumping up and down, throwing rocks and pebbles in all directions. It must have been two or three in the morning. The sky was flashing with the explosions of artillery. I helped Mạ grab hold of my sister's arms, then brought her back into the house. Diệu-Quỳnh refused to return to the bunker.

"It's killing me!" she screamed.

"It'll be over soon. Soon. Please come back—it's too dangerous out here!" my mother pleaded.

Diệu-Quỳnh covered her ears with her hands and began chasing around the house.

"What a time to have a crisis," said my mother's aunt, who was visiting us.

The next day Diệu-Quỳnh again screamed, "I can't stand it! I can't stand it!" It was the early hours of Sunday morning, however, and there was no sound of exploding rockets.

"She's getting worse and worse," my mother moaned. "What am I going to do?" Diệu-Quỳnh never explained what went through her mind. On the third day we took her to a doctor. He pulled a large insect, still alive, out of her ear. There was no way of knowing whether the bug that had been gnawing at her eardrum and her subsequent loss of hearing in that ear contributed to her mental illness.

We gave up the official residence next to the train station in 1969. Colonel Hinh moved in with his wife and two sons. General Lãm had found us a small house two blocks away from the school where my mother worked.

Compared with the spacious official residence, our new home

always seemed crowded. Built long before as one of many units housing French teachers at the local lycée, it had just two bedrooms and a living room. The kitchen was in a separate structure off the backyard. General Lãm provided carpenters to build an extension, which included a dining room three feet below the level of the living room area and a bedroom divided by a bookcase, which gave Diệu-Hà and me some privacy. The driver, Bác Thiều and our cook Chú Tuấn came with us, building their own wooden houses in the back. Chú Khử, the bodyguard, and his family took the garage. By this time they all had other jobs, and only rarely was Bác Thiều asked to drive us. The family car had been taken away, and my mother bought an old white Peugeot from her brother in Huế.

Diệu-Hà and I did not have our room long. The rockets kept coming at night, and when one of them landed in the school yard behind our house, Diệu-Hà moved into my mother's room. In any case, the corrugated tin roof installed on the extension made the room an oven, and I was more comfortable reading and studying in the bunker that had been built in the living room. With an electric fan and a small light, the bunker was my refuge every afternoon after school. On the shelves were some of my father's books. The sandbags protected me from the desperate heat as I learned about Richard Milhous Nixon, Pablo Picasso, and Mao Tse Tung, as well as the poetry of Baudelaire and the philosophy of Voltaire and Rousseau. There I first read and fell in love with the works of innumerable Vietnamese poets and writers, spending some of those afternoons memorizing the romantic lines of Huy Cận, Xuân Diệu, and Nguyễn Bính, Việt Nam's most famous prewar poets.

Diệu-Hà and I walked to the lycée each morning, coming home at noon for an hour and a half. The school day ended at four o'clock. My mother's school had the same schedule, though she usually came home closer to six. Diệu-Quỳnh now stayed at home. Her mental condition fluctuated. For weeks she would compulsively eat carrots or chew on ice cubes all day. At other times she would wash her hands every few minutes. Often she would suddenly laugh out loud without ever explaining herself. Whenever we took her to a shop she would spend hours trying on dress after dress, or one pair of shoes after another—but in the end always refusing to let my mother buy her anything. Shop owners came to know her, and indulged her with gracious patience.

For a few weeks my father's aunt visited us from his home village near Quảng Trị, north of Huế. "I know a man who'll cure her," my great-aunt declared one day. She brought home an ugly dark-skinned man with protruding teeth who was a member of a religious sect that embraced both Buddhism and obscure quasi-magical practices. He had come to discuss the details and set an "appropriate" day to carry out a ceremony that would supposedly heal Diệu-Quỳnh. "Your daughter is very special," he said. "The poor girl, she needs help. Heaven and the Buddha ought to love her, help her; she's very special. I'll do my best." He demanded that an altar be furnished with candles and incense, fruit, other food, and cups of tea, and pieces of a special kind of paper with gold and red markings painted on them. Of course, he had also arranged a fee with my great-aunt.

He came two days after his initial visit, put on a black robe over his military uniform—he was in the corps of engineers—and lit the candles and incense. He sat Diệu-Quỳnh in front of the altar, which was set up in the hall outside her room. He then went into a trance, muttering prayers and dancing into each room in the house, then outside. He must have had some training in martial arts, for his movements were precise and deliberate. He was outside a long time, sweating in the heat as he danced.

"How can you let him do that to her?" I asked my mother.

"Your father's relatives are pressuring me," she said. "I will bear the responsibility. Besides, what if it works?"

"You should stop it, Mạ," I pleaded.

"How can I? What will I say to your great-aunt?"

"It'll make Diệu-Quỳnh worse. That guy will drive her completely mad!" I said, starting to cry.

Coming inside again, the man sat with my sister before the altar, muttering inaudible words. My great-aunt stood next to Diệu-Quỳnh, who looked at the ground, expressionless. A few feet away, I stood alongside the railing that separated the original house from the extension. My mother rested her hands on my shoulders.

The man waved incense in front of Diệu-Quỳnh's face. She started to get up, but my great-aunt pushed her back down. Diệu-Quỳnh turned away from the man as he began chanting. When he finished, he began burning the pieces of paper, then put the ashes in the cups of tea on the altar. He forced Diệu-Quỳnh to drink from one of them.

"Mạ!" I screamed. The man gave me a cold stare. My great-aunt, normally cross-eyed, turned to me with a fierce look and pulled her lips downward.

Diệu-Quỳnh somehow survived the horrible afternoon. My mother paid the man, and my great-aunt went away. Mạ then turned to Western psychiatry. But the Vietnamese did not believe in such things, and therapy did not exist. In a war-torn country where practically everyone had experienced traumatic conditions and extreme loss, life simply had to go on. The only psychiatrist my mother was able to find was an American attached to the navy who was based on a military ship offshore. He agreed to see Diệu-Quỳnh, but gave up treatment after one session. "The language problem, the cultural gap, the environment—it just didn't work," Mạ said afterward. Diệu-Quỳnh gave signs that she understood the doctor's English, but she had refused to talk to him.

Friends and hobbies distracted me from Diệu-Quỳnh's problems. I enjoyed collecting stamps, and I filled aquariums with all types of fish. Later, as a young teenager, I traded them for tapes of the Beatles and Jimi Hendrix. I was close to Diệu-Quỳnh, but failed to give her the attention that might have helped. Weekends I spent with friends posing with our cigarettes in cafés, or at the flea market, looking for a pair of American shoes or perhaps an enviable colorful striped shirt to make me look like the hippies. A pair of straight-legged blue jeans my brother sent me remained untouched until I saved up enough money to have a tailor add triangular pieces of fabric to the legs to turn them into bell-bottoms. Emulating my friends, I wore a peace sign made of beads around my neck, which I hid inside my shirt when I got home. My mother would not tolerate this symbol of rebellion.

Bending to peer pressure, I also refused to get my hair cut. My mother would lecture me every few nights on the subject. When the chief of police called to say her son had been arrested for having long hair, she told him to keep me in jail for the night to teach me a lesson. My hair only just touched my collar, but having it even that long was a crime: it showed a lack of support for soldiers, who wore military crew cuts. The government deemed the long hair a symptom of a larger social ill. Getting arrested was proof of my rebellion, and my independence. The next day my mother took me from the jail directly to the barber and ordered me to get a crew cut—thus regaining a sense of control. But I relished the fact that, with my arrest, I could no longer be thought of as a young "prince" from an elite family.

During this period my mother's financial worries persisted. There was great inflation, and her salary from the school was barely enough to make ends meet. When the lycée closed down, she struggled to send Diệu-Hà and me back to Đà Lạt for one school year. The next year she was forced to enroll us in a public school. Along with family acquaintances, my mother and Uncle Phạm, a distant relative, started a private kindergarten in our front yard as well as a small specialty restaurant facing the street. An artist rented the kindergarten's office to sleep in at night. Sitting under the bamboo tree outside the office window, I would listen to his mournful rendering of Spanish songs on classical guitar. Even with all that had happened, life seemed peaceful. A degree of happiness temporarily dulled our awareness of the ugly reality of war and the gnawing absence of my father.

In January 1973 North and South Việt Nam signed the peace accord in Paris which formally ended American involvement in the conflict. Exchanges of prisoners began soon after at the Thạch Hãn River in Quảng Trị.

By now my father had been in captivity for five years. His civilian status was complicated by the games each side played. The Southern government did not want to release Việt Cộng cadres caught while on assignment in the South as civilians. Sài Gòn was certain that because they were to be exchanged on southern soil, they would immediately turn around and work as spies. Meanwhile, Hà Nội withheld numerous prisoners, including my father.

At the time of the prisoner exchange, my mother obtained permission for her and an uncle to accompany officials to Quảng Trị to look for my father. They were aboard a helicopter that had been airborne for about ten minutes, hovering noisily above the ground before the return trip to Đà Nẵng, when a just-released South Vietnamese soldier sitting on the canvas seat next to my uncle suddenly turned to him.

"Do you know a Mrs. Đãi?" the soldier shouted over the sound of the helicopter's engine, his loose uniform flapping in the wild wind generated by its blades.

My uncle was trying to keep his hair off his face. "The wife of the deputy governor? She's right here!" he shouted back. He turned to my mother. "Chị Đãi! Chị Đãi!"—"Cousin Đãi!"

The soldier reached into a bag. Struggling with the wind, he pulled out a pair of shorts and began to tear at the seams. By now he had caught the attention of the others on the helicopter, an army officer as well as six men wearing the same kind of loose uniform, without insignia or rank. Finally he found a rolled-up piece of paper, which he passed to my uncle, indicating that it was for my mother. The paper was passed from hand to hand until it reached her.

"It's from him!" my uncle heard her cry.

"Where is he? How is he?" His voice cracked with excitement. My mother, absorbed in the paper, didn't answer. He turned to the soldier. "He's my cousin. Do you know him?"

The soldier did indeed know him, and the piece of paper he had given my mother was in fact a letter from him. The soldier was among the thousands of prisoners being exchanged according to the terms of the Paris agreement.

Other newly released prisoners who answered my mother's frantic questions told of a white-haired man respected by his fellow captives both for his gentleness and for his principles, which allowed him to stand up to the prison guards. He was weak, but in the months before the prisoner exchange he was allowed a few Ping-Pong games in the sun. Other prisoners told my mother that they had met him in various camps, but none of them could say for sure where he was being held. He was constantly being moved from one prison to another. My father had written several letters and given them to various soldiers he had met in prison just before their release. But once they were exchanged, the prisoners shed the clothes the Việt Cộng had given them and replaced them with Southern uniforms. Most threw their prison garb into the river, and along with it, my father's letters, sewn into the seams. My father had written:

> I am lucky to be alive, and lucky that I am in relatively good health. You shouldn't worry too much about me, and I hope that you are able to take care of the children, a task that I am anxious to share with you. I think of you and the children, and my parents, every day of my captivity.

◦• Raindrops were beginning to fall from Hué's gray sky when the cortege left the front gate. Hundreds of people lined the L-shaped walkway from the front steps of the house to the street, obscuring the hedges and tea plants that defined the path. It was impossible to know who among them were relatives and who were simply curious. Over twenty professional pallbearers dressed in baggy white pants that stopped at the knee carried the coffin out. Some wore black boots, others were barefoot. The rain formed tiny streams that coursed down their red conical hats and mixed with sweat to soak their shirts, electric blue with yellow trim.

"*Hooo-ah! Hooo-ah! Aaah-hoo! Hoop!*"

Chanting loudly in unison helped the bearers coordinate their movements. For a quarter of an hour they struggled, some with heavy poles on their shoulders, some with ropes twisted behind their backs. The coffin, draped in a vividly colored cloth and weighed down by the brown clay used to seal it, was inched out the double doors onto the veranda, then hoisted over the railing and down into the front yard. The pallbearers had not been able to leave the house by way of the narrow front steps; it would be a bad omen if the coffin were not kept perfectly horizontal while it was being carried away. "*Hooo-ah! Hooo-ah! Aaah-hoo! Hoop!*" The leader yelled directions over the singing. Meanwhile, behind the coffin, a group of monks in saffron robes repeated rhythmic prayers in throaty voices, some tapping on small copper and wooden bells. In between I could hear the sobbing of my aunts, uncles, and other relatives, all in funeral garments made of coarse white fabric and without any buttons. Women wore hoods, men headbands.

In the courtyard facing the coffin, I stood transfixed for a long time, then began to fidget with the thick coconut rope tied around my waist. I was the only male member of the family wearing a hood. The neighbors' gaze seemed to bore into me.

Their children were gathered all around; some had climbed up in the longan trees to watch the spectacle.

"You'll walk backward, in front of the coffin," Uncle Vịnh had explained to me the night before. "Everyone else will stay behind it."

In my left hand I held a long, rough walking stick, in my right a small altar that resembled a miniature house with a sloping roof, painted gold and lined inside with purple velvet. Resting on it was a piece of gold paper on which was inscribed, in Chinese characters, my grandfather's name. He had died of throat cancer exactly a week before.

In his last months his health had worsened quickly. Unable to swallow, he could eat only a few spoonfuls of rice soup each day. With his emaciated figure curled up on the bed, he breathed with sharp, whistling sounds. His high forehead looked more pronounced than ever. My mother had taken my sisters and me to Huế a week before he died. My sisters went back to Đà Nẵng after a few days, Diệu-Hà to prepare for an important exam, and Diệu-Quỳnh because she felt uncomfortable with so many people around. Relatives visited all day, cooking, cleaning, sitting with my grandmother. She was frail and could only take a few steps at a time. She never said much. Her eyes seemed permanently glazed over.

There were relatives in every room, but, as though cursed by a hereditary disease, the whole family whispered. Many would stay over at night, and I could hear deep, tired breaths coming from various corners of the house. No one slept much. We listened to each other's sighs, stared into the darkness, and waited for daylight. And for my grandfather's delivery.

When it finally came, many of the relatives had gone back to their daily lives. Uncle Vịnh, forever a practical man, was out with Aunt Xuân-Liễu, arranging for the funeral and the legal process involved with the will.

"He's leaving," my great-aunt said softly. She had been sitting for most of the morning beside Grandfather's bed, where he lay with his back to the wall. He had not stirred for many hours. My mother and I helped my grandmother to the side of the bed. She sat down next to him, wordless.

Standing at the head of the bed, I touched my grandfather's shoulder. I didn't know how my great-aunt could tell he was dying. She was now at his feet. I expected her to wail, and I was surprised that no tears came to my eyes either.

"He's gone," my great-aunt said.

My grandfather didn't look any different.

"His feet have gone cold," my great-aunt announced after a moment. Tiptoeing to the dining table, I poured some water from a drinking bottle onto my hands and splashed it into my eyes. I started back toward his bed, paused behind the three women for a moment, then wiped my eyes dry.

The sobbing began slowly, short sounds that at first were indistinguishable from snorts of laughter. My grandmother sniffled, sighed several times, then broke into loud sobs. My mother remained silent, while my great-aunt began to recite what I took to be Buddhist prayers, but I could not hear the words. Father should be here, I thought to myself. That thought finally made me cry.

Relatives from Đà Nẵng brought Diệu-Quỳnh and Diệu-Hà to Huế for the funeral. The house was full of visitors paying their respects. According to custom, we kept my grandfather's body at home. The coffin was set in the dim area behind the living room, exactly in the center of the house. Traditional funeral scrolls lined the walls, some black and white, some brightly colored, and the metallic silver Chinese characters occasionally reflected the candlelight. My mother spent an afternoon with my great-aunt and Uncle Vịnh setting up an elaborate altar at the head of the coffin, arranging on it gold and white candles of all sizes around porcelain vases containing huge white flowers.

"It looks so real," said my great-aunt when Uncle Vịnh

brought out a pastel portrait of my grandfather. "When did you get it done?"

"At the beginning of the year," Uncle Vịnh answered. He had thought of everything. The portrait was placed in the middle of the altar, beneath images of the Buddha. Uncle Vịnh also had several three-legged brass urns, which my mother arranged on the lowest tier of the altar, behind the stacks of prayer books and copper bells used by the monks and nuns. My clothes started to smell like incense.

Covered with straw mats, the praying area extended from the altar through the rest of the living room. Buddhist monks performed endless rites. The most involved ceremony took place two days after my grandfather's death, when he was being dressed and readied to be laid to rest in the coffin. The undertaker's men spread a couple of inches of brown clay along the bottom and sides of the coffin, followed by a layer of flowers and dried leaves, which was covered with white cloth and then finally a piece of fine brocade. The wailing grew into a loud chorus as the men laid the body inside. Meanwhile, monks in brown robes draped with large pieces of saffron cloth kept up their chanting in front of the altar.

One ceremony followed another. Women from a Buddhist association took charge of the prayers said throughout the day, which were punctuated by complicated rites with six or more monks and nuns participating. Visitors and guests came to bow at the altar whenever there was a lull. Family members would line up on either side of the coffin to face the guests and bow back in gratitude.

"Stay in front, Cu Bé," my aunts and uncles often reminded me, scurrying with my mother and sisters to the back. After the first day I realized that they were waiting for me to lead the bowing sessions. Throughout the funeral, relatives asked questions of me: "We should light the candles now, shouldn't we?" "The monks are probably ready for the prayers now. You'll invite them

in, won't you?" "Do you think it's time to present the food?"
"Maybe you can tell your uncles to go to bed." At last I realized
the questions were actually orders. Tasks needed to be done, but
my relatives, deferring to tradition, pretended that I was making
the decisions. In my father's absence my brother was head of the
family, but since he was in Ohio, the role landed on my shoulders.
It was June 1971, and I was twelve years old.

Thus on the day of the burial, I led the coffin out of the
house. The blocks surrounding it were lined with pedicabs, each
bearing a wreath. The hearse was an old French van painted the
same electric blue and yellow of the pallbearers' shirts. The funeral
scrolls covered its sides, hiding the windows. Maneuvering the
coffin inside took half an hour. I was told to sit up front with the
driver and a monk. My mother sat with my great-aunt and Aunt
Xuân-Liễu in the back. My grandmother was too weak to make
the journey to the cemetery. Diệu-Quỳnh and Diệu-Hà were in
one of the cars behind the hearse, with other relatives. The rain
came down steadily as we moved along, rolling so slowly that
curious neighbors could keep up with us by walking alongside the
van and among the cars.

Turning from my grandparents' neighborhood onto the main
street inside the citadel, which wound along the series of lakes
encircling the old royal compound, we crossed through the arched
gates and emerged on the road going toward the river. The monks
kept up their prayers. High in the sky tiny raindrops formed a
dense veil that softened the cityscape in a blurred panorama.
There was hardly anybody on the streets, save for a lone cyclist
soundlessly floating forward.

Near the center of town we passed a cluster of schoolgirls
stranded under the narrow awnings of shops. The strands of their
black hair were lines above their flowing white *aó dài* and loose
trousers, as though they were bits of ink in the pages of a book
of poetry. Farther on there was a group of soldiers sitting on

stools in a riverside café, its roof a simple piece of army canvas. The soldiers' uniforms were tinged by the mist to a soft green that matched the flowing waters of the River of Perfume. The soldiers stood up, almost in slow motion, and lifted their hats as we passed. Some put their hands to their foreheads in a salute.

We progressed at our solemn pace past the shops and turned onto the restored Trường Tiền Bridge. Images of Huế four winters back flooded my mind, and I became conscious that I had tears in my eyes. How long ago it seemed, and how sad the city had stayed.

One step remained before burial to complete the traditional Vietnamese funeral: a stop on the way to the cemetery, during which the dead would make a final visit to a favorite place while the living offered Heaven and the gods a last prayer that the journey of the departed would be swift and tranquil. Walking up alongside the van, Uncle Vịnh murmured a suggestion to me through the open window. I agreed: the government guest house would be as good a place as any to stop. Though it would be hard for my mother, I had no other ideas. From there to the cemetery the road was the one on which my father would have traveled on his way to prison.

It was cold and raw when we arrived. The rain had not let up, and the wind was strong. While the others waited, my great-aunt, Uncle Vịnh, Aunt Xuân-Liễu, my mother, and I braved the gale to light incense sticks and follow the chanting monks to the crossroad outside the guest house. Other than the monks and our white figures, no one was about. We prayed and bowed, crying all the while.

"Make sure you do the bowing correctly," Uncle Vịnh said to me. "You're like your father now."

I repeated that phrase to myself all the way to the cemetery, and throughout the dismal afternoon until after we had covered my grandfather's coffin with the soggy earth of the Nam Giao

Hills, some miles outside of Huế. The rain made the rolling countryside in the distance look like a soft gray-blue mass, and the grass underneath my feet was slippery, uncertain.

"*Thôi, về, về chứ không thôi mưa, lạnh, đau cả nhà. Về cho rồi Cu Bé ơi,*" Uncle Vịnh called to me. "Let's go before the whole family catches cold in the wind and rain. Let's go home, Cu Bé."

I glanced around one last time. My grandfather's life, hardened yet fulfilled, had ended, and he was now buried beneath a heap of rain-soaked earth. Perhaps his spirit would travel on beyond this troubled world.

Turning back to the empty hearse, I mused about another journey, one that had started more than four years before from a holiday house not far from these hills. In the wind and rain, I wondered about the fate of a father whose role I had inherited, however figuratively. I remembered the way he had looked that night, hands tied and face downturned, standing under the indifferent light of the guest house's front porch at the start of his journey.

THREE

The Hồ Chí Minh Trail

In the darkness that began the second day of the lunar New Year 1968, the few incandescent bulbs illuminating the front entrance of the government guest house made the faces of the men gathered below look jaundiced. The more than two dozen prisoners were led away in single file, heads bowed and thoughts concealed.

My father's face probably revealed least. As a boy he had been quiet and gentle; now, at forty-four, he was an impossibly disciplined man whose emotions were always kept in check.

Of the journey's beginning he would later write in his memoirs:

The town seemed covered by a film of ash. There was something unnatural about a street so devoid of people, and it seemed broader than it really was. We crossed a bridge over a small river where a lone Việt Cộng soldier stood guard laconically and headed toward the hills of Nam Giao. Gazing at the leaves trembling in the late afternoon wind, the deserted streets of the dead town, and the murky water flowing through the river,

I thought of life's bitter upheavals and the effects of war. It was getting dark, and in the gloomy moments when daylight was giving way to blackness, a wintry feeling and a sense of doom penetrated my body.

My father's delicate Japanese sandals were meant for polished floors—hardly the rocks and pebbles of the roads that led off from the city streets. I am no different from these sandals, he thought, taking them off and walking barefoot for a long while. He remembered how in China, toward the end of the Ching dynasty, noblewomen with bound feet had walked for miles to escape worsening warfare. Wrapping his bleeding feet in pieces of cloth, my father put the sandals away in the plastic basket holding his few belongings. From now on everything he owned would be of incalculable value.

"Hurry up," one of the four Việt Cộng soldiers escorting the prisoners urged. She explained that they were "almost out of enemy territory," and "nearing the liberated zone." They traveled for more than a day, edging away from Huế, the soldier repeating that they were nearing Việt Cộng territory several times. Their march took them over hill after hill, and the prisoners had crossed several streams. At five in the afternoon they ascended one last treacherous hill to arrive at their first rest stop.

"The stream is over here; you have a few minutes to take a bath, and then you must come back here. We'll eat and sleep here for tonight," said one of the guards.

"At least we'll be able to rest for a night," a man whispered to my father. "I wonder whether anyone knows we're here."

"We can't be that far from Huế, or our own troops."

The tired men went to wash in the stream. At that altitude it was too cold to bathe. My father was thirsty but took only a small gulp from the stream, not sure what the effect of this unfamiliar, perhaps unsafe, water might be after such a journey.

The guards gathered the men inside a makeshift house hidden

under an immense tree. Chilling winds filtered through the gaps
in the walls, which were made of bamboo branches and dried
leaves, and swept up little eddies of dust from the dirt floor.
There was no window, and the single doorway, a flap propped up
by a branch, looked like an awning. Under it sat a bored soldier
bearing an AK-47 rifle. On the next hill, directly across from the
hut, stood the soldiers' quarters, a slightly larger shelter also made
of bamboo. It seemed sturdier and more comfortable.

Darkness came swiftly. Each of the prisoners was given a
fistful of rice the size of a duck egg, accompanied by some coarse
salt, which tore at my father's throat. While the soldiers relaxed
after dinner, he limped over to where another prisoner sat under
a tree. Hồ Thúc Tứ, a man in his fifties, had been the deputy
manager of the railroad station in Huế, which had been out of
operation for some time.

"They couldn't have attacked all our cities simultaneously,"
my father whispered.

"They said their forces were all over," his new friend replied.

"I don't believe it."

"There's been no gunfire. I don't think any of our soldiers
are in this area. No aircraft," Tứ speculated. "Do you think
anybody will find us here?"

"The Việt Cộng wouldn't stop here if they thought our
troops could find us. A lot of our soldiers were on leave, to be
home with their families for Tết," my father said. "It would take
time for them to mobilize for a counterattack. But if we have had
to move away so quickly, the Việt Cộng must be withdrawing."

"The farther from town we are, the less we'll know. Where
do you think we are?" Tứ wondered.

"Everybody inside!" a soldier shouted.

My father stood up. The sky was pitch black, with no moon,
no stars—and no airplanes. The surrounding hills were quiet. He
was among the last of the twenty-nine prisoners ducking under
the bamboo frame of the door. They packed themselves on a

single rough mat of woven bamboo sticks and branches. Two guards entered the hut and put shackles on most of the men's feet. A guard confiscated my father's glasses and ordered him and two others underground, each to his own pit.

The steps to the pit were carelessly dug into the ground. My father groped his way down, sickened by the stench of urine. The guard followed him down a moment later, aided by a flashlight, and swept a ray across the floor. My father braced himself for a night on the dirt, for there was no mat. Dropping his basket, he lay flat so that the guard could put the iron shackles on his feet. He could not see whether they were fastened to the ground or the walls of packed earth. He heard the sound of the brackets being locked into place and could feel the icy weight of the iron above his swollen feet.

The guard took the flashlight and left the cell. Alone in total darkness, my father joined his hands under his neck to support his head and prevent dirt from entering his shirt collar. Save for an occasional tennis or badminton game in Đà Nẵng, he was not used to strenuous activity. The journey had taken all his strength.

Above him the men murmured to each other, their unintelligible voices drifting down to the cell. The guards had left the hut. My father's companions were tired, and before long it was still. Straining to hear the rustling leaves outside, my father became aware of the cries of monkeys and the songs of owls and other night birds, which made a savage background to his thoughts. He worried that his family had also been incarcerated or perhaps harmed, and that my mother had been interrogated. He wondered about how his parents and his sister and her family had survived the attack. He also thought about my brother, who at that hour was beginning a new day half a world away.

The wilderness symphony carried on. My father thought of the questions he knew he would have to answer. How could he best maintain the dignity and composure of an official of the government of South Việt Nam, let alone be careful not to betray its secrets? As his watch ticked behind his ears, he felt the simple pain of knowing that time was passing. A minute in captivity was an eternity.

∾ "Please sit down. I trust you're well rested," the elder of the two men said. "We will work with you tonight. I represent the National Liberation Front."

My father thought how blatant it was that someone with this man's definite Northern accent should pretend to be from the Southern front. The men were facing him across a low table made of branches and split bamboo alongside the guards' hut. The prisoners had had a day of rest. It had rained intermittently, and until evening it was humid. My father was the first to be ordered over for his initial interrogation by the enemy just after dinner, which consisted of rice, wild vegetables, and salt.

"You must tell us all about yourself—your family back-ground, your duties and responsibilities within the machinery of the puppet government, all the agencies you have worked for," said my father's captor. "Cigarette?"

"Thank you," my father said as the younger man handed him a box of matches.

"Remember, you must report all details accurately. Your release depends on a complete and honest declaration." The man, somewhere in his fifties, was dark-skinned, and his khaki uniform was faded. A semblance of a mustache twitched above his lips. "We have a policy of amnesty for those whose attitudes are truthful and cooperative." His companion, thinner, also wearing a faded uniform, sat stony-faced next to him, hands clasped between his legs. The evening dampness grew with each gust of wind.

My father maintained a serious yet dispassionate tone. "I am a public functionary of the Republic of South Việt Nam. I think you already know that." He had heard the guards asking other prisoners about him. "I mainly encourage and monitor the implementation of the government's administrative projects. I don't know how or why they were first conceived, nor do I know the details."

He tried to gauge the reaction of his two opponents. All intercourse with his captors, he knew, would be an intellectual battle. His interrogators remained passive. "Give us some examples, concretely," said the older one.

"Well, we coordinate what is done at various levels of government, and work with different government ministries to build schools, roads, bridges—that kind of thing. Or we might help establish and manage rural health clinics and such. We—"

"So you do nothing but good work. It seems that you too are involved in revolutionary work!"

My father did not respond.

"I'm impressed that you do not abuse and oppress the People," the cadre said. "Or do you?"

"I can only tell the truth," replied my father. "I'm sure you do not want me to tell lies, even if they fit your viewpoint or expectations."

The two investigators exchanged glances. The older one spoke. "Actually, we are thoroughly aware of your activities. We already know all the details you're giving us. But go on."

From his questions about my father's travels in Europe in the 1950s, and his two later stays in the United States, the cadre apparently assumed he had some connection with the Central Intelligence Agency. In the North, only high-ranking members of the Communist party who had impeccable proletarian backgrounds dating back two or three generations, or members who had made significant contributions to the revolution, were permitted to go abroad. The two men believed that the Southern half of the country was, like other capitalist nations, a disorderly place plagued by rampant social ills which was completely controlled by the United States.

"That's enough for now," the Việt Cộng cadre said, standing

up abruptly. "Tomorrow you will write down the things you reported tonight."

When my father lay down on the dirt floor for a second night, he realized that if he were to write down what he had said in his oral statement the next day, it meant they would stay on for at least another day. The cold room with its odor yet provided some comfort compared to the pains of another march over rugged hills and humid jungles. *The longer I stay here, the better; our soldiers will rescue us*, he thought.

It rained again the next day, and no one arrived to rescue my father and the other prisoners. Sitting on a stool, he bent over sheets of paper on a plank of wood across his lap and began to write down the details of what he had said the night before. The awning that extended from the roof of the guards' hut barely protected him from the rain. A guard had agreed to give back his glasses. But now another guard questioned why he was not wearing them. "I thought you needed them to write."

"I mostly need them to see things far away."

"I'll reconsider the decision. Be prepared to give them back." The Việt Cộng disdained the wearing of glasses as characteristic only of members of the intellectual elite.

Around the compound, other prisoners were also composing their written reports. Some had been assigned to accompany soldiers and young tribal men to a nearby village in search of food. The Việt Cộng offered their frequent reliance on villagers for food as proof that they had ample support among the people. "The locals probably don't have a choice," my father whispered to a prisoner nearby. "They're so isolated they will believe the Communist propaganda, and be forced to give the Việt Cộng food or shelter."

The rain continued as my father went on with his task, stopping often to contemplate the yellowed sheets he had been given. The paper was thick and coarse, his pen a worn nib tied to an unpolished chopstick. An old vial held the thick ink. Though the soldiers habitually hid it, the poverty of the Hà Nội regime reached down to the fields.

Before dinner, a soldier asked for the report.

My father hesitated. "I am not done yet."

"I'll give it back to you tomorrow." The Việt Cộng did not want him to correct what he had already written.

The guards gathered the inmates in the hut after dinner and made them listen to exaggerated radio reports about the success of the attack on Huế. A Hà Nội writer and member of the Communist politburo spoke in support of the Việt Cộng. They sounded rehearsed. A woman identified as a peasant seemed unnaturally joyful as she talked, using phrases nearly identical to those of speakers before her, of the "glorious victory of our troops," her hatred for the "American puppet regime," and her "complete belief in the inevitable liberation of the whole of South Việt Nam." The program concluded with a student chorus performing a song with the refrain "I love my uncle, the liberation fighter."

The prisoners went on writing their reports. My father took his time, hoping to delay the continued trek through the jungle. After seven days they were ordered to pack up for another journey.

At the request of the Việt Cộng, the local people brought each of the men a dried hollowed-out melon to hold water for the trip. The prisoners assembled outside the hut. In the morning light they looked tired and pale. A young man asked, "Excuse me, have the rest of you had any bowel movements?"

"Nothing's going in, how can there be anything going out?" retorted the man standing next to my father.

"Perhaps they're moving us because there isn't anything to eat here. But there's only one direction, up the mountains and into the jungle. What is there to eat there?" said my father. He still hoped that Southern soldiers were near, forcing the Việt Cộng to move.

"Perhaps they'll bring us to a real liberated zone this time."

"I doubt that there's any food in the so-called liberated zone."

A Việt Cộng soldier called out to them to begin the march. "It rained so much last night, there are bound to be a lot of leeches," he warned.

My father contemplated the path leading out of the compound, which wound its way along the stream through thick bushes, roots and branches crossing it like a thousand snakes. There had been no medicine in the holding camp, and the cuts on the bottoms of his feet had not healed. He had found some string to tie his sandals back together, and he now again wrapped his feet in pieces of cloth. It was difficult to walk. The men's wrists were tied together with coconut rope. Then each was roped to another man, and they all marched away in single file.

Leaving the compound, they entered an area of dense foliage, with branches and leaves hanging low over the prisoners' heads. My father's labored steps made him and his companion fall to the back of the line. He was also attempting to stall, in the hope that the Southern soldiers he believed were on their trail would catch up. It was a mistake: leeches aroused by the passage of the men up ahead now attacked him relentlessly, sticking to his neck, his wrists, his bleeding feet, hanging inside his shirt and trousers. Pausing to remove them only made him a target for more. Since they did not sting, not until blood dripped from the places where they had attached themselves did he become aware of them. "I'll give you something for your wounds when we get to the new camp," a guard at the rear said. "That camp has everything."

The new camp turned out to be a set of dilapidated dormitories, also built of branches and bamboo sticks, facing each other across an empty yard, with a smaller shack used as a kitchen. My father and his fellow captives arrived at night, and met the

prisoners who were already there the next morning. The old and
sick were weaving baskets and mats; younger men were out
collecting manioc and dead branches to burn in cooking fires.

Once more the prisoners were told to observe the rules,
listening halfheartedly to the soldiers' counsel to apply themselves
to their reeducation—the content of which was never specified—
and to believe absolutely not only that the party would grant
them amnesty for their cooperation but that the revolution would
inevitably be victorious. My father began to doubt the idea that
if lies are repeated often enough, they become believable. It was
sad, he thought, that the cadres could not be trusted, even when
they spoke the truth.

In his first days at the camp he tried to learn more about
his fellow inmates, wondering why some had been arrested. A
man of over sixty presented himself as a "representative of the
people" from a small village. A young man complained that he
had been detained for two years, with no sentence passed, no
reeducation started. A civilian doctor thought he had been captured simply because the Việt Cộng needed medical help.

"You shouldn't ask too many questions about the people
here. Don't get too close to them," an old inmate warned my
father. Despite this warning, my father did befriend Võ Thành
Minh.

"Didn't you live in a tent in Geneva in 1954, protesting the
treaty dividing our country?"

The old man nodded, his few strands of white beard fluttering below his thin, pale face.

"I remember you from my primary school days. My teacher
was a Boy Scout leader and brought you to our class for a visit."

"It's been a long time," the man said. One of the founders
of the Boy Scout movement in Việt Nam, he had resisted Hồ Chí
Minh's attempt to incorporate the youths under his care into the
nascent Vietnamese Communist front in 1945. "I've heard a lot
about you, too," he continued. "But let's talk later."

~ "Go up to see the committee," a Việt Cộng soldier ordered. Interrogation sessions were to begin again before higher-ranking cadres. My father followed the soldier to a set of huts he had not noticed before on the other side of the hill, each large enough to house a table and a few chairs. Inside one of the huts was a cadre with large eyes whom he had seen at the previous camp, and who looked strangely familiar.

"Be honest," the man said after inquiring about my father's health. Neither he nor his fellow interrogator smiled. "The Revolution has eyes and ears everywhere—the Revolution knows all about you, and all about the puppet regime. That's why we're winning the war. Your release will depend on how honest you are. Tell us concretely about your background, and your activities in the Sài Gòn government."

While maintaining an appearance of attentiveness to the already well-worn introduction, my father observed the Việt Cộng cadre who sat facing him. He was a tall man of over forty, with a long face and loose limbs. As my father again described in an abstract way his work in the South Vietnamese administration, the man's face remained expressionless.

"Your report sounds like a class lecture on government. Give us the actual details."

"I will need time to remember where we built everything, the schools and roads and so on," he replied. "In any case, such details must be well known to you already, as you've said."

"You're being obstinate!" the cadre exclaimed. Such an outburst was unusual: it was rare that a Việt Cộng soldier revealed his emotions. The cadre now reverted to my father's early years, interrupting often to ask about rather intimate family details.

"I know you are from an antirevolutionary feudal family," he said.

My father's face reddened. "I take responsibility for my own actions. Please leave my family and my ancestors in peace."

Neither the cadre nor his partner uttered a word. My father

eyed his opponent. Suddenly he remembered where he had seen his face before: the Việt Cộng soldier was a distant cousin, Bình. His Quảng Trị accent should have given him away. He had joined the Việt Minh, precursor to the Communist movement, and gone north in 1954.

My father showed no recognition, however; family ties, he knew, must yield to party loyalty. The cadre would put himself in danger if he offered any sign of sympathy. My father mentally reversed roles, imagining himself as Bình's inquisitor. He was sure he would not hesitate to lend help if his cousin were imprisoned in South Việt Nam.

"Tell me about the Americans' intentions and secret plans, and the competition between political groups in the South," Bình said.

"The Americans' plans wouldn't be secret if I knew about them. If I had been working in the capital, with wide contacts, I might know a few things. But as you know, I have always worked in minor and faraway provinces."

Bình's face showed his frustration. "Well, you should rest," he said. "Tomorrow you will write it all down, in more detail."

Nightly interrogation sessions were always followed by the writing of the daily reports. The inmates were separated while they wrote. My father was alone most of the time. The questions asked in the sessions would often be the same, the answers given again and again. From what my father saw, the Việt Cộng did not use torture as a method of getting information. But the multiple reports were dangerous. No matter how one explained it, a discrepancy between two reports would be the subject of repeated, long-drawn-out cross-examinations. Prisoners who displayed any uncertainty, or whose minds and wills were not absolutely firm, would ultimately grow impatient or weary. They would lose control in the face of their determined questioners. At such moments the Việt Cộng would throw seeds of doubt into the inmates' minds, thus beginning the process of reeducation.

One morning as my father began writing his report, he was startled by mortar explosions coming from the back of the area where the Việt Cộng soldiers were quartered. "That was our firepower! Our cannon!" one of them yelled. "We did that!" Some moments later two helicopters appeared, circled the area twice, then flew off. "See, they can't see us—they didn't see us," the soldiers cried out.

Bảo Lộc, the thirty-three-year-old deputy mayor in charge of finance in Huế, came over, pretending to ask for ink. He had been captured the same night as my father.

"They lied. Fighting is still going on," my father said.

The prisoners had been told over and over that "the puppet army has been annihilated" and "the People have achieved total victory." The appearance of the helicopters refuted the Việt Cộng, but it also disappointed the prisoners.

"Maybe they won't come back," Lộc said and left.

My father returned to his report. A while later he heard female voices and laughter from the bottom of the hill. He lifted his head. Through the branches he saw a group of tribal women bending over the stream, looking for fish. They must have come from far away, since there was no village in the surrounding area. The women, the leaves still wet with dew, and the sunshine reflected on the water made a colorful, peaceful scene reminiscent of a painting by Gauguin. My father allowed himself a moment of optimism, reflecting that he was not completely cut off from the world. At the same time, the feeling of comfort the sight of the mountain women brought was quickly dispelled by the thought that though he could see it, he could take no part in such a tableau: ordinary, peaceful, and free.

The next journey was even harder. Along the trail my father was now following, the Việt Cộng—and their prisoners of war—had built a series of camps. "We're moving to a self-sufficient camp this time," a Việt Cộng soldier told my father. "They grow things there, and there is livestock."

The men headed west along rugged, hilly paths as they began the climb to the Trường Sơn Mountains, lying on a north-south axis, seemingly the spine of Việt Nam. The Việt Cộng had long used the country's jungles as a sanctuary, building a trail that would ultimately reach from the North to the South, crossing over to neighboring Laos and Cambodia in many places. Hundreds of thousands of men and women, carrying tons of weapons and ammunition, followed it southward. Soon becoming known as the Hồ Chí Minh Trail, it was bombed relentlessly by American forces. Under heavy foliage, my father and his fellow captives did not yet think of danger from bombs. The Việt Cộng pushed the prisoners through the jungle until a storm forced them to stop.

The prisoners sat leaning against the trees at dusk. The soldiers stretched out ponchos and hung hammocks from the branches. My father signaled to Minh, the founder of the Boy Scouts, to join him under a big tree. Minh held a raincoat over their heads.

"They won't hear us in this rain," said my father.

Minh nodded.

"How did you get arrested?"

"I was in Huế for Tết. I went with a Catholic priest and a Buddhist monk to the American military headquarters to ask them to stop the gunfire so we could bury the dead. The Việt Cộng accused me of surrendering to the Americans."

"Didn't you explain?"

"We had a white flag. A Việt Cộng came to my house, told me that I should meet with their officials, just for a discussion. Instead I am a prisoner like you."

"Do they know your background?"

"I guess. I've reported that Hồ Chí Minh wanted me to be part of his government in 1945. Actually, they wanted to use the

Boy Scout movement. They wanted to add 'National Salvation' to the name of our Boy Scout association. It was ridiculous. I left for Switzerland, later went to France and the United States, came back three years ago. Could have stayed."

"I'm sorry."

"I don't believe they can win the war. Yet our side is divided, and some people just don't seem to worry that we are at war."

The storm was subsiding. On one side of the mountain water flowed angrily downstream. A Việt Cộng soldier ordered the men to prepare for dinner. Minh whispered in French, "I'm going to escape."

"I'll come," said my father.

The prisoners gathered wood to make a fire. It took a long time to light the wet branches. "It's all right," said a guard. "A big fire would attract enemy planes." The smoke from the fire was heavy. Following it upward with his gaze, through the branches my father could see nothing but tears from heaven.

🔊 Bình again faced my father at the first interrogation session at the new camp. Accompanied by a white-haired cadre my father had never seen, he was now solicitous and jovial. Offering my father a cigarette, the older man explained, "This is local tobacco, produced by the tribal people from the region. Not as good as the cigarettes in the North, called Tam Đảo. You haven't tasted them, have you? They're good." The man turned to Bình. "Let's make sure our friend gets some when you get the next shipment."

The cadre took a drag on his cigarette. "You know, the South is so poor. In the North we're better off—we have everything, even during wartime."

My father listened in silence. Looking straight at him, Bình smiled. "Dear cousin, I have an idea."

The word "cousin" sounded sweet. My father expected a trap.

"You know General Hoàng Xuân Lãm well," Bình continued. "Perhaps you can persuade him to join the Revolution."

"What exactly do you mean?"

"We don't mean that he should move his troops away from the liberated zones, or stage a revolt against the puppet regime. Our proposal is simple. Let's say he were no longer to fight the Revolution so adamantly. He could distance himself from Sài Gòn; perhaps later he could take a neutral role."

"How—a military commander under the central government?"

"Well, maybe you could convince him to join the Revolution outright, then," came the reply. "It'll be your path to a pardon. The Revolution will recognize General Lãm's contribution."

My father tried another tack. "I am now in the hands of the Revolution. Who's going to believe me? It's not likely that in a short amount of time I would have switched sides. If I am released, however, everyone will recognize the Revolution's generosity. Maybe then I could persuade others."

There was a long pause before Bình spoke. "We'll discuss it." The soldier took my father back to his dormitory. The matter was never raised again.

One morning, a soldier named Thuần, who looked more like a university student than a cadre, said to my father, "I'd like you to translate these." My father glanced at the handwritten documents. They were in misspelled English. Reading the pages carefully when Thuần had left, he realized that the words were those of American prisoners. Someone had copied various parts of the "report" they had written for their captors, mixing unconnected paragraphs, but my father was able to glean some details about the two Americans in the camp. One was Weaver, a State Department official, who was once the first secretary at the American embassy in Tokyo and was later sent to Việt Nam as an adviser to the police in Huế, where he was captured. He had been brought to the camp before my father. The other was Godwin, an army officer stationed at the Huế airport.

The next day Weaver, a robust man of about forty, was sunbathing outside the door of his dormitory. Godwin slumped against a tree at the far corner, looking pale and sick. My father knew from his report that Godwin was thirty-two. He resisted the urge to approach the American and comfort him. Neither Godwin nor Weaver was included in the labor details required of the rest of the camp's prisoners. Besides the inmates' diet of manioc and wild cabbage, Godwin was given tinned food and milk because of his illness.

In the humid jungle, the prisoners had little food or clothing. All but the Americans were made to grow manioc in the clearings near the camp. Of the forty inmates, close to ten at any one time were so sick with malaria, tuberculosis, diarrhea, or constipation that they were unable to work and instead stayed in bed in a narrow room called the clinic. A nurse of dubious training complained endlessly about the lack of medicine; the small amount available inevitably went first to the cadres. The nurse alone decided whether a person could rest, and at times gravely ill prisoners were still sent to the fields. Coming back one day, an inmate dropped the logs from his shoulders and fell to the ground, coughing up bright red blood. He later died of tuberculosis.

Within his first week at the camp my father learned of two deaths, both of young men, whose bodies were borne to their shallow graves on a reinforced mat that was normally used for carrying rubbish. No sheet or mat could be spared to wrap either body. There was no service, no eulogy. The graves were left unmarked.

Minh was sure that, if he could escape, he could survive in the jungle. My father had doubts. He knew that they could not set aside any of the already inadequate portions of manioc or potatoes given to them each day, and without money they could not buy food. Villagers would turn them in as soon as they asked for food. My father wanted to delay any attempt to escape until after the rainy season. Peace talks had already started in Paris. If peace was restored, they would be released.

Two months later, in June of 1968, Minh appeared at my father's window. Heavy rain had prevented the men from going to the fields. Strong winds howled through the branches. "I'll look for your family," Minh whispered, then ran off.

By noon the soldiers were quietly looking for him. My father maintained a surface calmness, but could not concentrate on his daily report. Other prisoners went on with their tasks, weaving baskets or mats but whispering among themselves.

Late in the afternoon, a group of prisoners gathered near the kitchen as two soldiers dragged Minh to his isolation cell. He was soaked. He seemed tired, but his face exuded serenity. When my father heard the sound of the iron shackles, the pain he felt for Minh made him forget that he would have been in the same position had he gone with him.

The Paris peace talks had created eddies of excitement among the prisoners. In sending its delegates to the negotiating table, Hà Nội implicitly recognized the government of Sài Gòn, though it still insisted that the National Liberation Front was the sole legal power representing the people of the South. The beginning of talks meant that the status of prisoners was now an issue to be addressed in the dialogue, and the Việt Cộng would do well to be sure that their conditions did not become the focus of international outrage. Nevertheless, for my father and his fellow captives, things changed only for the worse: the farther they moved into the mountains, the more defiant of international law the soldiers became, and security measures became stricter. Moreover, because the manioc crop had been destroyed by the heavy rain, the prisoners' diet worsened.

My father had lost weight. He had little energy and suffered spells of dizziness. His left foot was almost paralyzed; he needed to use both hands just to slip on a worn-out sandal. "If the peace talks get anywhere and we're released, you'll be happy to crawl home," another prisoner said. Washing his face in the stream one morning, he was shocked to see that half his hair had turned white. He later remembered the day in a poem:

> *Forty narrow rooms, so much suffering;*
> *Separated by walls as thick as miles,*
> *We each glimpse a piece of blue sky above the trees*
> *And wonder in what direction our home lies.*
>
> *Someone remembers his white-haired father,*
> *Another a mother's tearful eyes,*
> *Another the single pillow of a wife made a widow,*
> *And the dry lips of children*
> *Who miss a loved one's kisses.*

A month had passed when one day a Việt Cộng soldier rounded up Tứ the railroad official, Lộc the deputy mayor, and my father. "Come with me—it's time for exercise," he said. Had there been a development in the Paris talks? Were they being prepared for release? What about Minh? Daily exercise sessions, consisting of long walks up and down mountain paths, continued for about a week for the three men. When the guards ordered prisoners to quickly weave a rattan hammock, my father could not restrain his curiosity. "Are we being moved?" he asked one of the friendlier officials. The man nodded.

"We must be close to the seventeenth parallel. Are we going to the North?"

"We are going where there is everything."

A few weeks after the week of strengthening exercises, my father was given a nylon hammock, a pair of canvas shoes, a hat, and a large piece of plastic to use as a raincoat. Supplies for a long journey, he thought. He wondered if he should try to check on what might be going on in the kitchen to see if extra provisions were being prepared. Before he could, however, a Việt Cộng cadre told him, "We may leave tomorrow."

Packing that night, my father thought, the farther away I am taken, the harder it will be to get home. He was able to say only a few words of farewell to Minh, who had just emerged from a disciplinary cell. In a cryptic line of poetry he had composed in classical Chinese, he expressed to Minh his regret that on this journey he would be deprived of a worthy companion and an ally.

At seven in the morning, Lộc, Tứ, and my father were gathered at the gates. My father wore his blue pajama trousers. "That's clever," Lộc said. Should they run into Republican soldiers, the sky blue pants would identify him as a captive of the Việt Cộng. As the two men were being tied together, Weaver waited beneath a tree. A few seconds later two soldiers carried out the rattan hammock. The young cadre, Thuần, one of the Việt Cộng who were to accompany the prisoners, called out, "Godwin!"

Leaning on a walking stick, the other American inmate stepped out of the clinic. By now extremely weak and emaciated, he took long moments to cross the narrow courtyard toward the others, then struggled up the steps to the gate. Thuần signaled for him to lie down on the hammock.

Once Godwin was lying flat, the two soldiers hoisted the hammock and the little group marched through the gate. The prisoners were reminded of the crude burials they had seen during their first weeks in the camp they were now leaving. With Godwin on his stretcher, the four other captives and their guards resembled a funeral procession. A funeral for a living soul, my father thought.

The prisoners forced their feet forward through the jungle, climbing up and down hills, the footpaths blurring in front of their eyes, on a seemingly endless trek. After marching them all day, the Việt Cộng would lead them to a rest stop for the night, usually a primitive shack inhabited by a tribal family. The prisoners would be allowed a quick meal before collapsing on a dirt floor or straw mat. The improved fare provided for the journey did not alleviate their hunger. Realizing he must keep his mind active, my father would construct scenarios in which he escaped or was released. He resolved, in the moments before succumbing to sleep, to learn more about the enemy. Mostly, though, he worried about his family and the progress of the war. In the morning the march would start again.

"Lie straight!" a frustrated cadre yelled at Godwin. "If you keep curling up like that, I'll lose my balance. You'll die before you can count to two!" He and the other soldier bearing Godwin's hammock wrestled with branches swaying in the wind, blocking the path, and strove to keep from sliding on the steep hills. Godwin was nearly unconscious, his eyes sunken, his constant moans the only indication that he was still breathing.

It was now the middle of July. Every day the sky was a mass of oppressive rain clouds the color of iron, and the paths twisting through the jungle were usually a mess of mud hiding dead branches and roots. The young guide frequently lost his bearings and led the men into wild parts of the forest, at times taking three-quarters of an hour to get back out, and longer to find the way again. Soaked from head to toe with rain and shivering in the wind, the prisoners were often whipped by thick bamboo branches. Water filled their canvas shoes. Tied in pairs, they would pull each other to the ground if one slipped and fell.

Godwin died at night, while the men were at a rest stop. No sound had come from him for several hours, and by the time the soldiers' suspicions were roused it was too late. Godwin had been a quiet man, always sick. He had survived his tour of duty making maps in Huế, away from the warfare faced by other American servicemen. He had been due to return to the United States, but decided to stay a little longer in Huế, for Tết.

"They shouldn't have moved him from the camp in this weather," my father said.

"He would have been sick all the same," Lộc replied.

"Yeah, but I don't think he would have died."

Thuần and the senior cadres whispered among themselves before writing out a death certificate, which they asked my father to translate into English. Tứ, Lộc, and my father all refused Thuần's request to sign their names as witnesses. Weaver too shook his head: "I am under orders from my government not to sign any document prepared by the enemy." Gathering the captives together, Thuần pleaded with them. "I realize that you have had nothing to do with this unfortunate event. The soldiers and cadres will take the responsibility. Tùng has signed for the technical end of things; he's a nurse who was brought along specifically to look after the American. You all saw that he died of illness—it was not an accident. Please sign your names, just to confirm a truthful report of his death."

My father and the other South Vietnamese prisoners relented. The nurse stayed behind to bury Godwin.

The next day's travels, in drier weather, brought the men to yet another camp, two thatched huts on a hill. Overhearing the camp officials and his escorts, my father learned that the camp was in his home province of Quảng Trị. Far from feeling the happiness of a man brought to the land where he spent his childhood, he was overcome with the pain of knowing the group was approaching the seventeenth parallel, which separated the two parts of Việt Nam. It would not be long now before they would be out of the Southern half altogether.

Six months after Việt Cộng soldiers led him away from the government guest house in Huế, my father had become a frail man, about to be taken into enemy territory. He could not sleep that night. At the same time, it was a moment to reaffirm his faith, as he later described in a poem he called "Crossing the Parallel":

March, march on, on this endless path
That does not cease its climb up the Trường Sơn range.
Leaves are woven into branches, the trees tall and taller still;
Sunlight, in bright pieces like flowers, chases my footsteps;
The angry water of the falls flows violently down and downward—
But to where, and does it not carry shades of the homeland?
And will it flow into the ill-willed river
That divides a nation in half, its water running in two different
    courses?
My feet fall apart; the walking stick I can no longer hold.
My throat has burned dry, lips melted into one,
While my heart beats fast and my breathing bursts my lungs.
Still the mountain pass is high above,
And my steps cannot be slowed.

Move, move on—I am forced from my mother's land,
My exile's steps bloodied, my heart wounded,
While around me are tides of enmity;
White into black, even absolute truths have been perverted.

The afternoon folds its wings over this desolate jungle;
Let us pause, this moment, where birds and streams meet like lovers.
I do not fear these formidable miles,
For I am this very night on the free shores still.

These flickering flames fail to make ashes of my sorrow;
The wind insists on blowing separation into my faithful soul.
My Southern land, will I ever return to you?
Or will my faith not blossom, red as the poincianas along the
    River of Perfume?

FOUR

Leaving Home

On the streets of Đà Nẵng in early 1975 I heard more and more people with a Huế or the stronger Quảng Trị accent. Visiting friends, I would find every corner of their houses occupied by strange faces. Every family was host to a dozen refugees from towns near the northern border. The American troops had left, and despite some heroic battles the Republican soldiers were severely demoralized. The corruption of their officers made their condition worse. The Việt Cộng were looking more and more like victors. They had overtaken Quảng Trị, South Việt Nam's northernmost province. Next in line would be Huế, where many members of both my mother's and my father's families lived; Đà Nẵng was just over an hour's drive farther.

Our house too was full of relatives. Diệu-Hà had gone to study at the University of Toledo, in Ohio, but my grandmother, frail and bent, came with my aunt Xuân-Liễu, my uncle Vịnh, and their two children to live with us. Others arrived within the next few days, their belongings stacked everywhere. There was no place where I could be alone—but by then I was never home myself, spending day and night at school.

An impatient mass of refugees gathered outside our school one morning in March, demanding that the classrooms be turned over to them as a temporary shelter. The handyman kept the gate locked while teachers and students rushed to carry tables and chairs out of the classrooms. The last time our school had been used as a refugee center, following a southern thrust by the Việt Cộng in 1972, our classroom furniture was burned as firewood for cooking. The refugees had stayed for over a month, and taught us plenty of lessons.

For two mad weeks, we students organized ourselves into groups to help the refugees. With virtually no leadership, we somehow divided up the tasks: some of us cooked massive pots of rice while others escorted the wounded back and forth between our school and the local hospital. More daring friends rode motorcycles to the outskirts of town, distributing bread and cooked rice. They came back with stories of being attacked by starving refugees who had been stuck for days in traffic jams on Highway 1. Buses, cars, bicycles, three-wheeled vehicles fashioned out of motorcycles, and people on foot piled over the Hải Vân Pass toward Đà Nẵng. Folks wound their way south, their clothes and valuables packed in bundles and tied on top of cars or on the sides of motorcycles already laden with three or four people. Some simply carried belongings on their shoulders.

Some students came back wounded. Many of us stayed in the school, never bathing or changing out of the clothes we had been wearing the day the mob of refugees appeared at the gate. The school uniform, a white shirt over dark blue trousers, distinguished us from the tattered refugees. For the first days at least, we also stood out as the only ones who had the energy to move about. The refugees took over the classrooms, then spilled over into the corridors and staircases, sitting on straw mats or sheets spread out on the floor. The school was host to a thousand zombies.

In the middle of that inert jumble of people, we rushed around, feeling useful and important.

"Hey, Thành! Get me some water!"

"Wait! I'll help you with the rice—you can't carry all that by yourself!"

"Lan, can you go get Professor Tiến? And get someone to bring some blankets, too." Lan, or whoever, would dash away and not be seen for an hour. It was easy to be distracted from one errand by another, more urgent task. With everything to be done, we became experts at everything. Girls fell into roles as nurses, applying bandages or spreading ointment on burns suffered by kids playing with the cooking fires. Boys went from house to house asking for donations: money, food, clothes, blankets. I spent a couple of hours one day distributing ice cubes. I'd bought a large block of ice, then chipped it into small pieces with an ice pick. In the extreme heat, dozens of kids had developed rashes all over their bodies. They kept rubbing the ice on themselves until it melted; then, dripping wet, they'd come back for more. Some chewed on the ice cubes, making cracking noises that gave me goose bumps.

On a couple of mornings I found myself chopping wood, cutting hair, or escorting the wounded and sick to Đà Nẵng's hospital, which was a few blocks away from the school and now overflowed with people. Instead of returning to the school, I was often drafted to help out at the hospital. Once I squeezed into the front of a flatbed truck for a lift back to the school, but two men already on the truck overruled the driver. I found myself an hour later on the edge of town, where dozens of severely wounded people needed to be transported to the hospital. We made it back past midnight, the truck full of injured refugees and soldiers. The highway remained packed with still more people making their way to Đà Nẵng. I stayed at the hospital for the next two hours, helping the wounded onto stretchers and carrying them inside. As I left, most of them were lying in the hallways. There were no more beds.

The wounded people horrified me. The bleeding of their injuries was difficult to stomach, and at sixteen, I learned to avoid people's eyes. More than physical pain, they reflected the mortification in having to lie exposed and helpless on the stretchers. Others who were helping out shared my difficulty. We worked in silence: no one knew what to say in the face of such enormous suffering. Yet we came back to the hospital again and again and did what was needed. The hospital scenes would return years later, vivid images in my nightmares. I would wake up thinking I once again smelled the odor of an overcrowded hospital, of human sweat and unbathed bodies, intensified by the tropical heat.

My prolonged absence from home began to upset my family. My grandmother felt neglected, and my mother was overcome with shame that none of us tended to her. My mother's school was also hosting thousands of displaced people, and she wasn't at home much either. Diệu-Qùynh's mental state had improved, but she remained shy and feared contact with most people. In that house full of relatives we managed to leave her a room where she could be by herself. She stayed there most days. It didn't occur to me that since I was gone, no one was around to calm her during her frequent tantrums at night. Diệu-Qùynh had a habit of waking up suddenly, crying or shouting. My mother would rush into her room, and Diệu-Qùynh would throw things at her. I was the only one who could coax her back to bed. But Aunt Xuân-Liễu later told me, "She never did act up during the nights you were gone."

One tiring day followed another, but the hectic pace kept us from reflecting on our situation. We functioned in long bursts of energy each day before collapsing in odd places. I lived just across the street from school, but because my bedroom floor had been appropriated by relatives, coming in late meant waking them up, stumbling over bodies and bags. I started to sleep at school, going home only in the afternoons to shower and change, then disappearing across the street within half an hour. "But take this," my grandmother would always say, handing me some food, which I would share with friends.

Tired as we were, we would stay up late. My best friend, Khủỏng-An, came back from a walk one night all excited. "Come on, come on!" he said to a group of us at the school. "There's a couple making love, over there!"

"Making love? You're sure?" we asked. "Where?"

"Come on! I just saw them!"

We rushed out to try to get a glimpse of the intrepid lovers. Later that same night, after everyone was asleep, Khủỏng-An and I wandered around the school.

"Have you seen your girlfriend lately?" Khủỏng-An asked me. The question was disconcerting. I hadn't even thought about Thu-Hảo, whom I had met a year before, for days. "It's your damn Boy Scout attitude. 'Help, help!' Yeah, go help all those poor people!"

"What's the matter?"

"They can take care of themselves!" he snapped. "And what're you gonna do when you leave? What about Thu-Hảo?"

"What do you mean—leave?"

"Aren't you?"

"I don't know!" In truth, I had not thought about leaving Đà Nẵng, and I was surprised at Khủỏng-An's sudden anger.

Our friendship had first grown out of rebellion against my family's wish that I befriend only kids from an elite background. Khủỏng-An's family was poor. I liked him because of his openness and his artistic nature. I spent time learning many poems he had discovered in books I never knew existed. Among my friends, Khủỏng-An lacked charm and social skills, but he was nevertheless popular because of his musical talent. As a singer, he could easily switch from French ballads to mournful Vietnamese lovers' laments to American pop songs, and he sang them all well. Even my mother, who disapproved of Khủởng-An's influence on me, was delighted by his voice.

Khủởng-An's love affair with Thúy-Loan, a classmate, was open and defiant in a society that frowned on youthful romances. Thúy-Loan and Khủởng-An often kissed and held hands in public, and they became close to me because I encouraged them. Thu-Hảo and I, by contrast, were shy, typical of Vietnamese teenagers in love. "Being in love" meant spending long hours every night carefully composing tender letters to one another, or copying lyrics for each other, lines from popular songs that moved us madly: "I Need You" by America, for instance.

We would calculate our morning walk to school so that we could pass each other, furtively handing over the nightly out-pouring of affection. Thu-Hảo and I were also in the same English class, which met in the evenings. We would revel in the few moments before class, during which we could stand near each other in silence on a balcony at the school. Afterwards we would ride our bicycles along the river, or up and down the small residential streets covered by branches of royal poincianas. Our love was expressed by lending each other tapes of those senti-mental songs, or making one another gifts of, say, a book of poetry, thoughtfully wrapped in rare Chinese paper. Though cer-tainly our relationship had a "puppy love" quality to it, we soon became so serious that her father forbade her to see me. After that, Khủởng-An served as a messenger between us.

During the second week of March I finally noticed that I had not seen many of my friends for days. When anyone asked, "Have you seen Thúy?" we would assume that our classmate was engaged in chores somewhere. But others went to look for friends, only to find locked doors: people were leaving town. Some were already refugees in cities farther south. Huế by now had fallen to the Communists, and Việt Cộng troops were gathered near High-way 1, at the foot of the mountains. Only the Hải Vân Pass stood between them and Đà Nẵng, and conflicting orders from Sài Gòn prevented local military commanders from mobilizing. What Khủởng-An had said about leaving now made sense.

🙢 "How much longer do you plan to live at your school?" My mother's sudden appearance startled me. I hadn't expected her to be home.

"I know, Mạ, but what do you want me to do?" I argued.

"Do you think you could come home sometimes? Do strangers mean more to you now than your own grandmother?"

My mother was fuming, but she kept her voice down. Before I could offer my defense, that I had only been trying to help people who were desperately in need, she gave me her news. "Get yourself packed—you're leaving tomorrow, for Sài Gòn." With her usual ingenuity, she had secured two seats for me and Diệu-Quỳnh on an American flight to the capital, where many of her siblings lived. She herself would have to wait until later to leave. I was not allowed to argue against the decision, or even to have an opinion.

"I don't have time to explain things to you. We're lucky the people down at the American consulate gave me any seats at all," she said. "How can I leave? I'm responsible for thousands of people camping at my school. Besides, your uncle is the superintendent of schools. Would he let me go? Even to be with my children? No!"

"Try to take care of your sister. And study hard," my grandmother said.

Someone helped pack a suitcase for me. I repacked it with my favorite clothes, and included a few books and some photographs from my albums. It was now midafternoon. There were two people I had to see before leaving. While my mother and relatives busied themselves getting Diệu-Quỳnh ready for the trip, I sneaked away from the house.

Finding Khủởng-An at school, I walked with him to a bench

outside the library to tell him the news. He showed no surprise as he silently shifted his feet back and forth beneath him, making patterns on the ground. He was from a large family, and they had no contacts, as my mother did, to help them find a flight out of Đà Nẵng. They didn't have the means to pay for any kind of transportation to a town farther south, or any relatives in Sài Gòn. Once I had told him I would have to leave, I too lapsed into silence.

Khủỏng-An sat, brooding. Finally, tucking his hands under his legs, he said, "I'm not going anywhere."

I avoided his eyes.

"See all those empty houses?" he asked.

"Yeah? What about them?"

"All those people are gone. They're never coming back to those houses. I'm going to loot them!"

In the indirect way that Asians communicate, Khủỏng-An had wounded me, implying that I too deserved to be punished for leaving. We both understood that in fact he would not consider leaving town because of Thúy-Loan. We also knew that besides wanting to say goodbye to him, I came to ask him to contact Thu-Hảo. Unlike him, I was prepared to leave my girlfriend.

That evening, Thu-Hảo and I rode our bicycles down to the river. There we walked along the bank awhile, not speaking. Thu-Hảo had already heard that I was leaving from Khủỏng-An. Reaching the edge of town, we turned into a deserted field off a pier.

Dusk hung over us. The dying sun cast a disquieting orange glow on the rusted pipes and tubing which formed a disorderly pile at our feet. We abandoned our bikes and climbed over a large heap of pipes, then walked to the edge of the pier. Thu-Hảo found a spot for us to sit. Neither of us could find the right words to say. She was crying silently. I found breathing difficult. Finally Thu-Hảo murmured, "Hold me."

I was mortified. She needed the comfort of my arms, and

she was ready to let me hold her, to strengthen our love, and yet I was insensitive to her. In the dying heat of the late March evening, I felt my heart sink. I felt utterly inadequate.

I touched her shoulders, I touched her fingers. I turned this way and that. It took a long time before we were fully embracing one another. I had never held her before. Holding her now meant making a serious commitment—which I was ready to make, but what could I commit to if I was to get on the plane in the morning?

A man came out of an office on the other side of the pier and shouted at us. "What are you doing there? Go away!"

I released Thu-Hảo, and we fled our sanctuary. It then dawned on me that I had never actually said the words I was supposed to say: I had not said goodbye. As we walked beside one another with our bikes, I couldn't break the silence. We wandered over our favorite streets, taking the longest way home. We would be unwelcome at each other's busy houses, and Thu-Hảo's father still terrified me. We stopped at a street corner where the roads to her house and mine separated. In the darkness, I gave Thu-Hảo my aunt's address in Sài Gòn. She gave me a simple necklace.

I tried to write a note to her later that night but couldn't organize my thoughts. I searched my shelves for a volume of prewar poetry, mostly celebrated love poems, which I hoped Khủởng-An could give to her the next morning. After thumbing through the text for some time, I signed it for Thu-Hảo and fell asleep. But I never got a chance to see Khủởng-An, or to ask him to give it to her.

We left for the airport early the next day, my relatives throwing Diệu-Quỳnh's and my bags into my mother's white Peugeot and rushing us off before my grandmother could work herself into a frenzy of worry and sorrow. My mother was calm during the trip to the airport, but I knew she was in agony. I kept quiet too, most of the way. Diệu-Quỳnh occasionally giggled.

The roads were clogged with cars and motorcycles. "Are all these people going to the airport?" I asked. "Do they have permission to enter the airport?"

"Do you think I have permission?" my mother retorted. I had not expected her testy tone. "What do I need permission for? Who's going to check? Everybody's leaving!"

In the event, we were met at the airport by an acquaintance who shepherded us through the crowd and took us to the area reserved for VIPs and foreigners. The room was deathly quiet compared to the reception area. Over the wall of dark wooden panels topped by dirty glass panes we could see women and children selling peanuts and soft drinks. Crates, boxes, and suitcases covering the benches and most of the floor. A mass of people overwhelmed the two Air Việt Nam agents at the main counter, adults waving papers and screaming, their children running back and forth. "A plane is coming in—look, it's landing!" a man announced. Part of the crowd turned to go toward the tarmac. A Western man appeared at the door, followed by a noisy group from outside. A mob descended on him, everyone moving together. The mass of black heads below his pale face and blond hair resembled a squid. The crowd stayed glued to him until two American marines, brandishing their black rifles, dispersed it. "Get away! Get away! Move!" they yelled. The agitated man was escorted to the VIP lounge.

Our guide accompanied us out to the airplane. My mother stood on the tarmac, sobbing. Diệu-Quỳnh gave her private laugh while I reached up to hug my mother. "Please take care of Diệu-Quỳnh. Tell your aunts and uncles I'll be in Sài Gòn in a day or two," she said.

☙ I didn't like Sài Gòn. On previous visits I had never gotten used to the sunshine; the heat was so extreme you could claw at it. The tall, square buildings were unwelcoming. At all hours the wide boulevards were full of people, and the exhaust fumes from thousands of motorcycles made it hard to breathe. It was always incredibly noisy. There was also the ever-present smell of decadence downtown.

Diệu-Quỳnh stayed with my aunt Diệu-Mai the few weeks we were there, while I shuffled between her house and Uncle Phồn-Anh's. When I stayed with him, my uncle would take me to visit Diệu-Quỳnh every day, and I spent my mornings washing her sheets. "I can't deal with them!" my aunt's maid had declared shortly after we arrived. About a year earlier Diệu-Quỳnh had developed the habit of urinating in bed at night. She refused to talk to us about the problem, and we were unable to get her to stop. We supposed it was another symptom of her mental disorder.

"Don't go out," Aunt Diệu-Mai said one morning.

"I was just going to stand at the front gate!" I protested, continuing to tie my shoes to show my determination to leave the house for a while.

"Things are getting bad out there," my aunt warned, but she was resigned to my going. Her eyes did not show anger, but rather retained the sadness that always marked her face. It was a touching sadness, a sadness that, I thought, made Aunt Diệu-Mai exceptionally beautiful.

She was right about the dangers in Sài Gòn. During the second week of my stay the Khmer Rouge had overwhelmed Cambodia's capital, Phnom Penh. A C-5A transport plane which was bearing 243 Vietnamese orphans to foster homes in the United States, blew up at Sài Gòn's Tân Sơn Nhất airport. The accident killed more than 200 of the children—some of whom were reputedly the sons and daughters of government officials and rich families—as well as 43 American officials. Then, just four days later, an air force pilot flying an A-37 jet dropped a bomb on the presidential palace, a few blocks from the American embassy. Sài Gòn went into shock. The Việt Cộng's clandestine radio claimed Communist responsibility, and the American intelligence community talked of political maneuvering by rivals of President

Nguyễn Văn Thiệu. It was enough for my aunt to want to chain me to my bed.

"Watch so you don't get arrested!" Aunt Diệu-Mai said as I sauntered down the back steps of her French-style villa. There were countless refugees in Sài Gòn, and the authorities assumed that the Việt Cộng had sent infiltrators among them. I was also a tall, overweight teenager. Even with my identification card, the military police might not believe I was only sixteen. They had been known to put young men they suspected of being deserters into uniforms and sending them out to the battlefield without checking records, let alone providing any training.

I borrowed a bicycle from my aunt's maid and made my way downtown to the offices of Air Việt Nam, where I asked anyone I could find from Đà Nẵng about my mother. No one could give me any comforting news.

I ran into my classmate Nguyễn Tuyền, who had arrived in Sài Gòn a few days before me, and at whose house in Đà Nẵng, which was a few blocks from mine, I had often spent the afternoon. Tuyền was glad to see me, but we both knew why we were really at the Air Việt Nam office. We shared a few cigarettes on the sidewalk amid the traffic noise, the beggars, and the Vietnamese youth called *yé-yés* who wore colorful Indian shirts and tattered bell-bottom jeans in imitation of American hippies.

"Look at those guys!" I said to Tuyền.

"What about them?"

"When the Việt Cộng get here, they're going to be in a lot of trouble. . . . I'm worried about Khủơng-An."

"For singing American songs?"

"*Yé-yés* like him they'll probably throw in jail," I said. "They'd kill your brother too." Like many young men of our generation, Tuyền's brother had been addicted to heroin for several years. Tuyền and I imagined horrible, torturous deaths for our family and friends left behind.

"Do you think they'll do it?" Tuyền wondered.

"Do what? Kill them?" I thought of the thousands of people who had been buried alive in Huế during the Tết offensive. "I don't know," I said.

"My uncle—remember him?—he said the Việt Cộng would punish guys with long hair, or women wearing nail polish." Tuyền flipped the cigarette butt onto the pavement.

"What about all the kids who went to the lycée with us?"

"I think most of them made it here. I saw Pháp yesterday. His parents aren't here, though."

I worried about my mother. She had two children in college in Ohio, and for two years she had been the head of the Vietnamese-American Friendship Association in Đà Nẵng. Even Tuyền had criticized her pro-American position, but in her prominent public role as a school principal she had to set an example of international goodwill. Her job also gave her the same status as heads of government agencies, which meant that she was required to join the Democratic party. Essentially the party was a machine that ensured President Thiệu's success at the polls— which in any case was guaranteed since he never allowed any other candidates to run against him. Newspapers derided him as Độc Diễn, "Solo-Performance." My mother had to attend events sponsored by both the party and the Vietnamese-American Friendship Association, and since my father was absent I had to escort her, a bored child among adults, for appearance's sake.

Tuyền was ready to leave. "Are you coming back here tomorrow?" he asked.

"Maybe," I said. "Let me know if you have any news."

After a few days at the Air Việt Nam office it was clear that there was no point in waiting for further flights. Đà Nẵng had fallen to the Communists a few days after I left. Phone lines were cut, and there was no other communication. Some people I knew had come south on cramped ships, a horrific journey during which Republican soldiers raped women and killed others to claim their space on board. No one I talked to had any news of my mother.

On the night of April 21 I was at my aunt's, watching President Thiệu on television. For nearly two hours he condemned the United States for abandoning an ally at its greatest crisis. He announced his resignation, complaining that he could not carry out his duties without the support that Presidents Nixon and Ford had promised. My uncle Hải, who had once been private secretary to President Ngô Đình Diệm, threw a hammer at the television set. President Thiệu's image shattered in a split second.

The villas on my aunt's street bustled with people moving furniture, bags, and suitcases into trucks, small vans, and even pedicabs. Two blocks away was a row of elegant residences rented by the various embassies. Here too porters were carrying out crates and suitcases and placing them in waiting trucks. Military men walked up and down the blocks, their rifles at the ready.

At my aunt's house, relatives and visitors debated about leaving the country. "Go if you like. Leave like cowards!" roared Uncle Hải. "My plans are not dreams, they're not senseless!" He believed that even with the collapse of the Sài Gòn regime a coalition government would be formed.

"You'd work with the Việt Cộng?" my aunt asked. "They'd cut your throat first."

Uncle Hải ignored her.

"If we're going to stay, I hope you're right," Aunt Diệu-Mai added. "The only way we might survive is if there's a coalition government."

"*Dans ce cas, ce serait mon devoir—d'être là, prendre un rôle. Il faut bien faire quelque chose!*" he replied. He always spoke in French when servants were present. Forever the mandarin, Uncle Hải yearned for a role in any new government which might allow him to revive the social programs once espoused by the slain president Diệm.

Even though I had a brother and sister in the United States, I had no thought of leaving. I went to sleep at night with the impossible thought that the next day might bring news of my mother, or even my father. The enemy was now the victor, at least in the central part of the country. Would my father at last be released?

◦◦ As the situation worsened, my relatives became more strict. I was not to leave the house alone, and could no longer see my friends. A few days later some of them came to my aunt's to announce frantically that a former teacher was looking for me. Monsieur Donikian was a Frenchman of Armenian descent who considered me among the better students in his class on French literature. He wanted to help me get to France. My aunt and uncles thought this would be a good opportunity for my sister and me to get out of the country. I felt the rush of blood through my body as I pedaled to my old teacher's apartment. Shivering in the air-conditioning, I listened to the possibilities he arrayed before me.

"I'll sign any papers, support you while you're in France," he promised. "You must go back to school!"

"What about my brother and sister in the States?" I blurted out, realizing too late how ungrateful the question sounded.

Monsieur Donikian was unperturbed. "Don't worry—I'll pay your way to Ohio if you want," he said. "You've got to get out of here, to continue your education!"

When I mentioned Diệu-Qùynh's condition, the gentle teacher assured me that she could be treated—once we were in Paris. But at the end of two hours, we had gone through all the options for getting there and rejected each. He could not adopt me—he was single, and I was one year too old. No one could now be found to forge papers claiming that he had a wife and had adopted me some years before. "You know, I only have a few days left here," he finally said. "I should have asked some friends to send papers offering you a scholarship. It's too late now; even a fake one would take months."

He was leaving Việt Nam within the next couple of days. If I could find a way to Laos I was to let him know, and he would come there to help me.

"*Ça doit être possible du Laos,*" he said.

It would be possible from Laos. But how was I to get there? I thanked him, crying as I said goodbye.

I spent the rest of the afternoon biking through the unfamiliar streets of Sài Gòn. I did not want to face my relatives and my sister. It might simply be better to wait for the final hours, I thought. I was sure I would meet my mother again, and of course, my father. If Sài Gòn fell, peace would come. Prisoners would be released, and we could live together again as a family.

I went back to my aunt's house to tell her that there would be no trip to France, and that I was determined to stay. Before I could tell her what had happened at Monsieur Donikian's apartment, however, Aunt Diệu-Mai said I was to go immediately to my uncle's house. It was now nearly five o'clock. The date was April 24, 1975.

The maid came in from the front gate as I got back on the bicycle. "Some girl's asking for you out there," she said.

It was Thu-Hảo. Her family had found its way to Sài Gòn and was staying with relatives.

"I'm so happy!" she said, her face glowing.

I stood with her at my aunt's gate, not daring to bring her into the house.

"Guess what?" Thu-Hảo's eyes were brilliant.

"What?"

"My parents want to see you! Will you come?"

"They want to see me? Really?"

"Please, you have to come! Come now!"

Thu-Hảo turned her bicycle around. I stood still, fearing my uncle's wrath if I didn't show up at his house promptly. "Let me ask my aunt," I said, leaning my bike against the half-open gate.

"Đức, please, come see my parents," Thu-Hảo repeated as I turned to go into the house. When I came back out a moment later, she was gone.

🐌 "We're leaving tomorrow. Maybe tonight," said Uncle Phồn-Anh. He was at the gate, announcing the news before I could roll the bike into the front yard. "Go inside and pack a bag."

"We brought Diệu-Quỳnh down to say goodbye," my aunt said as Uncle Hải pulled me up at the front gate in their car, a comical machine called the Anglia. It was now seven o'clock. Other than Aunt Diệu-Mai and her family, all my Sài Gòn relatives were leaving Việt Nam, and my uncles had decided to take me along. If they got to America, they would send me to Ohio, to my brother Đinh. But they didn't want to take responsibility for Diệu-Quỳnh; she would remain with Aunt Diệu-Mai. At some point the adults had reached this decision without telling us children. I never found out which one among my numerous uncles and aunts had the American contacts that made it possible for us to leave.

My uncles and aunts gathered inside the house, deciding what to do with the precious teapots and vases my mother's father had collected until his death in 1965. Diệu-Quỳnh and I walked over to the ancient mango tree. I was choosing words in my head when she gave her nervous titter. The sound made me choke with tears. Later, as my uncle pulled away in the Anglia with Diệu-Quỳnh inside, my sister moved a few hesitant fingers. She had not said a word.

I stayed up all night and left with my uncle Phồn-Anh and his family at dawn the next day. One of my uncles had secured seats on an American flight from Sài Gòn to the island of Phú Quốc, known for its atrocious heat, its famous fish sauce, and a massive prison camp holding thousands of Việt Cộng soldiers. There I became part of my uncle Thịnh-Anh's family, which included his wife, his three sons, and my step-grandmother. We slept on straw mats in abandoned army barracks, washed in the sea four miles away, and for food walked three miles of sandy paths down a few naked hills to a tiny island market. I went there the first day but found only some meat lying on dirty shelves under the sun; flies hovered over it. I came back with a few tins of sardines. None of us had much of an appetite anyway.

For the next few mornings we sat outside the entrance to our barracks to wait for news of the American ships that were to take us away. Each afternoon we lined up to receive a few liters of drinking and cooking water. At all hours, officials from the crumbling Sài Gòn government and others connected with the American forces in Việt Nam arrived on the trucks that shuttled between the airport and the camp. All feared a Việt Cộng blood-bath. Performers from a CIA-sponsored anticommunist radio sta-tion were ensconced in the barracks next to ours; at night Việt Nam's well-known traditional fiddler Lữ Liên played sorrowful tunes. "That music is enough to rot the inside of my stomach," I complained late one night when my uncle found me sitting outdoors on the steps to the barracks.

When helicopters began landing in the cleared area behind the camp, we knew our departure was near. That evening, tribal soldiers hired by the Americans took us down to the docks. Small boats would take us to a ship moored in the bay. The soldiers ordered us to leave our luggage behind, assuring us that the bags would be brought to our boats. Later, they told us that refugees from a nearby holding camp had stormed our compound and stolen our belongings. I lost all my clothes, my books, and the photographs of my parents, sisters, and grandparents. I still had a handbag, a discarded military container designed for mines, which contained a toothbrush and some underwear. I looked in the pockets. The necklace Thu-Hảo had given me was not there; I remembered that I had taken it off in the shower at Uncle Phồn-Anh's bathroom and left it behind.

Crouched in the darkness, we waited on the beach. The

tribal soldiers exchanged gunfire with Republican sailors trying to board the American ships. It was near midnight when the soldiers took us onto a cargo ship, the *Pioneer Challenger*. Standing, sitting, squatting, lying curled up against each other, people covered every inch of space on the steel deck. They looked like worms. My relatives and I were dazed. We stared at each other in silence, suddenly aware that we had been on the losing side and now were ignominiously deserting our homeland and our ancestors. Images of my mother and sister swirled in my head. My chest and stomach burned with shame.

It was April 30, 1975, the day Việt Cộng tanks rolled to victory in the center of Sài Gòn. The war had ended. My life in exile began on the dark blue waters of the South China Sea.

For hours a flotilla of small boats brought more people out to the ship, each fighting the wind and waves to climb the iron steps that swung precariously down its side. High up on the ship's deck, I couldn't hear the shouts of the men below as they struggled to tie their boats to the larger vessel, or the cries of mothers as they passed infants and small children up the ladder.

Dozens of people fell overboard. Helicopters circled overhead, taking turns landing on platforms extending from the side of the ship. More hordes of refugees emerged from each helicopter before it was pushed off the deck, an ugly mass of empty smoking steel sinking slowly into the ocean.

Squeezed on the *Pioneer Challenger*, I sat frightened and utterly alone. No one in my family had thought it necessary to talk to me about the plan to leave our country. I had obeyed my uncle and was now accompanying him as a refugee. All I had were the clothes on my back. My father was in prison in the North, my mother stuck in Đà Nẵng. Diệu-Quỳnh I left in Sài Gòn, deep in the seclusion of her ailing mind.

FIVE

Authentic Hué Beef Noodle

"I must say, Sister, it sounds like you're just about per-fect—always fair, just, reliable . . . a solid leader . . . What else has been said here this afternoon? Ah, yes—consci-entious, and kind, and . . . well, I am impressed, most impressed."

The man from the People's Committee sat at the head of a conference table, his eyes shielded behind a pair of sunglasses. Half squatting, he had one bare foot on his chair, his knee near his chin. With the other foot he toyed with his brown plastic sandals on the floor. He looked up from his notes and turned toward my mother, who was sitting to his right. He waited.

"I am far from perfect," my mother murmured.

"Oh, come now," the man interrupted, scratching the top of his crew-cut head. "I doubt the Revolution could have had much to offer a person like you. You could probably teach us a few lessons, couldn't you? Listen to everyone in this room. Not one person—not one—has spoken negatively of you. I am impressed. Not one person in this room," the man repeated, waving his arm. Scanning the faces of the more than fifty teachers and administrators sitting two rows deep, he allowed a moment of silence, then removed his sunglasses, not without a theatrical touch. "Now this lady here, our Sister, is a saint. . . . Is that what everyone here is saying to me? No one here wishes to change his or her opinion, I presume."

Another moment of silence passed. Those in the audience averted their eyes. The man began tapping his sunglasses on the surface of the table. "Well then, what are doing we here? Should I dismiss you all? Should I bring this meeting to a close?" Pointing to my mother with his glasses, he continued: "Should I allow Sister Diệu-Liễu, our saint here, to continue in her job? Should the Revolution give her an award? Tell me. Tell me."

No one spoke. The man's use of my mother's given name was insulting. My mother had lowered her eyes, but her look conveyed that she ignored the slight.

The man consulted his watch, then methodically gathered the papers in front of him and arranged them in a folder. Finally, after lighting a cigarette, he said, "The People's Committee will decide. We thank you, and urge you to always keep in mind your duties. The people put their trust in you to educate their children. Under the Party's wise guidance we will ensure them a happy, safe, and productive future."

There had been only a perfunctory interval between the time the soldiers wearing National Liberation Front uniforms took over Đà Nẵng and the time the Communist party took control. The new authorities still referred to themselves as "the Front," but did not hide their allegiance to "the Party." As the head of the education section of the People's Committee, the man at the conference table could make life troublesome for any of those present in the room. He now dismissed them and shuffled away, nodding to a few people as he left. He made a point of ignoring my mother.

"Madam Principal, I'm afraid you ought to quit," the librarian whispered to my mother on the way out of the meeting room. "Volunteer to leave before they take your job away. It will be a mark on your record if you fight them."

"I was thinking exactly the same thing," my mother replied. "And please, under the circumstances, don't call me Madam Principal anymore. Thank you for speaking up on my behalf anyway."

Other teachers followed my mother out and stood around her in the school yard. She noticed a few had tears in their eyes. She turned away. Others put a furtive hand on her back or shoulders, without speaking. In the heat of the May afternoon, she stared at the back of the man who had created the turmoil. He was walking his bicycle past the flower bed that encircled a flagpole in the middle of the school yard, his shadow merging with that of the red flag with a yellow star which sagged from the top of the pole.

"They've won," my mother muttered to herself. She too left the school a moment later, in midafternoon—"It doesn't matter now," she thought. She walked the two blocks home, and avoiding all relatives, locked herself in her room for the rest of the afternoon and cried.

The next day, two months after the Communist flag was first flown over the bright skies of Đà Nẵng, the man from the People's Committee told my mother she had lost her job as principal of the girls' high school. Her background alone would have been enough to get her fired: member of President Thiệu's Democratic party, head of the Vietnamese-American Friendship Association, the mother of children who had attended French schools and then gone off to American universities, wife of a former South Vietnamese government official—no matter that he was now in a Communist jail, or perhaps even no longer alive. The man said she was fired because she had deserted her duties at the school when the Communists arrived. The fiery temper my mother had inherited from her father briefly flared. "Look, my husband and I have always put our jobs and responsibilities ahead of our children!" she spat back. "It was an extraordinary time! The war had just ended, and I had no idea where my children were. Let me tell you: my daughter is mentally ill; she needed me. I had to find them! You may think that contrary to party policy or attitude or whatever—but even dogs and cats care about their puppies and kittens—"

"There's no need to shout," the man said.

My mother had decided not to fight the case, but she could not control her emotions. "You heard everyone yesterday. I take my job seriously. In twenty years of teaching, I've always fulfilled my responsibilities! I had to go to Sài Gòn—Hồ Chí Minh City— to look for my children—"

"Sister, please, we can discuss this calmly—"

"Discuss what? I am—my husband . . . daughter . . . my job . . ." Her voice trailed off incoherently.

The day after Diệu-Quỳnh and I left, Đà Nẵng, the second largest city in South Việt Nam, had been effectively abandoned by the central government. Demoralized officers fled their posts and took their families to Sài Gòn or safer cities, using whatever military transport was at their disposal. The streets of Đà Nẵng were littered with Southern army uniforms as soldiers sought to escape, hundreds forcing their way onto the navy vessels and cargo ships provided by the Americans to evacuate refugees. Officials from the U.S. consulate and the local branch of the Central Intelligence Agency organized desperate boat trips and helicopter flights to ferry out government employees and their relatives. Thousands of people jammed the docks along the river. Yet others rushed to the beaches, all hoping for a trip south. Meanwhile, Communist forces gathered at the edge of town and shelled the airports for days.

On the last days of March 1975, World Airways lent its help to the airlift. When the boarding ramp of its first Boeing 727 aircraft was lowered onto the Đà Nẵng tarmac, five thousand people stormed it. Women and children were trampled on the runway. Dozens were still hanging on to the wheels, hatch, and wings as the plane took off. The next day the president of World Airways, Edward Daly, went with two Boeing 727s from Sài Gòn to Đà Nẵng. One of the planes wasn't able to land, while the other was overwhelmed by nearly three hundred soldiers trying to board. One soldier, unable to get on, threw a hand grenade at the plane. The sound of its explosion blended with that of the rockets falling farther down the runway. Daly's was the last flight out, saving the soldiers, two women, and a child, though it crushed several people under its wheels when it taxied out on the runway. Many in the crowd on the hot tarmac tried to grab on to the wings, falling to their death as the plane took off. Others clung inside the wheel wells and were killed moments later when the wheels retracted.

My mother was among the thousands trying to flee, rushing from docks to beaches to airport in search of any kind of transportation south. But though she was unable to fight through the mobs to gain a place, her white Peugeot, left at one of the docks along the riverbank, convinced friends that she had succeeded in getting out of Đà Nẵng.

Ultimately realizing that she could no longer escape, she made her way home on foot, where she had the flag of the Republic of South Việt Nam, which had been painted on our gates under government order, covered over. Having lost both husband and children, and with immense fear in her heart, she prepared to deal with the new masters of Đà Nẵng.

The first Việt Cộng cadre with whom she had any extensive contact came to ask her a favor. In the delta region, south and southwest of the capital, the Republican military commander,

General Nguyễn-Khoa Nam, had refused to give up the fight. shooting orders to halt deserters on boats and barges floating down the nine branches of the Mekong River and out to sea. General Nam was able to keep up morale within his ranks and to hold off Communist advances. The Việt Cộng decided my mother could talk to him.

A man turned up at the house unannounced one evening, wearing a short-sleeved gray shirt that wasn't tucked in and faded brown trousers. In his forties, he had a haggard face but gentle manners. He did not appear to be someone who held a position of power. His thick lips forming a modest smile that revealed nicotine-stained teeth, he presented himself as "a man of the National Liberation Front," failing to give his name.

"But how do you know about me?" my mother asked.

"It's of no importance. The Front has its eyes and ears," he replied, sitting in our living room in Đà Nẵng. "The most essential thing is that we need you. You would earn the Revolution's permanent gratitude—and think of all the lives you will save.

"If you accept the task, we'll provide you with all that you need to travel south," the man went on. "It will not be an easy journey, but we'll protect you. Even if you fail, it will still be a great contribution to bringing peace and reconciliation to our nation."

"I am happy and honored that the Front is seeking my help," my mother said. In the circumstances, she thought, the lie was warranted. "I'm not sure I'm up to the job, but please allow me to think about it."

"It's critical, if you should accept the assignment, that you leave tomorrow or the next day," he said.

Stalling for time, my mother excused herself to bring tea for her visitor. The unexpected proposal had some advantages. She would, she knew, be accompanied south by Việt Cộng, but perhaps once she was near enough she could flee to Sài Gòn to find Diệu-Quỳnh and me. Before returning to the discussion of the man's plan, she asked for news of my father.

"I don't know about his case personally. If he is with the Revolution, he is in good hands," the man said.

"Will he be released soon?"

"That would, I suppose, depend on his attitude. If he has seen the wisdom of the Party, and agreed to work with the Front, there should be no problem. But again, I don't know much about his case."

"Surely, if you know about me, if you have come to me with this task, then you must know about him."

"Perhaps. Do consider how helpful it will be to your husband if you were to provide the Front with this help. It would show that you have mended your ways, that you have seen which side is right, which side is wrong."

"Please trust that I know which side is right and which is wrong."

"All you have to do is convince the general either to stop fighting, or not to be so adamant. Our forces will win in the end, so it would be better for everyone if your brother—"

"That's what I was going to mention," my mother interrupted. "He isn't my brother. I have a brother of the same name, a doctor in Huế."

"Are your sure?" the man asked. "Your family name, Nguyễn-Khoa, is uncommon. He has to be a relative—"

"Indeed, he's a cousin. Not a brother. I don't know him well. In the end, don't you think he would take out his gun and shoot me on the spot if I were to approach him with your proposal?"

The man stood up. "Well, I'd still like you to think about it. There is no better way you can help the Revolution. And I'll be sure to bring you any news I hear about your husband. We'll be in touch, in case you change your mind."

Travel to the south will be very dangerous as long as the fighting is heavy. I'll go if they release my husband first, my mother told herself.

Within two weeks of the man's visit, Việt Cộng tanks rumbled through Sài Gòn. On April 30, 1975, a general named Dủởng Văn Minh, in his painful position as the last president of the Republic of South Việt Nam, surrendered on the front steps of Independence Palace to a Việt Cộng colonel, Bùi Tín. Over forty years earlier the colonel had been my mother's classmate in primary school. Her cousin, General Nguyễn-Khoa Nam, put a bullet through his temple.

After the shock of Sài Gòn's defeat wore off, my mother made her way to the former capital, now Hồ Chí Minh City. It was this trip that the People's Committee used as evidence that she had neglected her duties at the high school. She wept when she was reunited with Diệu-Quỳnh at Aunt Diệu-Mai's house, and fresh worries immediately arose about me.

"Who knows where Cu Bé is now?" she said to my aunt.

"Oh, don't worry. He's with Phồn-Anh and Thịnh-Anh. They'll take him to Đính and Diệu-Hà in America. His brother and sister will take care of him."

"I'm worried that Đính won't be able to afford to feed both Cu Bé and Diệu-Hà, along with his own family," my mother sighed. "Will Cu Bé listen to his brother? Maybe he'll have to work, abandon school—"

"*'Trời sinh voi, trời sinh cỏ,'*" Aunt Diệu-Mai said, quoting a Vietnamese proverb. "'Heaven creates the elephant, Heaven will make grass.' You should worry about Diệu-Quỳnh."

Despite the broiling sun of Sài Gòn, my sister was pale. Now a frail woman of twenty-five, she weighed no more than eighty-five pounds. With her stooped posture—back bent, shoulders pulled forward, chest and stomach caved in—her body, like her mind, arched inward. She was taciturn most of the time. No one knew whether the end of the war meant anything to her.

"We will go back to Đà Nẵng soon," my mother said to Diệu-Quỳnh. "You'll have the whole house to yourself now that Diệu-Hà and Cu Bé are gone. Maybe Cha will come home soon."

☙ My grandmother and other members of my father's family had left for Huế by the time my mother and Diệu-Quỳnh returned to Đà Nẵng. Two weeks later my mother lost her job. She was unable even to resume teaching since there was no longer any need for French language teachers—only teachers of Russian. Feeling isolated and alone, she began to think that perhaps she and Diệu-Quỳnh should leave Đà Nẵng for good.

Uncle Phạm, my mother's partner in opening the kindergarten in front of our house, turned out to be a collaborator with the Communists; he was now a member of the People's Committee. Though she knew about his pro-nationalist sentiments, my mother had always had enormous affection for him, and it was shocking to her, when he showed up at the house wearing a Việt Cộng hat, to realize that the quiet man had actually been involved with the other side.

"You shouldn't have let Cu Bé go to the States," said Uncle Phạm.

"His uncles took him. I had nothing to do with it. In those days—"

"Our country is unified now. He could have gone on to be of great help."

"Well, he's gone now." My mother started to cry.

Uncle Phạm had been close to us during the last years of the war. Not only did he teach French at my school, but he and his family lived around the corner from us, and he would often come over after dinner to accompany us to the movies at the French cultural center, or to drive us in my mother's car down to the river, or just walk with us in the evening breeze. Thinking of those times, my mother suggested that perhaps, as a member of the People's Committee, he could help her find a job.

"With your background?" he retorted.

My mother was stunned. Uncle Pham went on to say that he wanted to close down the kindergarten. "There's no need anymore for private schools—the Party and the government will provide education for everyone," he explained. He hinted that possibly she would like to donate the kindergarten building to the People's Committee.

The decision to move away from Đà Nẵng firmed up in my mother's mind. She knew she would have to act quickly; once the kindergarten was taken over—and since the idea had been proposed, it was a certainty—she would also lose her home. With the two younger children gone, the house would be considered too big for just two women, and anyone who might be assigned by the People's Committee to live in the house with them would certainly act as a spy for the authorities.

She was detained in Đà Nẵng to acquaint her replacement, a former student at the school as well as a Việt Cộng agent, with her duties as principal. Afterward, my mother was ordered to report for reeducation. The program lasted only a couple of months, during which she was allowed to stay at home. She did not believe a word of the talks about "the wisdom of the Revolution," the "class struggle," the "drive for socialism," the "road to communism," or the "superb and visionary leadership" of the Party. By this time, my mother had learned to control her temper and barely said a word. In the numerous sessions in which participants were required to recant any of their actions that had obstructed the revolution, she willingly invented crimes she had committed against "the People," admitting to a blindness that drove her to try to move against the tide of history.

 Early in 1976, on a humid afternoon in Hồ Chí Minh City, Aunt Diệu-Mai opened her doors again to receive her sister, a tired woman of fifty with no means of support, accompanied by a daughter with an ailing mind.

"'*Trời sinh voi, trời sinh cỏ,*'" my aunt said. "You'll survive."

"Heaven did not create communism," Mạ replied. "Cruel men did. What will I feed Diệu-Quỳnh? Grass?"

"Watch what you say," my aunt responded softly. "Communism has created a lot of spies."

Making the arrangements to travel to Sài Gòn had been an ordeal. My mother was required to obtain permission first to make the trip and then to buy bus tickets, giving as her reason Diệu-Quỳnh is needed for emergency medical treatment available only in Hồ Chí Minh City. Despite her submitting a document signed by a relative on his doctor's letterhead, suspicious authorities asked a myriad of questions, a few even touching on Diệu-Quỳnh's illness. It was incomprehensible to my mother how a trip within her own country could need official sanction. She did not see how a woman traveling with her daughter could be a security risk. She failed to think of how the North Vietnamese had used exactly such disguises to relay information, smuggle arms and ammunition south, and carry out acts of sabotage and terrorism during the war.

When her temporary permit to stay at Aunt Diệu-Mai's expired, my mother joined my Uncle Anh-Anh, the last of her brothers remaining in Sài Gòn. He had taken over the house vacated by her other brothers. The mango tree under which I had spent my last moments with Diệu-Quỳnh still drooped in the Sài Gòn sun, but behind it there was now a loudspeaker attached to the concrete pole supporting electric cables. It blared socialist slogans from dawn to nightfall. The metallic voices of the broadcasts made my mother's headaches, worse, while the reports extolling the Party's vision and leadership sickened her heart.

Beginning in the early postwar days of 1975, South Việt Nam had plunged into a nightmare. Offices and agencies stopped functioning since many intellectuals, technocrats, and professionals had fled the country. Those who stayed behind either were distrusted, or themselves shunned the new government out of fear or disgust. Hundreds of thousands connected with the defunct government or the armed forces of Sài Gòn were marched to concentration camps to undergo reeducation in programs that would last for years. Aunt Diệu-Mai's husband, Uncle Hải, at first thought he had been spared: he remained free for a year or so after the Communists came because he managed a bank that would simply not function without him. Once the new regime gained control of the bank's finances, however, he was sent off for reeducation. He never came back, dying of an unspecified illness, according to the papers furnished by authorities.

The detainees included corrupt people who had profited from the war or abused their power. Yet their mistreatment could hardly be justified. The camps turned out to be a massive system of prisons run by Việt Cộng who, for most of their adult lives, had fought in the jungle and lived in wretched conditions. They believed the Communist party's accusation that the detainees, those "lackeys of the American imperialists," had been abusing the people while they indulged their taste for luxuries. Anger and envy drove them to torture these former enemies. None of the inmates was allowed visits for months. Their families did not even know where they were being held. When contacts were finally established, horrendous stories began to filter out about men being tied to poles, or locked up in metal boxes that had been used to transport bombs and ammunition and left to perish in the heat. It was the guards in each camp who determined whether their prisoners had changed their ways enough to be released. High-ranking South Vietnamese officials and military men disappeared in remote camps in the North, and untold numbers died in detention.

The economy of the South, which had been propped up in large part by American aid during the war years, collapsed. The Communist party imposed a centrally controlled economy; there was nothing available in the markets. While the party newspaper *Nhân Dân* (the *People's Daily*) offered staid articles about the "extraordinary above-quota output" of state factories, the numbers did not translate into consumer goods or food. Bustling with energy just months before, the former capital became a dead town. Where once there was uncontrollable traffic, now nothing moved. Only once in a while could one see a truck, which would roll along at the speed of a bicycle, a column of smoke rising behind it. Since there was no gasoline, such vehicles were powered by steam engines, and men would dangle from the side or the back, stoking a coal fire. Across town, a worker would receive a medal for overcoming a "modern technological problem" by replacing electricity with candles.

Colorful clothing and the *aó dài* disappeared, along with sentimental songs and rock-and-roll. Black and brown became the colors of choice. Hair-styling boutiques, cafés, restaurants, cinemas—anything hinting of bourgeois hedonism closed down. The Việt Cộng took pride in announcing again and again that they had brought peace to the country, and independence. They also brought about such a degree of austerity that their foreign minister, a man whose bittersweet wit exemplified the Vietnamese sensibility, declared that "at least the revolution had succeeded in spreading poverty all around."

Hồ Chí Minh City's administrative jobs were being offered as rewards to retired soldiers and peasants from the countryside who had supported the Việt Cộng. They brought a warped logic to their functions. My mother and her brother Anh-Anh humored officials, begged, pleaded, fought, and did everything in between in order to keep their house. They finally bribed the authorities to issue them a residential household registration—a sad-looking piece of paper that meant everything in socialist Việt Nam. One could not stay in one's house or buy food or other goods without it. One could not receive visitors or mail without it. One did not count without it. Public security agents could come into private homes at any time and ask to see the form. Anyone in the house whose name was not on it would be detained immediately, along with the head of the household. My mother went to bed each night fearing a knock on the door.

During the first years of Communist control in the South the government repeatedly devalued the currency. People hoarded gold, making it the real currency on the streets. Public security men once came to search my mother's house for hidden gold and stayed for an hour, looking in cupboards and pillows and inside books, but came up empty-handed. "I know you're hiding it somewhere," one of them said. "We'll be back." They had not looked inside the pot of rice sitting on the brick stove in the kitchen.

Twice a week my mother and my uncle Anh-Anh and his wife trotted off to political training sessions. Public security agents and neighborhood authorities would come to quiz my uncle's children and Diệu-Quỳnh about the family and whether there was any gold in the house. At school, children were asked to report on activities in their homes as teachers aimed to shift their loyalty from family to the state and the party. My mother and my uncle were no longer able to speak freely in their own home.

 "*Bún bò Huế, bún bò Huế đúng điệu đây!*" my mother called, sitting on a stool on the sidewalk. "Huế beef noodle. Authentic Huế beef noodle!"

Outside Aunt Diệu-Mai's house, pedestrians ignored my mother's invitation. Huế beef noodle is extremely spicy—not the most appealing dish on a hot afternoon in Hồ Chí Minh City. And who had the money for a bowl of noodle soup? Selling on the street had been Aunt Diệu-Mai's idea, and she had taught my mother to make the soup. "Just so you can say you have a job," my aunt said. She helped out so that she could say the same.

In a socialist country, everyone was supposed to have a job; if you didn't, the state would provide you with one. A state job would allow you to buy goods in state shops, at state prices. But my mother's antirevolutionary background precluded her from obtaining a state job. Her choice was the soup stand or joining the thousands sent to "new economic zones."

The zones, or NEZs, were an example of an idealistic Communist innovation gone utterly wrong. Interpreting the notion of a job for every person literally, the party did provide things for people to do. For months in the late 1970s the government compiled lists of the unemployed in every district of Hồ Chí Minh City and other urban areas, who were then systematically sent by the truckload each morning to the countryside. City folks who could not distinguish a garden rake from a hoe were suddenly turned into farmers.

At first, many people were naive enough to believe in the scheme. Impressed that the state would allot each of them a plot of land, some actually volunteered for the NEZs in the early days after the war. Packing their families and belongings into the waiting trucks, they later disembarked on barren pieces of land they were to try to cultivate. Many were killed or maimed by the American and Việt Cộng land mines left underground. Others found that before they could be self-sufficient they were required to meet state production quotas. Pigs, chickens, and other livestock had to be sold to the state at ridiculously low prices. Though the new farmers shed tears under the sun, they still did not have enough water for their manioc and potatoes.

This massive social engineering program was born in the dark corners of a few politburo minds. It succeeded in shifting a mass of the urban unemployed to the countryside, but instead of producing green fields and utopian socialist farms, the program backfired, creating a homeless population in urban areas where there had been none before. After disastrous seasons or mere weeks in the NEZs, people simply returned to the cities, where they were not welcomed back into their former homes. They became illegal aliens in their own country. They slept in parks and on sidewalks, begged, stole, and smuggled goods, and helped to proliferate the black markets. When caught, they were sent to

languish in reeducation camps, where conditions were worse than
in the NEZs. Going from misery to misery seemed to be the fate
of the entire population of Việt Nam.

Humbling as it was, the sidewalk noodle stand was still a
stroke of luck for my mother. Often teased as a woman who,
instead of words, would "yell out fire" during her days as a high
school principal, she now meekly called out, "Huế beef noodle,
authentic Huế beef noodle," to indifferent pedestrians. Sometimes
a trace of her old defiant, "bourgeois" spirit vented itself. Once
in a while, tired of riding a bicycle from her house to my aunt's,
she would sit back in a pedicab and allow herself to be driven to
her spot on the sidewalk. At such times Diệu-Quỳnh would often
ride along and stay with my mother for the day. Otherwise she
never left the house. In a rare show of compassion, the local
authorities exempted Diệu-Quỳnh from the requirement either to
work or to attend a political training program.

Diệu-Quỳnh kept giggling to herself, compulsively washed
her hands every half hour, and still liked to chew on ice cubes.
Occasionally she would ask my aunt Hồng-Khuê, "Can we have
deep-fried shrimp tonight?"—which my kind aunt would take as
a hint that Diệu-Quỳnh wanted to talk, although rarely would
she say anything else. In the chaotic world of Hồ Chí Minh City,
my mother thought perhaps it was better that Diệu-Quỳnh was
unaware of the uglier sides of life. But no one could tell what she
saw, what she thought, how she felt. She continued to wet her
bed. O Thia, a cross-eyed servant from Đà Nẵng, had agreed to
stay on, living in the house in Hồ Chí Minh City and taking care
of Diệu-Quỳnh.

O Thia, who had been recommended to my mother by an
acquaintance in Đà Nẵng, had no known family. With a bribe to
the appropriate officials, she went on the residential household
registration form as a cousin of my mother's. Though grateful for
her help, my mother at times regretted having her around. The

woman was slightly mad. She would come back from the market with randomly chosen groceries that could in no way be put together to make a meal. She had an uncontrollable and dangerous desire to comment on anything and everything, and she would do so cackling loudly.

Once during a political training session, from which O Thia was not exempt, the careless woman let out a loud yawn.

"Did you want to say something?" asked the neighborhood political commissar, who was giving a lecture on building socialism from the grass-roots level. O Thia stared at him, though one eye appeared to be gazing at the portrait of Hồ Chí Minh above the man's head. "You are displaying a hostile attitude toward the Revolution!" the man exclaimed.

Anyone else would have remained silent. But not O Thia.

"But you always say 'the People this,' 'the People that'— 'The People dictate,' 'The People are all that count,' 'The People are all-important.' Well, if the People are so all-important, how come you won't let me yawn? I am the People!"

The assembled neighbors roared with laughter while the commissar gaped, at a loss for words.

On most afternoons O Thia would squat on the ground in the courtyard, seemingly observing the mango branches intently with her crossed eyes while toying with her long thick strands of shiny hair. In this posture she would make pronouncements on life under communism.

"Before, you never had to stand in line. And there was always something to buy. Now no one has any money, everyone's always standing in line, and there will never be anything to buy," she commented. Or, "During the war we could go anywhere. You didn't care about gunfire or bombs. Now you can't go anywhere. In peace you fear not having permission papers."

On one occasion O Thia aptly glossed Hồ Chí Minh's best-known maxim, "Nothing is more precious than independence and liberty": "A third of that phrase is true," she declared. "We don't have independence, and we don't have liberty. But we have the 'nothing' part."

My mother or Aunt Hồng-Khuê would signal O Thia to be quiet, but to no avail. Nothing ever happened to her, however, although it was certain that people in the neighborhood heard her comments. Some might have reported them; others would only have relished them.

"We're the bourgeois people who must now become blind, mute, and deaf. O Thia is the people. She can say anything she wants," my uncle whispered to my mother. "The party lies, the insane speak the truth, the people suffer."

꿍 Late in 1978, news began to filter into Hồ Chí Minh City that thousands of people in the western cities had been killed by the Khmer Rouge. The government gave few details, and never hinted at an invasion. When fighting broke out Uncle Anh-Anh said, "Our country can never be at peace for long. There will always be men in uniform."

My cousin Nguyên-Anh, Uncle Anh-Anh's oldest son, was now sixteen. Because his family had an antirevolutionary background, he would not be allowed to continue his education beyond high school unless my uncle paid an immense sum of money to a state university, in which case Nguyên-Anh would become a ward of the state. If he did not go to the university, he risked being drafted and sent to Cambodia on "international duty." The only remaining choice was to try to leave the country by boat.

"I'll come with you," my mother said. She had given up running her noodle stand because it was losing too much money. She and Uncle Anh-Anh had both found work in a chalk factory. Their wages were inconsequential, but at least they could stay in the city.

"And what about your husband? What if he comes back?" Uncle Anh-Anh asked.

"I don't know," said my mother. There had been no news of my father since the end of the war. "I'll wait for him until the day I die. But maybe I should be with the children in the States—take Diệu-Quỳnh out of this hell."

"You make it sound easy," he replied.

"Thousands of people have done it."

"Yes, but thousands get caught. Thousands die. Do you think Diệu-Quỳnh could survive any of the things that might happen if you tried to escape?"

"Living here is worse than being dead." She sighed deeply.

By writing to relatives in France, by 1977 my mother had established contact with my brother in Ohio. Đỉnh began sending money home, and later Diệu-Hà also chipped in. Against Đỉnh's and Diệu-Hà's salaries, she then borrowed enough money to add to what she had to buy two seats on a boat for Diệu-Quỳnh and herself. She turned to a cousin to help organize the trip. The man took the money—nearly a thousand dollars—and went away. He was gone for weeks. He came back empty-handed, claiming that he had been duped and lost the entire amount. Hồ Chí Minh City was full of con artists in those days. My mother was never sure whether her cousin had truly been duped, or whether he had cheated her. She lost everything.

How many times can a person's fortune be reversed in a lifetime? she asked herself. Tossing in her bed at night, she had nothing but her own sighs and tears for an answer.

Nevertheless, again and again she found the energy to start life anew. Somehow she always found a solution. Within a few months of those sleepless nights she had borrowed enough money to install a Ping-Pong table in the courtyard, which she rented by the hour to neighborhood youths. Her family had always been respected as one that produced scholars—never anyone with the least bit of interest in business or aptitude for it. Somehow in the dark days of socialism she found she had the acumen to make a living and to support her daughter, albeit with help from Đỉnh and Diệu-Hà.

Diệu-Quỳnh's mental condition was improving. She wrote loving letters that were extremely coherent to her family in the United States, and she proved helpful to my mother in handling the Ping-Pong customers. Though she wouldn't talk to the customers, she kept track of the rental fees that were due. Unaware of Diệu-Quỳnh's obsession with cleanliness, customers found it odd that she never touched the money they gave her and were amazed at how she deftly handled the coins and bills, using a piece of paper to shield her fingers. Within the family Diệu-Quỳnh would occasionally carry on a conversation, but she talked only about inconsequential matters. She never complained about life under communism or said she envied her siblings in the United States. She never mentioned our father.

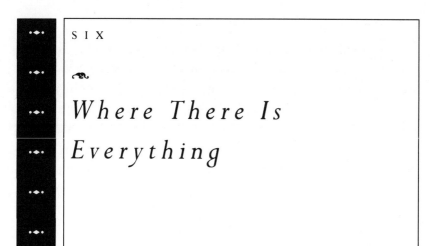

SIX

Where There Is Everything

"We'll have to sleep in those bunkers tonight," the cadre named Thuần told the prisoners. "You wouldn't believe the bombing raids in this region."

In the diminishing light of dusk, my father made out the dunes of packed earth where the cadre pointed. Brought to the largest of the subterranean chambers, the men piled in one after another. The air, thick with humidity, felt like a heavy weight on each man's chest. There was a stench of urine. Mosquitoes attacked them. Whenever he stuck out his hand and closed his fingers, my father caught several of the relentless insects.

"Damn American bandits. They make life so difficult!" a soldier's loud voice echoed back.

"We won't let them win this war," another answered.

My father had just drifted into sleep when the roar came. It sounded like hundreds of ocean waves all breaking at once. The soldiers immediately moved farther into the cave. The roar grew louder. Suddenly the bombs rained down, shaking the entire jungle. The cave became an earthen box in the hands of a giant gone mad. The walls seemed about to collapse as flashes of light pierced the darkness. The men panicked but they were unable to move. Outside, trees were crashing on top of each other. Fireballs shot up in the air, searing the leaves and branches and entire tree trunks. The bombs pounded down for a long time, near, far, everywhere, and it did seem like the end of the world. For the first time my father became aware of the gravity of the war.

During a lull in the attack a Việt Cộng guard named Hiền warned them not to move: "Never run out. It's always safer under here, and it's not over yet. They always come back to drop a second round."

My father sat up to avoid dirt getting into his eyes. In the blackness of the underground chamber he could make out the glowing hands of his watch; it was three in the morning. The darkness reminded him of lines in a poem describing the cold and gloomy interiors of coffins deep underground. He would relate in his memoirs: "The idea of death did not stay with me for long, although I was bitterly aware that the cave was fragile protection against the bombs. Being blown to pieces here would put an end to the terrible hardships I had suffered, but to be killed by an ally's bomb would be a painful mockery."

The men waited for the next round, feeling their profound powerlessness. The silence continued. At last the cries of roosters surprised them.

"That's it. That's the full extent of the power of the mighty American air force. It didn't kill me!" said Hiền.

The Việt Cộng soldiers did not venture out until past seven o'clock, returning about an hour later with a pot of rice and a few bits of dried fish. Weaver was singled out to sample a few slices of jackfruit, the region's pride.

"First time I've had this. Tastes like cheese. It's good," he said. As with anything Weaver uttered, the comment had to be translated. My father struggled to explain to the Việt Cộng what cheese was.

The men were led outside onto a road winding below a mountain range that extended to the horizon. The massive trees along the side of the road were devoid of leaves, killed by defoliants dropped from American planes. Twisting upward, their dried branches silhouetted against the sky looked like bones from some prehistoric animal. Here and there a few charred, lifeless trunks still stood, oddly and grotesquely, between bomb craters scattered at random over the flat fields. Each cavity had the same circumference and gave the appearance of having been meticulously bored into the ground by patient hands. The winds carried down the distressed cries of wild birds as they circled over the forest for prey.

A convoy of trucks caught up with the prisoners. The contents of the trucks were hidden beneath green canvas covers and the trucks' exteriors meticulously camouflaged, making the convoy look like moving columns of trees and branches against the dead and dreary landscape. The Việt Cộng tied the prisoners' hands and pushed them into two of the trucks. My father tried in vain to find a comfortable position among the cans of fuel on the oily floor. A long time passed, the trucks remaining motionless. The soldiers did not seem to be in a hurry.

"All armies are the same. Always rushing, rushing you, and then they make you wait forever," said Weaver.

"We should thank the Việt Cộng," said my father. "They're training us to be patient. Just in case they put us in prison."

When the trucks did get underway, my father was shaken and thrown about with the fuel cans until he grew sick. Finally a gunshot signaled the convoy to halt. Thuần announced that the road had been blocked. The driver turned off the dim lights. The bound prisoners were allowed to climb out of the trucks.

"Is it a mine?" asked a soldier.

"Looks like one of those delayed-explosion bombs. We won't have to wait long," Thuần said. "The Forward Youth are working on it."

Along the Hồ Chí Minh Trail, the Forward Youth were volunteers whose most frequent task was to help the Northern army's engineers rebuild paths damaged by mines and bombs. Where repair was impossible the Việt Cộng would build new roads that skirted around the bombed areas. The Hồ Chí Minh Trail was in fact not a single trail but a series of roads and connecting branches.

The delay provided my father with time to contemplate the actions of the enemy and the Americans:

> The men labored frantically under the dim stars. I could hear voices shouting, and the sound of shovels, rushing feet, and earth being dumped into craters created a sense of urgency. Every few moments we would look up at the stars in the black sky, frightened that the bombing raids would resume. The indifferent stars twinkled on as they always had done, yet they also appeared to be mocking the warring men on earth. With sophisticated technology from across the Pacific Ocean, one side attempted to obstruct the incursion of men and weapons, while the other tried with crude tools to undo the damage and continue the invasion. How long could both sides carry on the unending task?

Another gunshot rang out in the darkness. Prisoners and soldiers crawled back into the trucks. When the convoy stopped again it was daylight. The men disembarked in an area with no vegetation other than tall stands of bamboo. While Thuần lit a cigarette for him, my father ventured a question. "How far north are we?"

"We haven't been traveling north," Thuần said. "We've been on the Lao Bảo Pass; we're now in Laos."

The evening meal came early, and included a surprise: along with rice, the men were served wild bamboo shoots. Thuần gave them some water and announced that they would be leaving again within a quarter of an hour. The wind gathered while the men waited under a clump of bamboo. The searing wind was a reminder that the worst of summer was just beginning. The memory of hot, dry summers under just such winds from Laos came to my father's mind: of the sunny days of his youth in Quảng Trị province. He had not seen his home village in twenty years. Established along a saltwater river, its land was poor and arid, yet so overplanted that the earth had lost all color. Other than a temple with a roof of red tile, most structures in the village were thatched-roof dwellings. There was no garden of trees with rich leaves "green as jade," but only a few tattered and lonely banana trees, wild ivy growing along the dirt roads, and parched bamboo fighting to hold its own against the Laotian wind. People's eyes and skin showed the marks of their struggle to survive.

My father broke off a bamboo leaf and toyed with it. He missed his sunbathed, windswept village. He would have given anything to be sent there now.

↦ The trucks climbed and descended more mountains over the next few nights, and the exhausted prisoners took naps during the days. Overhearing the Northern soldiers talking about their impending reunions with their families, they realized that they had crossed into enemy territory. At the end of the night the convoy abandoned them on a jungle road. They marched on through the following nights, resting during the days in abandoned churches, or in random homes where the Việt Cộng quartered them in villages they passed through. In most towns the population consisted mainly of women, children and the elderly; the war had claimed all men and women over sixteen. Stopping in a villager's house while the soldiers went off to look for food, my father talked to a woman whose laments he related in a poem called "Halfway into Exile":

Before dawn we halted our march, already long;
Bamboo shadows fell heavy on my shoulders gone wrong.

The hamlet slept in the murmuring breeze of the hill,
The bombs had gone quiet, and all was still.
Banana trees, cassava, hedges—
All the plants had fallen dead.
In the thatched hut we could light but a hesitant flame;
Hammock hung, I shook the journey off the dusty cloth that had
*   long covered my frame,*
And felt the wreckage of war between the sides.

We were guests, all ears to the villager's tale.
"My grief is braided into more mourning;
My misery too is entangled with further sorrow.
I had a young brother, fallen west of the Trị Thiên Hills,
And two older ones, now but bones in the jungle belly of northern
*   Laos.*
I wait from the moment daylight fades until the stars die out,
Through the time the moonlight straddles the Bến-Hải River.
Yet my anguish remains, while rice and corn wither
In my husband's absence, and lament my warrior's wife's fate in
*   silence.*
Who caused our separation? Who authorized
The bombs over there, and tears on this side?"

The hammock swings my heart heavy
While the rooster's crow proclaims the pain
Of my march into exile, and its halfway point.

The people never seemed to have any rice or meat; manioc and
potatoes were the only foods available. Aside from the low pro-
ductivity of the region, which had always been known for its
harsh climate, the war contributed to their poverty. But the rise
of communism seemed to have restored the austere conditions of
a previous century. Progressive ideas had not improved things.
The equality of men and women, for example, had somehow

robbed the women my father met of their femininity and char-
acteristically Vietnamese graciousness.

When American flares would momentarily turn night into
day, soldiers and prisoners would take cover under trees or in
patches of tall grass. After darkness returned, the soldiers would
fight among themselves over the parachutes attached to the flares,
which were prized as gifts for the young women of the Forward
Youth. My father wondered whether, in their offices on the
Potomac, U.S. military planners ever suspected that their parachutes were being used to help enemy troops win the affection
of young women.

The march north continued. Usually they would walk in
total darkness, with nothing but the buzzing of crickets to suggest
that anything around them was alive. During bombing raids the
men would throw themselves to the ground. The journey took
them past towns in the provinces of Hà Tĩnh, Nghệ An, and
Thanh Hóa. The destruction by American bombs became more
apparent. Fields pitted with craters, burned villages, and ruined
bridges dotted the land. Children gathered near Weaver once as
he was washing in a stream, yelling, "It's a Russian!" The soldiers
quickly chased them away.

"You need to be careful. People here consider you the enemy,
and they may attack you," Thuần explained to my father.

"That can't be true," my father later said to Tứ. "If it were,
wouldn't the people be more respectful of the soldiers guarding
us?"

"Who knows?" Tứ replied. "After years of propaganda—"

"But I've talked to some of the villagers," my father inter-
jected. "They're pleasant enough. I think the soldiers just want
to keep us from learning too much about life here."

"I guess you're right. They've stopped boasting about life in
the North, 'where there is everything.'"

The first time my father had gone to the North was by train,
as a student about to enter the university. He was in high spirits

then, and his luggage seemed inflated with confident youthful dreams. Later, in 1948, he went to Hà Nội at the beginning of his life as a married man. There he worked for the Ministry of Education of the Vietnamese nationalist government that had been established that year. Twenty years later he made his third trip north, hands tied, in the back of a truck or marching through thick jungle.

Now the truck driver pulled to a stop in front of a brick gate that was dimly illuminated by a few kerosene lamps. After the iron gates closed behind the truck, Thuần took the prisoners into a waiting room and immediately left with Hiền. My father didn't see the two cadres again.

Another cadre came into the waiting room with a set of keys and a flashlight. "Come with me," he said. "I'll be in front; one of you, take hold of my shoulder. The rest will do likewise— put your hand on the shoulder of whoever is ahead of you. Follow me; it's not far."

The captives marched from the nighttime darkness to the darkness of prison cells. The truck driver had delayed their arrival so that they would not be able to see, and perhaps recognize, where they were held. They were led through three locked gates, past a series of cells with unpainted steel doors, and down a short alley before arriving at the building. My father did not notice how the cadres had separated Tứ, Lộc, and Weaver from him. By the time he was led into his cell, his fellow captives had disappeared.

The cadre shone a dim ray on the plank of wood attached to a wall in the rectangular room, on one end of which was an enamel pot. Otherwise the cell was bare. After informing my father that he would be allowed to wash up the next day, the cadre stepped outside. Darkness enveloped the cell as my father heard the sound of the lock catching. Dropping his woven bag, he pushed it beneath the wooden plank. He turned in the dark, then sat hesitantly on the platform, then stretched out on it. He listened for noises from outside. The cells on either side were quiet. Footsteps and disembodied voices filtered into his cell for a few minutes. Using his hands as a pillow, he fell asleep with the thought that his life in isolation was just beginning.

☙ There was neither sound nor sunlight to greet him when he woke up the next morning. He did not know what time it was, for his watch had been confiscated. There was nothing he could do in the narrow room, and he continued to lie on the wooden plank, which was more comfortable than any floor or mat he had slept on in eight months. How long would he be held in this tiny cell? He now saw in the murky gray within the cell that its iron door had bars over the upper half, which had been left open during the night. Approaching, he could see through the bars the top of a wall about five feet away.

A gong announced wake-up time, though it was not until half an hour later that anyone came to the cell door. My father could hear doors opening and closing, the sound growing louder and closer each time. Arriving at his cell, a guard marched him quickly past five others to a basin of opaque water.

"Don't wash your towel," the soldier said. "Another time. Just wash quickly today."

On his way back to his cell my father was able to see that there were about twenty others in his row. The sorrowful gray doors were all shut. Prisoners could look out but could not see to the right or left. They washed separately. The isolation was complete.

For hours after being allowed out to wash, my father was left alone with nothing to do but wait for something to happen, for a guard's harsh orders, for anything. His boredom was relieved for a few moments when a guard appeared to hand him a blue uniform, a blanket, and a mosquito net.

"No nails. Hang the net on the strings," the guard instructed tersely. "But at night only." My father found the strings were stuck into cracks in the walls with tiny bamboo sticks. The Việt

Cộng did not want the prisoners to have metal objects in the cells.

The guard disappeared before my father could ask any questions, but the uniform told him he was to remain in the prison a long time. Likewise, it would be a while before he would need the blanket to keep off a wintry chill. He began to study the cell again. The domelike curve of the tall ceiling prevented any attempt to get out through the roof. It was dark and gloomy even at this morning hour, and the grayness of the walls reflected my father's desolation.

Doors were opening and closing again, one by one. Finally my father's opened.

"Come get your food!" a guard said.

Several enamel soup bowls were laid out on top of bowls of rice on an old table in a large room. My father carried his portion back to his cell. His door was closed and locked behind him. The soup was salted water boiled with a few strands of cabbage. The rice was an improvement over the manioc the prisoners had been eating for weeks on end.

The meal over, the guard came to walk my father back to the hall to return the bowls. There he was allowed a few cups of water, using the inner shell of a coconut as a scoop and a glass.

Silence and boredom returned. On his trip to and from the meal hall he had glimpsed a few other prisoners, criminal convicts in brown uniforms who looked as though they were helping the guards. They said nothing to him. Prison rules forbade any contact between inmates, and the blue uniform of a political prisoner held in isolation probably deterred them even more.

My father's busy life in freedom had allowed him only infrequent moments of introspection. He feared he would be unable to deal with the isolation, and was aware that a strong mind was essential for survival. But he had no choice other than to face his own self, and his loneliness. The Việt Cộng had brought him to this prison. Did they think Southern troops might have rescued the prisoners if they had remained in the jungle camps? Were they afraid the men would have died there? Were they holding the prisoners for exchange with their own men incarcerated in the South? Would the captives be left to languish in their cells until they died, so that the Việt Cộng could avoid accusations that they had executed the prisoners?

His questions were unanswerable. Perhaps the daily routines of the prison would help explain and structure this existence. A gong interrupted his thoughts, but this time no one came to the cell. Through the upper portion of the door he could see a man in brown pajamas carrying buckets of water back and forth. Turned into a blind man within the cell, his hearing grew sharper. He listened to the laborious footsteps, the water being poured into some sort of container; after a while he could recognize the change in the sound of the water as the container filled up. The man finished his task and left; my father regretted his absence. He did what all prisoners in isolation cells do: he paced his narrow room—two steps one way, two the other.

There were prisoners in the cells on all sides of his. Back again from the hall with his bowls of rice and soup, my father tapped on the side and rear walls. Someone knocked back from each of the three walls. Behind him must be another set of cells facing the opposite direction. He was thrilled to hear the knocks, but quickly sank into depression. He had never learned Morse code and couldn't communicate with other prisoners.

Later, after the evening meal, a guard came to the cell and handed him a kerosene lamp through the iron bars. The lamp brought a semblance of warmth, and my father sat up again on his wooden plank. One full day of isolation had almost passed, but it would still be a few hours before he could sleep.

"Hang up your net," the guard said from behind the bars. My father stood up quickly, hoping to engage him in conversation, but the man abruptly walked away. My father realized that the guards left the upper half of the door open so they could keep watch on him. They had brought him the kerosene lamp for the same reason. He would be observed even during his sleep. Annoyed, he put up the net and stretched out under it. Turning his face to the wall made him feel claustrophobic, but he kept his back to the door. He heard the guard's footsteps about a quarter of an hour later, and turned to see his face looking through the bars. It wasn't cold this September night, but he pulled the blanket over his body, trying to create a distance between the eyes and himself.

For days nothing happened. Then one morning a one-eyed man with an air of self-importance and an unfriendly face came to the cell and said, "Come!" Was it time for an interrogation session? My father had even begun hoping that they would start up again. He was surprised to be brought to a man wearing a stethoscope who examined him cursorily, gave him some vitamin tablets, and said, "You'll be allowed to rest for a while, to regain your strength."

After the exam Sử, the one-eyed guard, took my father to a building near a courtyard with a longan tree. He was put in cell number 12, which was as narrow as the first but had more light and a proper, if ancient, bed. The doctor had recommended that he be moved because of his poor health. From his new room he could look out to the courtyard: the uneven ground, the water tank, the longan tree with its green leaves, and beyond that, a wall not tall enough to hide the red-tiled roofs in the distance. Prison officers, ducking through a crude hole in the wall to enter the compound next door, provided him with some distraction.

He was given a sheet of paper. The handwritten prison rules on it were already familiar to him: he was not to contact other prisoners, use a foreign language, sing, read; he was required to observe set times for eating, sleeping, and washing. Other than those basic rules there were others that could be interpreted creatively. Prohibitions against "spreading unreliable news," for example, or "demoralizing other prisoners" hung like a rope over prisoners' heads.

The meal routine did not vary, except that the cell doors were opened in random order, thus preventing prisoners from knowing which inmates had picked up their food. My father needed allies, and unable to see any, he turned to poetry.

Nightfall with its shadows heightens my ordeal
And sets my sorrow down under the longan tree.
Wind and rain swirl under the eaves
Where a hurricane lamp swings and spreads its jaundiced light.

Somewhere in the forty tiny cells behind heavy bars
Someone heaves a sigh of distress.
This group of men,
Helpless birds from all around, battered by a tempest,
Are cast here, far away from home, with broken wings.

Each night, watching my shadow, I feel solitude deep in my soul
And hate the strangeness of my bed.
Each morning I wait for the birds' early song and the first cock's
   crow
And remember I have too much time
To spend in too little space.

Footsteps are confined in a two-meter cell,
In which I take one step forward and stop after the next.
I imagine the vast expanses of my country
And long for my freedom like a tiger for his jungle.

Not only days and months cease to elapse;
History also stops in its tracks.

The peace talks have not broken the icy barrier
And the intense heat of the war has not subsided.

We are only a few inches apart,
Separated by the thickness of a tarnished brick wall.
Through the wall a faint noise
Can resound with communion
Because we flow in the same stream,
Stand on the same frontline,
Hold the same beliefs,
and cling to the same dear dreams.

In the shadow of the bamboo curtain
I crave for the Fatherland's liberty,
The sweetness of love,
The gentle nature of the people,
The multiple scents of the land.
I can feel from distant oceans
The waves of struggle in the hearts of an entire generation.

As tree leaves await a breeze from afar to rustle,
Our cause will sail on a sweeping wind across the sea.
Vivaciously my soul tickles and my heart throbs
Viewing the moonlight in the prison as a dawning ray of hope.

The few things he could see through his cell door continued to comfort him. Half a dozen hens would run about catching bits of bread thrown out from different cells. There must be Americans held in the compound, whose portions of food were generous enough that they could spare some for the chickens.

One moonlit night as he stared out at the brightness of the courtyard, he thought of the verse of poets like Shakespeare, Edgar Allan Poe, Baudelaire, and Hàn Mặc Tử which spoke of the sadness of moonlight. In his imposed solitude, the moon instead became a soothing presence.

A guard interrupted his reverie. "Can't you sleep?" He appeared to be in his mid-twenties.

Encouraged by his sympathetic tone, my father replied, "Maybe I slept too much today. The moon is so wonderfully bright and the weather is pleasant, not too hot or cold."

"It'll get colder next month. Does it get cold in the South?"

"Not really; only in a few places. We must be near Hà Nội, no?"

"That's right—this is the Thanh Liệt camp, in the province of Hà Đông. Try to sleep, won't you?"

☙ The period of rest lasted three weeks. Then the interrogation sessions began. The words about my father's health, the party's generosity, the offer of amnesty and early release for cooperation were as old and tattered as the banana leaves outside the interview room. The Việt Cộng interrogator had short hair and a round face with sharp eyes; his army shirt was old, but he wore it with an air of dignity. He smoked as he observed my father.

Again my father answered questions about his family background and his career within the Southern government. The cadre never used harsh words; his speech was that of an educated man. He was adept at making the interrogation seem to be a friendly dialogue, joking innocently here and there. At other times he would try to show sympathy: "I understand. In the tough conditions of the South I would have done the same."

For all that, he failed to gain my father's confidence, and the answers were no more specific than those my father had given in the sessions en route north. My father refused to disclose information about the central government in Sài Gòn. When the man switched tactics, asking tougher questions about particular political and military situations in the South, my father prefaced his answers with expressions like "I guess . . .,"

"I assume . . .," "I may be mistaken but . . .," "I can only venture this thought . . ."

"Tell us only what you know. If you're not sure, don't bother," the man said.

"What happened with the Paris peace talks?" my father asked.

"Oh, nothing concrete yet."

"When do I begin reeducation?"

"You'll receive books and magazines that will explain to you the superior characteristics of the socialist North. Talk to your guards; they'll bring you reading materials."

The first session went from morning past lunchtime, then took up most of the afternoon. Afterward my father was taken back to his cell. Someone had gone through his belongings, though it was impossible to hide much in the empty room. My father checked that whoever had come into his cell had planted no incriminating objects.

A young guard accompanied him back and forth from his cell to the interrogation room for the next four days. He again wrote down the answers he had already given orally. He wrote slowly, carefully choosing his words. He had also become terrified of the empty unending days in his cell.

During the weeks of rest he had once glimpsed a tall American prisoner pacing furiously in the courtyard. "I want company! Put me with an American!" the man yelled.

"Go inside first," a cadre said.

"No. An American!" The prisoner screamed louder. "I want to be with my people!"

"We'll consider your request—just go inside."

"You never keep your promises!"

More guards arrived to help subdue the enraged prisoner. For a while his screams echoed in my father's cell. He worried about his own sanity, his ability to withstand his isolation. For many years he had contributed essays and poems to literary magazines, wishing he had more free hours in which to write. Now he had no paper or ink, deprived of everything but time. Yet he found that composing poetry about his captivity oddly enough let him escape from that misery. He spent hours molding words and rhymes in his mind. At night he recited the poems back to himself, always hungry for freedom:

> *The silvery silk glitters across the window,*
> *Catching a declining ray of sunshine that longs for unbounded*
>   *expanses.*
> *The iron bars having already confined my footsteps,*
> *Is the spider spinning its web to arrest my thoughts?*

The hours and days dragged on; the months stacked up on each other; autumn came and went. When the winter winds began to chill the nights, he could not complain: the upper half of the door was to remain open so that the guards could always monitor his movements. He paced his cell or curled up on his bed, composing, reworking, and memorizing lines of poetry. He forced his mind to re-create books he had read, chapter by chapter. He waited for new orders that never came; he was not charged with any specific crime, did not appear in any court, and received no sentence. His days were dreary and cold and interminable. Then came Tết, when the Year of the Monkey was succeeded by the Year of the Rooster, and a small treat:

A few improved meals marked the Tết holiday, supplemented by candies and a pack of cigarettes made from strong black tobacco from Albania, which I especially treasured since I had been deprived for such a long time. I smoked my first cigarette after breakfast, studying the package, which was imprinted with the image of a castle, perhaps a historic landmark in Albania. The paper was neither pure white nor smooth; the corners were folded untidily; the picture was unfocused and crudely printed. Yet I did not tire of looking at it, simply because of the few words TWENTY CIGARETTES and MADE IN ALBANIA, and particularly because the picture of the castle brought to my mind images of life out in the world. Those few simple details lightened my mood, and then I felt again my yearning for normal life.

After the evening meal I wrapped the blanket around me and leaned against the wall, looking at the dense darkness of the night falling quickly over the prison and holding me down. The darkness brought back a familiar feeling: since my capture I had lived in darkness, including the days on the trail taking me to the North. On this side of the parallel it was dark, on the other light. In the past year I had simultaneously led two existences: the physical life of a prisoner in the land of hatred, and an inner life turned toward the freedom of the South, where there is compassion and sunshine.

Thinking of the South, I turned to the past, my mind filled with the memory of the different periods of my life before my imprisonment. On that New Year's Eve, as the wind howled frightfully, it took a while before I could clear my mind and examine all my actions. Unwittingly I ignored my achievements, remembering only my mistakes and failures. I regretted occasions when I was weak and had wasted time or had not accomplished my goals, when I had failed to help or somehow mistreated others, and when I had not responded to the affection of friends. I found more faults with myself than with others, and I wondered whether my suffering hadn't made me kindlier, more generous. I regretted not having acted on my aspirations, and promised myself to make up for past wrongdoings when I regained my freedom. This year-end introspection helped me understand myself and others better than I had before.

Two days later I was still contemplating the pack of Albanian cigarettes, longing for days past, for my family, my friends, and my homeland, and grieving over my prisoner's destiny. The pack of cigarettes was, in the end, much more precious to me than the special food that the camp provided to the prisoners for the New Year.

A guard named Lam surprised my father with a quick visit. He normally dealt with the Americans.

"Are you well?" he asked with a warm smile.

"Not so well, as you can see."

"Well. You know the war of aggression is escalating."

"You mean . . .?" My father hesitated.

"Concretely, I mean the Americans could bomb this complex. They've done it before. Are you afraid of dying?"

"I've been through terrible raids on my way from the South. It's so easy to die, but it's also difficult. Would they bomb here, even with the American prisoners?"

Lam smiled again. "In any case, the Party and the government will protect you."

Halfway through the night he was awakened and taken out to wash. The cadre responsible for him gave no explanation: "Get ready to move immediately. Leave the net and blanket; the prison shirt as well."

"It is cold," my father said. "I propose that the cadre allow me to keep it for the road. Immediately after arriving in the new camp I will endeavor to return it to Thanh Liệt."

"No, you must leave it," the guard said, then tied a black cloth tightly over my father's eyes. He was led on a ten-minute walk before the guard ordered him onto an army vehicle with flaps covering its sides, its back divided into two separate cabins. My father heard Lộc talking to a cadre as he climbed into the other cabin; perhaps Weaver and Tứ were also being moved. They traveled throughout the night, my father sick and dizzy. A flap blown up by the wind revealed a street corner with many people, possibly in Hà Nội. His sickness grew worse the farther they went. The roads in the countryside were especially hard on him. His bones ached, and the blood pressure in his temples and at the back of his head was unbearable. He also suffered from a tooth that had begun hurting some months before. By the time they arrived at a river and stopped to wait for a ferry he had nearly fainted. The sun was now high up in the sky, and the vehicle sped past empty fields and forests, stopping at last near a field of tea plants where they waited for darkness before entering the camp.

The sentry at the front gate methodically completed paperwork while a guard took my father across an open yard, along a set of single-story houses, and down a couple of unpaved alleyways before they arrived at an inner compound. Inside the two encountered five sets of locked doors before the cells came into view.

Locked up in his new cell, my father collapsed on a damp bed, too tired to eat the piece of bread the guard had given him. From the middle of the tall ceiling a single dim bulb cast a sickly amber light over the room. He closed his eyes but could not sleep.

For the next few days he stayed in bed. His cell was slightly larger than the ones he had occupied at the previous camp, and instead of bars the steel door had a square hole at eye level. The wall outside was not tall, but the sky beyond it was obscured by the eaves. Standing on his toes, he could see a corner of the courtyard, which was always dark. Somehow he no longer craved hearing a voice through the hole in the door, or seeing a face. He fought to regain his strength and his will, fearing that he would come to a state of complete and lasting desolation. He told himself over and over that the Southern government would finally come to victory.

Meals, water for washing, and an aluminum can to be used as a chamber pot were all brought to him in his cell, making his isolation even more severe than in the previous prison. Only after many months did the camp authorities allow him out once a week to wash, sit in the sun, and exercise a little. The courtyard was immense compared to the cell, and the bit of blue sky he could see comforted him tremendously.

More months went by. Most of the time the guards who came to his cell maintained silence, and he routinely went for weeks without an occasion to say a word. His ability to withstand these harsh conditions in stoic silence was his only weapon: he would deny the Việt Cộng the perverse pleasure of hearing him lament his plight. The only time he succumbed to the desire to talk was a conversation he had with Đoàn, the cadre in whose charge he was, which took place at Tết, almost a year after his transfer to the new prison. The cadre came to his door with some candies, some small cakes, and a pack of cigarettes. "Some gifts for you, for Tết." He turned on the light.

"What's the date, cadre?" my father asked from the bed.

"The last day of the year. You'll be given special rations for three days."

It was now two years since his imprisonment. In the South, celebrations would resound in every home. Were his loved ones celebrating too—his parents, his wife, his children, his sister and her family? Were they even safe and well after the Tết of 1968?

Draping his blanket over his shoulders, he went to the door. Đoàn entered, bearing a tray on which were a teapot, a couple of small glasses, and a bottle of wine.

"Let's drink a bit together to greet the New Year," the cadre began. "Try this tea. We produce it here, in this camp."

"Thank you. I know this region produces good tea." Seizing on Đoàn's openness, my father asked, "This is the Phú Sơn camp in Thái Nguyên, isn't it?" The name was painted on the bottom of the can he used as a chamber pot.

"Yes."

Việt Cộng cadres were trained to treat inmates according to the policies of "the Party and the government," so the tea ceremony inside the cell was surely ordered by the central authorities. But whereas during Tết it was Vietnamese custom to abandon old grudges, the Việt Cộng carried out their fiercest, most ruthless attacks then.

"Is the cadre from this region?" he asked.

"No. From Lạng Sơn."

"Isn't the cadre going home to visit his family?"

"No, unfortunately. But I went home this past summer. Oh, well . . . It's sad not to be home with my family at this time."

"This is my third Tết away from my family. I wonder when—"

"Concretely," Đoàn replied, "reeducation cases take at least three years before prisoners can be released. The central government sent you here; we're only supposed to feed and house you. Decisions about your future will come from the central government."

My father sipped a bit of tea. "I hope the Paris talks will bring some results before too long."

"Me too. But so far there's been no sign that they will conclude anytime soon." Đoàn raised the bottle of wine. "Have a glass, won't you?"

"Thank you, cadre. I don't drink."

"Oh, but this is just a light plum wine. I thought you people . . ." Perhaps Đoàn believed the newspapers' reports about the decadence of the South. He asked again, "Is it really true you don't drink? Come on, have a glass."

"If I did, the cadre wouldn't have to invite me a second time."

Đoàn was silent a moment. "In the South, what food quotas do you have?"

"We don't have quotas or rations. You eat whatever you like, according to your budget. There are no food shortages, so there's no problem."

"Do you have transportation?"

"What kind?"

"Oh, like bicycles."

"They're used a lot by people in small towns, and in the countryside, especially by students and public functionaries. High-ranking officials often use motorcycles or cars."

"Are people assigned motorcycles and cars according to cylinders or liters?"

"Well, neither, actually; you buy whatever you want, if you have the money. There's no quota."

Đoàn grew pensive. "I don't understand life in the South, just as you don't understand life in the North," he said.

My father had no solution to this puzzle, but he seized the opening. "In my circumstances, if I could read things—anything, newspapers, books, magazines—I'd be more informed."

"I'll lend them to you, when I have any," Đoàn said. He stood up to leave.

The visit was no more than an official formality, but the contact cheered my father in his solitude. This conversation of nearly thirty minutes was an extraordinary event.

The rest of Tết passed by in dullness, though he could hear other prisoners practicing for a performance he was not allowed to see. Their singing entertained him, while a violinist rehearsing the "Blue Danube Waltz" brought him moments of unexpected happiness. It was the first time since his capture that he had heard music, a moment preserved in his poem "In Harmony":

The plaintive sound of a violin
Flows like a spring of melody,
Its notes scattering as if suspended in scented air.
The nimble bow glides on the wailing strings
And brings to mind a colorful fluttering of waves.

The beauty of my motherland's blue river is unequaled,
Its river on which boats shuttle to connect its two faithful banks.
Who brought war on this stream of love?
Oars disturb the sunset's reflection on the water
And rouse dormant feelings in the lonely woman.

The muted song still lingers
To voice anger at the gunfire of yesteryear's spring.

The music seems to recall the river of a distant country,
On whose stream festival lights glimmer in the eddies
In the shadow of an imposing castle bathed in glorious sound.
My soul exults in the evening song;
I think of the white statue whispering to the rosebush
In the prolonged sunset that gives lovers more time together.

Memories of the cherished airs of old
Bring yearning for a time now past,
When sweet dreams flowed like morning sunshine.
Enraptured by the warmth of spring, the sparrow rests on the
windowsill.
Now that the dead leaves have fallen, who can give me back my
young days?

The music defies the bounds of time
And crosses innumerable miles,
While here my prison cell is dreary, like an abyss;
I can confide only in the stars high above.
The melody longs for a faraway horizon
Where the bow freely dances
And the strings fully vibrate
To transport my thoughts to boundless expanses.
Sustained in adversity by the same hopes,
Nightly we are in communion through the harmonious notes
That fly through the windows to find those in similar straits,
Those who cherish similar vows in their hearts.

Once when Đoàn came into the cell with lunch, he handed my
father some salt on a papaya leaf. My father had requested the
salt for his aching teeth, but now he nearly forgot the pain in his

mouth and, dumping the salt on his towel, began to stare at the leaf with its bright veins. The half of the leaf that was still green suggested the clear water of a lake in autumn; the other half, turned a faint yellow, reminded him of sunlight.

He had been living in a world of gray. Before eating his lunch, and before thinking about his teeth, he took a bamboo nail and stuck the leaf into a crack in the wall. He studied it for hours; each jagged tip, each vein was a brushstroke in a mental painting of life and freedom beyond the cell door.

"What are you doing with that leaf?" Đoàn said on returning to the cell in the evening.

"I haven't seen colors for the longest time," my father explained.

The cadre removed the leaf from the wall, examined the crack, then let my father hang it up again.

 Winter arrived, yet another winter in solitude.

> *As my crossed legs freeze to the thick stone floor,*
> *I no longer feel the spinning earth.*
> *I have sat motionless for two years in one spot,*
> *Night after night watching the moon wax and wane,*
> *And constellations bloom in their season*
> *Beyond the trellis of thin bars on the jail window—*
> *An indelible image of stillness*
> *Undisturbed even by the drifting clouds.*
>
> *In pain and sorrow I sit here,*
> *Placid amid the moon and stars.*
> *No ocean storm or hurricane*
> *Can trouble this high hilltop.*
>
> *I sit in this temporal world*
> *While moonlight purifies my soul.*

The terrestrial pink dust that settles outside the prison gate
Does not stain my gray prisoner's shirt.

I sit here while my numb and cold heart
Continually kindles its fire of faithfulness,
Even though my flesh and bones might turn to stone,
Like that rock resembling the fabled mother holding her son
To watch for the return of her forever-gone husband,
Frozen in her eternal wait atop the mountain.

On sunny days my father could go outside. He took immense pleasure in observing a few ant colonies. Sitting by the hour, he came to know the different kinds of ants that crisscrossed the courtyard: red, black, and yellow ants, big ants, small ants, ants that stung, ants that did not; worker ants that carried food, overseer ants that kept the others in line as they went back and forth from one corner of the yard to another. He watched them attack other insects, watched them build new homes; he could tell what the weather would be by their activity. He noticed that none of them stopped to eat any of the food they carried to their nests. He observed how they would put their heads together, their antennae twitching as they exchanged information. He knew black ants avoided red ants, and that red ants stayed close to the ground whereas black ones would crawl on walls. Once, putting a few grains of rice at the opening of a nest, he blew softly until the grains fell inside. Later he found that the ants would come toward the opening whenever he blew into their hole. Unexpectedly, the ants taught him lessons of discipline and of patience. He thought of them as his small friends. After it had rained he tried to help them clear the collapsed entrances to their anthills, but they would always beat him to it, carrying specks of dirt away one by one.

✎ Toward the end of that winter, early in 1971, he was ordered to dig his own hole: a one-man air-raid shelter. Perhaps the peace negotiations had stalled, or had broken down altogether. Perhaps the United States and the Southern government were escalating the fighting to force concessions. Pointing to a circle he had scratched in the ground in one corner of the courtyard, Đoàn dropped a shovel at my father's feet.

Starting in the early morning, he dug throughout that day and again the next until midafternoon. When the shelter was finished he fell on his bed, exhausted, only to be awakened after a couple of hours of sleep.

"Get ready to move. Immediately," Đoàn ordered. "Bring all your belongings, along with the mosquito net and your blanket."

My father felt sick at the sight of the small olive green truck. The trip took ten minutes, during which the truck kept turning left and right. It crossed a small bridge and, after a few more turns, pulled up to the gate of a prison compound. The woman guard who came to meet Đoàn and my father led them inside by the dim light of a hurricane lamp to a cell built into the side of the hill under the main compound. It was darker, smaller, and more humid than any of his previous ones. The high walls were filthy, and the floor was badly stained. A concrete platform served as a bed. There was no window or air vent. It smelled bad.

After lighting a lamp in the corner, the woman left with Đ oàn. My father wrapped his blanket around him and, sitting on the platform, slowly leaned back against the cold wall. A couple of cockroaches climbed up his legs, tickling him to the bone. He chased them away. Questions were swirling in his head. Why had he been moved again? What was happening in the world outside? Finally he fell asleep.

When he woke up he heard voices chattering. For a moment he thought he was near a market, but then realized that the prison would not be located near a populated area. The voices were mostly those of women; once in a while he also heard the higher-pitched voices of children. He was unable to explain the voices to himself. When a woman in a prisoner's uniform brought him a chamber pot, it dawned on him that he was in a women's prison—the women's quarters of the prison he had just left. The noises he heard in the morning were made by women gathering for labor detail, and the children were theirs, kept in prison with their mothers since they had nowhere else to go. The Việt Cộng apparently feared that the bigger camp might be mistaken from the air as a military compound and bombed.

When he was taken out of his cell to get his evening meal, he saw several other portions laid out on the table—presumably for his former companions Lộc, Tứ, and Weaver. He heard women singing, practicing for the coming Tết celebration. The next day his usual rations were not only increased, but he was also given a pork dish along with candies and a pack of cigarettes. It was his second Tết in Thái Nguyên.

That spring, while washing his feet on the paved area of the courtyard, my father fell and suffered a slipped disk. He was forced to stay in bed for weeks. When it rained, the roof leaked over his bed and soaked him, but he could not move to another spot. To relieve his pain, the prison nurse gave him a shot; within a day, the site of the injection became infected. Đoàn lent him a book to read while he recuperated.

The American bombs did not come until summer. My father had sufficiently recovered to be able to walk again, but Đoàn always had to accompany him to the courtyard in case an air raid began and he needed to be brought back to his cell quickly. Mornings and evenings he sat alone, listening to the explosions of firebombs. Some days the raids were carried out by B-52 bombers; on others smaller aircraft would swoop down like iron thunder to unleash their rocket fire. He couldn't tell from their sound what or where their targets were, but he could hear Việt Cộng missiles flying upward in retaliation.

Later an old newspaper brought depressing news: Quảng Trị, his home province, had fallen to the Communists in May of

1972. Thousands of people had been displaced; hundreds had died. The peace talks had dragged on for four years without results.

Late one evening Đoàn entered the cell, saying, "Come with me!"

"Do I bring my clothes?"

"No need."

My father shuffled behind the cadre through an alley to a small house. Another cadre in civilian clothes, old but healthy-looking, stood up from his desk and greeted him warmly. No cadre had ever shaken hands with him before. The man offered him a cigarette. After first inquiring about his health, he brought up the subject of my father's home village.

"You can probably tell from my accent that I am also from Quảng Trị. Since we're from the same place, we can talk as friends."

"I couldn't hope for more."

"Let me ask you a question, then. If you were to be released, where would you resettle, and what would you do?"

The question took my father completely by surprise. He hesitated before answering, then spoke carefully. "When I was captured my parents were living in Huế, my wife and children in Đà Nẵng. But I have had no news from them for all these years; I don't even know where they are. I have no idea where I would live after being released. As for a job, you can see I am now very weak. If I were allowed to go back to the South, it would take a long time before I recovered my health. I don't think I could go back to work right away."

"Once you had regained your health, though, what would you do? Would you work for the Southern government again?"

"Does the cadre think that the Southern government would employ someone who had been in reeducation for five years?" Việt Cộng soldiers captured in the South would certainly not be trusted after being released and returned to the North. My father was fascinated that the cadre had used the words "Southern government" instead of "puppet regime."

The cadre thought about the question, then replied, "It depends on your own attitude once you return to the South."

"It also depends on the political situation there."

"You're right. If you go back to Quảng Trị, we'll meet again. Your cousin Bình says hello. We'll meet him again also, in our home province."

Back in his cell, my father tried to guess what the exchange meant. The cadre's questions were undoubtedly dictated from above, and the political concerns of that higher authority changed according to the situation. The Communist government must be looking forward to a time when he would be released—released but watched. He began to dream of freedom and of home.

◦• As always when my father was moved, Đoàn rushed him out of his cell and into the back of an army truck. But this time, as he climbed in he found Tứ and Lộc already there. The cadre got in with them so that the men could not talk. There was no sign of Weaver. Once the vehicle was rolling, Tứ scratched French letters into my father's leg: P-A-I-X. Peace.

The men could not stop looking at each other. Tứ and Lộc both looked even thinner than when they had arrived in Thanh Liệt, and miserably old, their faces wrinkled; Tứ's hair had gone white. The years of captivity had dulled their eyes. My father could tell they were shocked by his appearance as well. His jaundiced and flaky skin covered bones with virtually no flesh, as though he had sat under the chisel of a sculptor who kept carving away, making thin lines of his cheekbones and shoulders and limbs, exaggerating his eyes and forehead, and replacing the smooth chest with a row of ribs.

From the women's prison they were driven past the men's compound. My father glimpsed buildings lying in piles; the compound had been bombed. He was lucky to have been taken away, but he did not know the real reason he had been brought to the women's prison. After an American rescue operation at a prison in the northern region the Việt Cộng had decided to hide Weaver, Tứ, Lộc, and my father in the women's quarters at Thái Nguyên. My father had no way of knowing that he was the highest-ranking South Vietnamese official the Việt Cộng held, and they meant to make the most out of that fact.

In Hà Nội the three prisoners were each treated to a bowl of beef noodle soup, a specialty of the Northern capital and one of the best Vietnamese dishes. This night its watery contents betrayed the poverty of the country after the years of war. Nevertheless, my father was sure their being given the soup was an omen marking a turning-point in their lives as prisoners. For the first time since 1968, he truly believed he was about to be free again.

SEVEN

They Don't Sit Around in Cafés Here, Do They?

"Say hello, Donnie," Đỉnh commanded. "That's your uncle Đức. He'll be staying with us from now on."

I crouched down to Donnie's level. He stared at me, arms bowed out from his sides. He was three years old and had never seen me before. Now I was going to stay with his family.

"Cu Bé, this is Becky," Đỉnh said. He had left home in 1966, long before most people stopped calling me Cu Bé. My brother stood tall, big and confident in his polo shirt and khaki pants.

I stood up to face Becky, who had just taken off her sunglasses and was squinting slightly in the sunlight. I shifted my eyes from her blond hair to the pale skin of her arms, back to her gray-blue eyes. The warm May afternoon was pleasant, with a breeze stirring the new leaves in the treetops. We were standing in my brother's driveway in the suburban village of Sylvania in the fine state of Ohio. It was a long way from Việt Nam.

"Hi, Đức. Welcome ta Ohio," Becky said.

"Hel-lo, how-do-you-do-to-day?" I said. I couldn't

bring myself to say her first name. She was my elder, and in Vietnamese, I would have had to precede her name with the word Chị, "Older Sister."

"I'm fine," Becky said. "D'yuhvagood flight?"

I opted for a smile. I had been in the United States for exactly one week, and my English was limited to slow, formal sentences. I had arrived in Ohio half an hour before. Đinh picked me up at the Toledo airport in his red BMW while Becky was shopping with my nephew. They had just now turned up in the driveway and gotten out of Becky's car. I tugged at my blue-and-white striped shirt. Its collar points looked like the turned-down wings of an airplane beneath my chin—very American, I'd thought when I bought it at the flea market in Đà Nẵng and had the side seams taken in. Becky couldn't see the part I had tucked in, which came midway down my thighs. My bell-bottom jeans were filthy, torn at the hems, but not by design.

"Whad'you buy?" Đinh asked his wife.

"Nothing," Becky said. "Why are we standing here? Why don't we all go inside?" She and Đinh walked off.

I crouched down again to Donnie's level. I wanted to get to know my nephew, but more than that I feared going inside. I was sure Becky would see my shoes, which had lost their heels in the last hectic week, and I wasn't sure about how to behave with my brother, whom I hadn't seen in almost ten years. Our conversation in the car coming from the airport had been awkward.

Donnie ran into the garage and wheeled out his tricycle.

"Ah," I said. "I-think-you-are-going-to-ride-on-your-tricy-cle, are-you-not?"

Donnie merely waved his hand at the tricycle, then at me.

"Is-this-your-tri-cy-cle?" I asked, edging toward my nephew. He did not reply.

"This-is-your-tri-cy-cle. Would-you-like-to-ride on-your-tri-cy-cle please?" I tried, taking a few more steps toward him.

He waved his arm again at the tricycle and at me, then turned and ran inside. I too would have to go in.

  The USS *Pioneer Challenger* had taken a week to sail from the southern coast of Việt Nam to the island of Guam—seven agonizing days.

    My uncle Thịnh-Anh had said, "Don't—you'll lose your space," when I got up from the piece of cardboard we had been given to sleep on our first night out. I couldn't breathe, I told him, and left the hold, stepping over the mass of bodies and negotiating the staircase up to the deck. Hundreds more bodies covered its surface. Massive floodlights shone on them, bright as the midday sun. I crawled up another set of stairs to the dim upper deck and looked around for a place to sleep. I felt nauseous as I stretched myself out on the damp and oily floor, but I was too tired to care. For half an hour, without any kind of cover or blanket, I shivered in the cold wind as though I were feverish. Suddenly I felt a hand touch my crotch. I bolted upright. "Shhh," whispered the man next to me, trying to hold me down. I kicked my foot free from his grasp and quickly made my way back downstairs, my heart pounding. My arms and legs were covered with goose bumps, and I was sweating badly.

    When I reached the hold, my uncle and his family were asleep. There was only enough room among the sleeping figures for me to sit in a curled-up ball, arms around my legs, head on my knees. That was how I slept my first night away from my country.

    By morning the *Pioneer Challenger* had sailed around the southern tip of Việt Nam and was moored in the bay of Vũng Tàu, taking on still more people arriving on small boats. Hundreds fought to get on board; dozens failed and drowned. Parents saw their babies handed up the ladder to the big ship while they remained stranded on their sampans. I would later read that the *Pioneer Challenger* ended up bearing a total of three thousand men, women, and children away from South Việt Nam and the Communists.

As the ship set sail again, I put my head on my knees and cried, oblivious to everything around me. My relatives left me alone. When I had no tears left, I fell asleep. I woke up later as a man handed me a cup of bitter-tasting instant coffee obtained from an American soldier. He had managed to boil water in two empty milk cans over a fire stoked with note after note of South Vietnamese currency. Those around him watched with glee as he burned the money, unconcerned about the danger of setting fire to the overcrowded hold.

For the rest of the sea journey I stayed on deck to avoid the heat below, standing for hours at the railing, where I would gaze at the water foaming up from under the ship and let the salty wind caress my sunburned skin.

Camera lights blinded us as we disembarked in Guam. Uncle Thịnh-Anh and I turned away, as if by reflex. My uncle pushed his wife and children back against the tide of people pouring forth. The bright lights of the camera crews recording our arrival seemed to shine deep into our hearts to reveal the shame of losing a war, and of fleeing home.

~ We were brought from the dock to an American military base called Orote Point. Dry, orange-red soil stretched for miles, and a ferocious sun shone above. In the odd moments when the wind had accumulated enough to put out a few miserable puffs of air, dust would get in my eyes and blind me. My hair, drenched with sweat, was a matted mess. The thousands of refugees went to sleep on canvas army cots in a tent city. The heat would wake them up early each morning. On my first day in Guam, I ran into my friend Tuyền. Together we roamed the camp for hours. We both avoided talking about our mothers. Two days later we were delighted to find Linh, another school friend from Đà Nẵng. I greeted him with a bear hug; Linh fell to the ground, weak and exhausted from a sea journey that had been worse than mine.

"I can't imagine what you do out there all day in the heat," exclaimed Uncle Thịnh-Anh. "Haven't you reached your brother yet?"

"I tried," I lied, "but there were so many people at the phone office." In fact, I had already made a collect call to Đinh and told him I had left the country, and that our mother and Diệu-Quỳnh were still in Việt Nam. "Call me when you get to California!" he had said.

Uncle Thịnh-Anh had warned that at any time we might be called for a flight to a camp in California. "Get some new clothes. You can't go to America looking like a hippie." He gave me $50, which I spent trying to impress Tuyền, Linh, and their families. At the American commissary I bought several packs of Pall Malls and some round ground beef sandwiches wrapped in foil. I didn't know that individual packages of ketchup and mustard were available—they would have not made any difference to us anyway, then—or that the sandwiches should be served hot. My first hamburgers in Guam must have been the worst I ever ate, but I didn't realize it at the time. The excitement of finding friends and of speculating about what life would be like in America dulled gloomy thoughts about our homeland.

The days began to blend into one another, and I didn't know whether it was Friday or Saturday night when the sound of a rock band drew us to the beach. Under a tin roof held up by thin poles, Americans and Guamanians were twisting their bodies to the music.

"Look," Linh said, "that American girl is dancing by herself!"

"Heck, do you see those two boys dancing with each other?"

"If that's only dancing, what do they do when they make love?"

The Americans had introduced rock dancing in Đà Nẵng in previous years, but we still preferred older ballroom styles. A dance in Việt Nam was a formal occasion; the casual clothes and atmosphere we saw that night on the beach in Guam amazed us. During one long song the dancers would bang their hips together. A woman pulled me onto the dance floor. "It's the bump," she explained. "See, you swing your hips like this . . ." I tried a few moves, then offered the woman a helpless smile and walked off the dance floor. "Let's get out of here," I said to my friends.

The heat remained relentless. I could not stay still, however, and soon ran into three uncles and three aunts, all siblings of my mother's. With their spouses and children, altogether there were twenty-two of us preparing to go to the United States. A week after we arrived in Guam I was with my uncle Thịnh-Anh's family on a flight to Camp Pendleton in California. Once the plane was airborne, however, the pilot announced the camp was over-crowded and the flight would be rerouted.

I first set foot in America on a May afternoon in 1975, in the middle of flat miles of rain-blurred green fields around Fort Smith, Arkansas.

America's image has changed for me in the years since my first steps on its soil. I've enjoyed New York City, both its summer excitement and its picture-postcard wintry beauty after a snowfall, and the idyllic golden hills of northern California that roll toward the wine-growing valleys. I have lived many years among the faultless architecture and steep, wind-swept streets of San Francisco, but I have never had reason to go back to Fort Smith, Arkansas. At times I have thought of the soft green fields I saw that afternoon as though they had been a part of me all my life, and sometimes, for brief moments, I have missed them the way a person misses his home, his memory of it filtered and made attractive by time away. In that May afternoon the light rain over the fields, the expanse of space, the softness of time—all of these things soothed me. For the first time since my chaotic departure from Đà Nẵng, then Sài Gòn, Phú Quốc, and the ocean journey and the days of harsh sunshine and exhaustion in Guam, I felt a sense of comfort. It might have been just another ordinary May afternoon in Fort Smith, but it embraced me in the fragrance of something I had not known until then in my life. It was peace.

From Fort Smith we were taken to nearby Fort Chaffee for a week, during which the heels of my shoes finally broke off, American soldiers tried to put DDT powder on my head, and immigration officials gave me a form stating that I was a refugee with "parolee" status, "employment authorized." Trying to reach Đinh, a volunteer worker got Becky on the line and asked if she wouldn't kindly sponsor me. Becky agreed. After saying goodbye to my uncle, his family, and the friends I had found in the camp, I was on a plane to Toledo.

When I changed planes at O'Hare, a young man with long hair and a beard approached and spoke to me in halting French. He showed me some beads and a picture of George Harrison, and tried to sell me a booklet containing the words of an Indian guru. "I only have a few dollars," I said.

"How much do you have?" he asked. He took ten. I had five left.

Ten minutes later I was even more bewildered when a man at the boarding gate for the plane to Toledo offered me money. After making sure I had the right place, I answered his question about where I was from. He then tried to give me a five-dollar bill, saying, "I hope you like it here." I thanked him and declined the money. During the flight he jotted down his name and invited me to his home in Defiance. "Not far from Sylvania," he said. "Just ask for Dr. Burke." He offered me more money, which I again declined. My loud words of thanks and refusal to further offers of money caught my brother's attention when we descended from the plane. On the drive to Sylvania, I told Đinh the story of my encounters with the man from Defiance, but not about the ten dollars I no longer had.

When my sister Diệu-Hà later spotted the booklet and asked me where it came from, I said I had found it in Arkansas. Diệu-

Hà lived with Đinh at the time, studying to be a pharmacist at the University of Toledo. With no job, she was a financial burden on my brother, and my arrival only made things harder. Đinh enrolled me at the local high school for the summer term, and I spent most afternoons looking for work as a dishwasher or gas station attendant.

"He said he'd keep my name," I reported one day after making the rounds of prospective employers.

"They always say that!" Diệu-Hà said.

"No, he said he would call me when—"

"But that's what I'm trying to tell you! Why don't you ever listen? They never call!"

"But if they need people—"

"Well, go sit by the phone then."

I walked up and down Monroe, the business street near my brother's house, trying all the restaurants, the fast-food places, the hardware and automotive stores, the Exxon and Shell stations. I'd never held a job, my English was minimal, and I had no idea what would be expected of me if I did find work in a restaurant or gas station, but I kept trying.

I had long heard about the value Americans placed on independence and self-sufficiency. Now, living in their midst, I wanted desperately to prove that I could be self-sufficient. The Vietnamese too value independence; millions had died defending it. Though foreigners often marvel at the acceptance by the Vietnamese of their prescribed roles within extended families, self-reliance also is cherished.

The phone did not ring. I stayed home, and young as he was, Donnie became my best friend. The language barrier faded away. We played soccer, and I became a willing baby-sitter. Donnie had a natural kindness, and much of his affection was directed toward my parents, the grandparents he had never seen. "I'll go take a nap, and I'll close my eyes, and then I'll wake up—and then you can show me Granddad and Grandma's pictures," he would say. Sometimes he would close his eyes for just a few minutes and then call out from his room, "I'm finished—I'm finished! My eyes are open now. Show me the pictures!" "Showing the pictures" was the cue for me to tell stories about my parents and the country his father came from. He showed me a brocade jacket my mother had sent that he had never been able to wear. "Too bad. It came from far, far away, and it diddint get here for a long time, and then I grew too big, and then when it got here, well, it diddint fit me anymore. But don't tell her that, will you?"

I smiled and shook my head. I wasn't sure how to tell him that I couldn't have told her, even if I had wanted to. I didn't even know where she and Diệu-Quỳnh were. I stared at that question in the darkness every night.

In my first weeks in America, Diệu-Hà asked about her friends and people we knew in Đà Nẵng, and Đinh and Becky were curious about my departure. I found it hard to answer their questions. Đinh's memories of Việt Nam were of the sheltered and peaceful life our family had led in Đà Lạt before the war escalated. Because of my parents' position, he had associated only with others from a small urban elite, and the wartime suffering of the villagers and peasants in the countryside were too far removed from his world to touch him. I failed to find words to describe Việt Nam after he had left: the nightly bombing raids, the occasional Việt Cộng grenade in the markets, the Tết offensive. Đinh's impressions of the war back home were strangely enhanced but also sanitized by television. His interest in his homeland was strictly historical. When he came to the United States he had concentrated on his studies, and now he devoted himself to his career as a biologist and to his family.

When everyone was out of the house and Donnie was asleep I would sneak into Diệu-Hà's room to play tapes she had brought from home. Listening to the songs on headphones would plunge me into hours of intense depression. I would never be able to return to see the schools I had attended, the houses I had lived in as a child, my old friends. I would never be able to eat the food of my country, breathe its air, smell the earth during the first rain after months of tremendous heat, wake up to the chatter of women selling noodles, or go to bed hearing others hawk half-hatched duck eggs. I would never see my parents and Diệu-Quỳnh again.

The search for peace, safety, and freedom justified my departure from Việt Nam, and I found them all in the United States. The voice of reason nagged at my conscience, reminding me to be grateful that I had survived the war, and that I had found the door to America open. But like a scorned lover, I could not believe any future happiness was possible. On the streets of Sylvania, Ohio, I kept looking for heads of black hair. American coffee disappointed me, the oranges were bitter, the people had no style or sophistication, life was bland. Oddly, I never blamed "the Communists" for robbing me of my homeland. I had once feared them as ruthless enemies, but somehow I could never hate them.

❧ "Mow as close to that tree as you can, and then when you get over to this side keep going back and forth in straight lines," Đình explained, flinging his arm out to accentuate his words. I was being initiated in the suburban ritual of "mowing the lawn."

It had turned hot in June. I pushed the mower around languidly, sweating in the afternoon humidity. Every two weeks I would pull the mower out of the garage and strive again to get as close as possible to the tree, to cut perfectly straight swaths across the yard. At those times I hated the heat and the lawn mower, and the sound of the two girls next door splashing about in their swimming pool. I hated my self-pity and my tears, which were mixed with sweat. I began eating great quantities of ice cream every afternoon, as if the pleasure I got from its milky substance could take away my frustration and sorrow. I hated feeling guilty about leaving my parents and sister behind in Việt

Nam. I hated not being able to find a job, and not having any friends to talk to or things I could relate to. I hated being dependent on my brother, for food, money, rides, everything. I did not like the tidiness and the hyperefficient ways that made life in America so artificial; I hated Ohio. The smell of fresh-cut grass even now brings back to me the memory of the heat of a midwestern summer, and the sadness of life in exile.

At those times I also came to fear what my future in America might be like. Đinh would leave for work at the hospital at six in the morning and come home at three in the afternoon, an hour after Becky had left for her own job. When she came back around midnight, Đinh would already be asleep. During the week they never saw each other with eyes open. Though I fretted about having a job, I couldn't accept the notion that work could make spouses into strangers. "They don't sit around in cafés here, do they?" I would say to Diệu-Hà.

"Nope," she would snap. "This is Sylvania, Ohio. No cafés here, that's for sure."

From my brother's front lawn I could see the other houses up and down the street. Nowhere in sight was there anything but cars in various colors and houses in shades of blue and gray. No one ever walked on the prim sidewalks. And there were lawns: neat, clean lawns, big and small, rectangular or square, flat or graded; weed-free Sears-brochure lawns, simple or imperious or "ornamented." Sylvania was lawn country. For me the lawns began to stand for all that was sterile and uniform and conformist in America.

By July I had finished summer school, a half-hour bike ride from my brother's house. I never really got to know any of the students. At the beginning a few curious ones asked where I was from, then came up with general questions about the war. Others asked whether we had electricity or television in Việt Nam. "Yes," I said. "'Gunsmoke,' Wednesday night, and 'Bonanza' on Sunday. Also 'Batman' and 'Get Smart' and 'Wild, Wild West.'"

Someone said, "Cool, man." I didn't know what that meant. Denise Cousino was the only classmate who became friendly— not that we talked much. She'd bum a cigarette each morning as an excuse to sit with me on the school steps until class time. We smoked our cigarettes in silence and smiled at each other a lot. She didn't ask for my phone number, and I was too shy to ask for hers. Once I looked up her name in the phone book but there were too many Cousinos listed to know which might be her family. A couple of weeks later Denise stopped sitting with me. She merely showed me her own pack of cigarettes, then rushed off. The other kids must have said something about her hanging around with me.

After that, every other day or so I'd find that someone had loosened the bolts on the wheels of my bicycle. I started taking a wrench to school. I didn't want trouble, and I didn't want my brother to know, since it was his bicycle. Then one day I came out of class to find the front tire lying beside the bike, the bolts gone. While I stood looking down at it, considering whether I should try to carry it in pieces on my shoulder all the way home, some schoolmates swung by in a station wagon and one yelled out, "Hey, wanna ride?" They loaded my bike on top of the car and drove off with me in the backseat. Moments later they lit a cigarette and passed it around. I assumed it was tobacco; in Việt Nam my friends and I routinely took turns smoking from the same cigarette. By the time I noticed the peculiar smell, it was too late. My saviors dropped me off at a gas station near the house. The attendant kept shaking his head as I looked dazedly about, then loaded the bike on my back and grabbed the front tire in one hand. Carrying my books in the other, I wobbled the few blocks home. I put the bike in the garage, sat down next to it, and before I could rehearse a story for my brother, fell asleep.

"What happened to the bike?" Đinh asked when he came home that afternoon. I decided that from that day on I would walk to school.

✍ "Maybe you should join the marines," Đinh suggested. He was half joking, which meant he was half serious. It was a Sunday, and Đinh was washing his car in the garage, where I had a cot and a desk. "They'll pay for you to go to college. You speak French—they may station you in Paris." Where there were cafés, people on the streets, shops instead of malls, beautiful houses without lawns.

"I'll think about it," I replied, but Đinh knew I wouldn't. I didn't tell him I had seen a few marines in Việt Nam. Đinh hadn't seen the young girls thrown off their bicycles when marines reached down from their passing trucks to yank their hats away. He hadn't seen the masses of olive green steel transporting marines on the streets of Huế and Đà Nẵng, or seen what they did in countless villages, firing mortars and burning huts. He hadn't seen the six- and and nine- and fifteen-year-old boys bolting up from their sidewalk naps, pushing and punching each other to grab the marines' legs, yelling, whining all the while, "Okay, Salem, I shinin' yo shoes. . . . Take you good Mama San, ten do-la boom-boom. Wan good fack, okay, okay? GI numbah wan! Come for wan good fack, numbah-wan-fack!"

I was grateful to Đinh, and he remained willing to help even when I showed no appreciation of Sylvania. But I wrote to tell Tuyền in Montreal that I wanted to leave Ohio, to find some more lively place where I could earn money, be independent. "If you want cafés, there are lots here," Tuyền wrote back, "and you can stay with me." Tuyền's boss had agreed to hire me to work in his jewelry shop.

One week in August when Đinh was away on vacation, Diệu-Hà's friend Thuận came to visit from Washington, D.C., and offered to drive me to Montreal. I threw the few bits of clothes I had on the sheet of my cot, bundled it all up, and put it in the back of Thuận's Volkswagen station wagon.

Thuận broke into laughter when he saw me lacing my shoes. "Hell, these are the only shoes I have!" I said. The old-fashioned

two-tone gangster style shoes had been brown and white when
Đình gave them to me, but I spray-painted them black. They
didn't exactly go with the light blue trousers and pink shirt I was
wearing, also gifts from my brother. I didn't have anything I could
wear with spray-painted gangster shoes. A zoot suit would be
about the only possibility. It didn't matter. I'd get something new
for my feet in Montreal with my first paycheck.

We drove to a neighbor's house where Diệu-Hà was baby-
sitting.

"Try to get into school," she said.

"I will," I promised. "All right, take care," I added. That
was how I had said goodbye to my other sister. Armed with $100
a refugee assistance agency had sent, I rolled away. The August
sun washed the Sylvania morning and shone on the green-and-
white reflective signs on the Ohio and Michigan freeways. Thuận
got lost in Detroit, where we drove around aimlessly for hours. I
was appalled by its burned-out and abandoned buildings and its
illogical streets, and terrified of the drunken and menacing black
men shouting who knows what outside the car window. By the
time we reached the Windsor Bridge and got out of the car to
talk to the border patrolmen, it was beginning to get dark.

"You can go," said the Canadian immigration officer. "But
if you can't find a job, we'll kick you out."

"Go ahead," said the American one. "You're free. But once
you leave you can't come back."

"I'd have to live on that bridge, huh?" I said.

"No, sir," said the straight-faced American. "We'll deport
you."

"To where? I can't go back to Việt Nam!"

"We will still send you. Duh-unt matter whether they take
you." As a refugee on parole, I had no citizenship, no passport.
And there was no going back to Ohio.

Thuận parked in a rest area off a freeway, and we slept in
the back of the station wagon. In the morning we began our

journey south along back roads winding through bleak coal-mining towns, past golden fields and delightful small towns.

"In Washington, do people live like machines?" I asked Thuận.

"This is America," he said. His voice was a tad irritated. He had graciously agreed to drive me to Canada. Now he had to bring me back with him to his own city. "They live the same way everywhere. Nine to five: work. Six to seven: eat. After that TV, sleep, and work again at nine the next day. Everybody does the same thing every day."

"Yeah, and wash your car and mow the lawn on Saturday and go to the mall and eat at Kentucky Fried Chicken on Sunday, right?"

"What do you want? You're not gonna escape it."

I dropped the subject and let my benefactor drive. After a while he said, "I have some friends from college—they share a place in D.C. Maybe you can stay with them. Whoever works pays rent."

"Thanks," I said. "I'll find something." I waited for a word of encouragement that didn't come. "D.C. must be big," I said.

"You'll see. Plenty of time. Big monuments and museums."

"I meant lots of jobs."

Thuận didn't answer. I smoked cigarettes; he chewed gum.

"You hungry?" Thuận asked a few minutes after we entered Washington. It was midday.

"I'd like something to drink maybe," I said, eyes darting from one tall old building to another, with their elaborate facades and sculptures on their roofs. Car horns honked while people rushed about, taking up all the sidewalk. They didn't wear blue jeans.

"I should have stopped in Maryland. It'll be impossible to park anywhere here," Thuận said.

"Should we stop at your friends' house first?"

"There won't be anyone there now. Let's eat first."

We drove a few blocks farther, and I remained absorbed in the urban scenes. Thuận finally maneuvered the station wagon into a parking spot. "Let's go to Roy Rogers."

"Fine," I said, not knowing what Roy Rogers was.

As we were getting out of the car Thuận said, "Wait—why don't you apply for a job here? It's not far from my friends' place, and they usually have openings. I'll give you my address; just put it down on the application form for now."

Inside the restaurant Thuận stood in line while I asked for an application. I filled it out as he ate his hamburger.

"Think they'll hire me?" I asked when we left.

"I don't know. What did they say? Any openings?"

"The guy said he'd call."

Whether anyone called I never knew. That afternoon, before going to his friends', Thuận took me to a refugee assistance agency. A social worker there, a former admiral from Đà Nẵng and an acquaintance of my family's, immediately called my uncle Phồn-Anh in Alexandria, Virginia. Thuận's Volkswagen was soon speeding south along the Potomac. I barely had a glimpse of D.C.

"You're lucky the general recognized you," Uncle Phồn-Anh said when I got to his house. "What did you think you were doing, leaving your brother's?"

"I was going to Canada."

"And what would you do there?"

I thought I was going to work in a jewelry shop, but I didn't say anything. I had no idea what I was going to do in Alexandria, Virginia, but I knew I couldn't escape. Uncle Phồn-Anh would never allow me to.

"Thôi cứ ở đó đã, mai xin vô trường đi học. Chuyện khác tính sau. Rửa ráy đi rồi ăn cơm," said my uncle. "Just stay here; tomorrow we'll get you enrolled in school. We'll figure out the rest later. Now wash up—we'll be having dinner in a while."

I said a respectful yes in Vietnamese but didn't move, keeping my eyes on my spray-painted shoes. Then I went to look out the bay window at the front of the house. The last rays of sunshine had given way to darkness. I glanced left and right. For as far as I could see on either side of the street there were darkening patches in front of each house which I knew to be nothing else but lawns.

In September, along with Uncle Phồn-Anh's two older sons and a young daughter, I made the daily walk to Mount Vernon High, a few blocks from the house. Another daughter was in college, while a third son was in primary school. I had escaped being a burden on my brother only to become one on a jobless uncle with a large family. His wife was sponsored by a former boss in Việt Nam, a U.S. Army colonel who helped her get a job at the Pentagon. It was because of the colonel that a family of refugees had found its way to this conservative, subdued, and exclusive neighborhood.

My cousin worked at a fried chicken place, his brother at a Pizza Hut, and I cooked hamburgers at a nearby Roy Rogers—having shown the manager my immigration form and convinced him that the word *parolee* meant I was a refugee, not a criminal fresh out of prison. I earned minimum wage, $2.10 an hour, but I was proud to have a job. Roy Rogers had a western theme, and I had to wear a cowboy outfit: red-and-white checkered shirt, blue jeans, cowboy boots, and a plastic Stetson-style hat to hide my black hair. The customers didn't laugh out loud—not until I greeted them in my accented English: "Haoodi pahedner, may ah heop you?"

I spent most evenings of the first month of my first winter in the United States in the hot kitchen of Roy Rogers. Every few hours I'd push an industrial-size trash bin on a dolly out to the Dumpster in the back of the building, where it was cold and often snowy. I'd feel sorry for myself, and cried a few times. I cried also because I always seemed to do the wrong thing: I'd drop the burger trays or forget to save the fat for the company to sell to a soap factory. I didn't understand why anyone would want to save stinking, grimy black grease that looked like tar.

My boss was a pink-faced southern cowboy, stern and mean, with a crew cut and prominent sideburns. Often I couldn't understand his Virginia accent. His lips never seemed to move when he talked. "Rapid need, rapid need," I heard him say over my shoulder one evening. I looked at the nearly empty counter, but quietly set half a dozen burger patties on the grill. I did not dare question the boss.

"Now, what are you cooking all them hamburgers for?" he asked a moment later. "There ain't but them few folks here!"

"I thought you—" I started, but dropped my protest. I was already in enough trouble. I never explained myself to him, even after I realized he hadn't said there was a "rapid need" for more hamburgers. What he actually said was "wrap it neat." Once I learned the word *neat,* and that my boss didn't believe in adverbs, I tried hard to show that my hamburgers were indeed carefully wrapped in the thin pieces of paper marked ROY ROGERS. It was too late.

"Say, why don't you bring in your shirt the next time you come in?" said my boss a few days later.

"Pardon me, you want my shirt?" I asked.

"Uh-huh."

I thought he had suddenly turned kind and was offering to get it washed for me. The next day at school a classmate and co-worker said, "Heard you got fired."

"What do you mean?"

"He told you to return the shirt, didn't he?"

As soon as I got out of school, I jumped on my cousin's bike, raced down to Roy Rogers, and cornered my boss in his narrow office. He was leaning back with his shiny black-booted feet on the desk. He looked up from the accounting book on his lap and looked down again when he saw me.

"Did you fire me?"

"D'you bring in your shirt?"

"You can't fire me!" My anger made my English better. "How can you do that? What am I going to tell my family? What do you think I'm going to do now?"

"Don't know."

"You can't say that!"

"Look-it-here, son," said my boss, swinging his feet to the floor and turning to face me. "You're fired. You cain't even cut an au-nee-un without cryin'."

He pulled a check out of a drawer and handed it to me, wordless. I threw it back at him. It landed on top of his cigarette in the ashtray and started burning. My boss stared at it for a while before rescuing it. "Fine if you don't want the money," he said, handing me the check. "But ain't you needing it fer yer tax records?"

I kept shouting, then reached for my cowboy hat hanging in a row with others on a hook outside the office door. I threw it on the floor in a way that John Wayne might have approved. After that there was nothing to do but walk away.

I felt suffocated in the silence that followed me out the double doors of Roy Rogers. The boss didn't call me back, and for a fleeting moment I wanted to kick a few chairs and throw the napkin and sugar containers off a nearby table. My rage turned to shame. My ears burned red. I recoiled from my co-workers standing quietly in the kitchen, who had never seen me angry. I resented the attention from the customers around me. I hated the afternoon light outside. I hated America.

My wounded pride was restored two weeks later when I was hired as a paint salesman and stock clerk at a Sherwin Williams store. It felt fabulous. My hourly salary would be $2.55. But that first job was my most important introduction to America: hamburgers, western clothes, a mean boss. Since those Roy Rogers days I've come to detest hamburgers. They bring back not so much the memory of the cold burgers I first tasted in Guam as the greasy atmosphere of the Roy Rogers kitchen, and I can always smell the fat. I don't care much for the cowboy style either. It reminds me of my pink-faced boss—and besides, wearing a plastic Stetson wouldn't make me any more American.

Even without the cowboy clothes, I did start to become Americanized during my time in Virginia. The change was subtle and superficial enough, and I later dismissed it as part of a youthful need to fit in with the crowd around me, homogeneously white and upper class though it was. At seventeen I had possessed the adolescent insouciance that had allowed me to survive the war and leave home without my family; now it helped me adapt to life in Alexandria. I stopped thinking so much about the past and the fact that I was a refugee. At my uncle's, at least, I could speak Vietnamese and eat Vietnamese food. My homesick longing for familiarity was readily gratified as I became a part of an immigrant community that included relatives and friends in the area.

Gradually I confined my activities within that community to the weekends. Vietnamese friends and I would iron our clothes for hours on Friday evenings and then parade into Georgetown coffeehouses. On Saturday nights we went to clubs and massive parties in a university cafeteria where Vietnamese bands played sentimental songs and adults shifted their bodies across the dance floor in a tango embrace, temporarily recapturing the life they once knew. The weekend over, they surely resumed worrying about relatives left in Việt Nam, or their as yet uncertain futures in the United States. I worried about homework, and dates with American girls.

I wasn't exactly the hottest date around. I spent more of my free time with other boys, becoming a typical American youth in suburban Virginia. That meant turning up WPGC on the radio in the red-and-white Mustang belonging to John Turner's father, singing along to the lyrics of the Eagles and Jackson Browne, and cruising to the Krispy Kramer for doughnuts and the 7-Eleven for a Coke and a pack of Pall Malls. Chris Heine took me to art supply stores and poster shops in his mother's Ford LTD, and Lee Majeski drove me to record shops in search of jazz albums I had never heard before.

The parents I met, either at my friends' houses or when they came to Sherwin Williams to buy paint, wallpaper, or curtains, treated me with respect. They teased me about my formal ways and polite manner. Along with my friends, they would nag me about taking this or that schoolmate out on a date and suggested relentlessly that I attend class parties or school dances, but never with the aim of "introducing" me to American youth culture. They merely made suggestions because to them I always seemed shy.

I missed a formal dance midway through the school year. When the next dance took place, I agreed to go. Wearing my uncle's dark brown three-piece suit and my platform shoes, I left the house feeling sophisticated. Marie Lundy was waiting for me over at the school. As I approached the building, lightning struck.

Everyone else was wearing western outfits.

I shot back to my uncle's. Somehow I had failed to notice, and no one else had mentioned, that it was a square dance. Marie waited patiently while I changed. I was hopeless on the dance floor, jumping and kicking completely out of step and unable to hook arms in the right way or follow the dance leader's calls. We abandoned the dance, and Marie took me to a Pizza Hut. Sitting in her red blouse, short white skirt, and white boots and ignoring the stares we got, she soothed my embarrassment with her big eyes and managed the kindest smile.

Other incidents disturbed me profoundly. I could not get used to the American habit of complaining about one's parents. Perhaps my not having my parents made me resentful. My classmates also seemed undisciplined. Even the achievers resisted spending long hours studying or preparing homework. Students walked in and out of classrooms in casual clothes, slouched in their chairs, and addressed teachers and school officials in overly intimate tones that would have offended Vietnamese educators. Kids held hands, embraced, and kissed in the cafeteria and corridors. A friend who was distraught over breaking up with a girl this week might be in another relationship by the next.

Even as I adopted their ways, I observed my new friends through Vietnamese eyes. It struck me that the permissiveness of Western culture allowed the premature evaporation of adolescent innocence. The war had likewise robbed us Vietnamese youth of our innocence, giving us a sort of ageless sorrowful wisdom, and yet compared to American teenagers we remained curiously ignorant and naive. By the time we reached our teens, many of us were certain that our futures would be cut short on the battlefield. Nevertheless, we listened to our elders, nurtured our faith, and studied for a tomorrow we weren't sure would come. American teenagers baffled me. I became reproachful of children from such a privileged community as Mount Vernon who failed at school, smoked dope, or were generally unappreciative of their wealth and opportunities. Others were adamant and impatient about being independent and away from their families. In the end, the friendships I formed with American classmates could not be sustained because of the quiet force of the cultural differences that divided us.

Mount Vernon's graduating seniors packed their bags and went to private universities, mostly in other states. I moved out of my uncle's house, supporting myself with longer hours at Sherwin Williams, and enrolled at the community college of northern Virginia.

☙ The nightmares started during this period. No particular event provoked them. My mother always appeared in them, either sick, wounded, dying, or about to be taken away. I would be too late getting to her side. Sometimes I would rush in panic through floor after floor of a hospital, stepping over the dead in corridors and stairways, always searching for her. In many of these nightmares I would reach the floor where she was, only to hear the swirling blades of a helicopter taking off and carrying my mother away. If I did succeed in reaching her she would be on a stretcher, in a coma. She was never able to talk to me.

On other nights my dreams involved clandestine trips back home. I would be in hiding, climbing from rooftop to rooftop or slipping through narrow doorways, or riding a bicycle up hills and down valleys, always being chased. My legs felt heavy, my knees and heart about to give out. I could feel men chasing me, but rarely saw them. When I did, I could recognize the faded green uniforms of the Việt Cộng. The men had neither faces nor voices. I was never caught, and never had a confrontation with them. I would escape, but only just.

I did not know how to stop the horrifying dreams, and I simply came to expect them each night. When Diệu-Hà called and told me she had received a letter from my mother, I was thrilled. I hoped the nightmares would end. They didn't. My mother continued to write by way of relatives in France. The letters were censored, and she sometimes used euphemisms too obscure to decipher. Still, there was no mistaking how much she was suffering, and it was wrenching to write back. What could I tell her about life in America that would not fill her with envy? But painting a dark picture would worry her. I tried to convince her that I was doing fine on my own, and that I was continuing my education. I doubted that she fully believed my words about how secure my future was. I did not believe them myself.

꙰ Linh didn't argue with my explanation that I wanted to move to California because I wanted a chance to go to a university. "I'll find a job," I assured him over the phone. I didn't explain that I also wanted to be with him and other childhood friends. In July 1977 Tuyèn and his two brothers had come from Montreal to visit me in Alexandria, Virginia. He talked me into joining them on a bus trip to California. I regretted the six days and nights in the confines of the bus, traveling over endless freeways running through the flatlands, getting off to wait in dingy Greyhound stations with the inevitable filthy bums, drunkards, and drug dealers in places like Memphis and Dallas and Tucson. At roadside diners obese bikers and truck drivers didn't care to be friendly to four long-haired Asian boys. Waitresses bulging out of yellowed uniforms pretended not to understand our English. We ate greasy grilled cheese sandwiches, wishing it were fried rice instead. I had not imagined the summer heat could be so terrible in America: with the temperature always just below a hundred degrees, it tore at your skin and gave you instant headaches, and the sun burned and burned our eyes.

In San Diego the weather was milder, and the trip seemed worthwhile after I was reunited with Linh, his cousin Bình, Nghị, and Hân, all friends from Đà Nẵng. Back in Virginia I had missed having my old friends of many years to talk to. It was wonderful, though sad too, to remember with them our home, our other school friends, and the things we used to do. I decided to move to California, arguing to my doubting relatives that I would establish residency and get an education at a good university for next to nothing.

The sunny and bright days of San Diego buoyed my optimism. I found a job at Montgomery Ward, and although I had to mix, smell, and sell paint again, I could afford my own studio apartment. It was over an hour by bus to work in National City, but I felt proud. I stayed with the job and the apartment for the next two years, studied broadcasting at San Diego State University, and enjoyed the company of my boyhood friends on Friday evenings.

I moved to San Jose in 1979 to take a job as a social worker, meeting refugees from Cambodia, Laos, and Việt Nam at the airport and taking them to low-rent apartments across the city.

The relief agency for which I worked provided blankets, pillows, and household utensils, along with donated clothes. I sent hundreds of newcomers into the fluorescent-lit, bare-walled assembly workshops of the booming electronics companies in Silicon Valley. I helped others register for English and vocational classes.

I never questioned the fact that I was helping create instant Asian ghettos and a massive bottom-rung work force serving the electronics industry. I didn't quite believe in the American Dream I was prescribing for the refugees, but enough of those I aided did eventually succeed. Many are still in the industry, some owning their own firms, and others have completed college and university degrees. Some opened up small businesses and later became a vocal part of a community that was expanding in size and influence in the San Jose area. Once in a while I would recognize a face in an advertisement in Vietnamese magazines: someone I'd picked up at the airport and placed in an electronics firm in the late 1970s, now a real estate or insurance agent. Those who failed I would not see again; they showed up in statistics in some government report, or in mug shots in police files.

≈ I abandoned refugee work for a year to produce a Vietnamese radio program in the area, then returned to it for another year when I moved to San Francisco in 1981. By this time I had become a bureaucrat, and when I was tired of that I accepted an offer to work in a refugee camp in Indonesia. The only problem: to fill the job, I had to be an American citizen. I decided in one short moment to get U.S. citizenship. Until then the thought of formally becoming an American had always pained me. I had filled out a few applications since 1980, the year I became eligible, but I always discarded them. It would simply be disloyal.

I had come to dislike America for what had been done to the Vietnamese and Việt Nam during the war. Even as I lived in its cities and among its people, I remained alienated from American culture. The most powerful force preventing me from submitting the application was the feeling that acquiring American citizenship would forever sever my link to Việt Nam. I took comfort in the fact that I was applying for citizenship only to return to Asia to live among my own people. Yet shame clung to me like a heavy summer shadow.

I succeeded in having the application process speeded up, and within three weeks I was summoned to the Immigration and Naturalization Service in San Francisco. At seven-thirty in the morning, hundreds of anxious immigrants were already gathered there. People in line volunteered facts and more facts about U.S. history and government while others flipped through thick books, reviewing for the all-important citizenship test. I had studied next to nothing.

I waited two hours. The woman who met me smiled gently, her white blouse, blue blazer, and red neck bow making her look the part of a civil servant. She wanted to start the test right away. Panic set in with her first question. Did I know who designed the American flag?

"Calvin Klein?" I ventured. He'd designed everything else in America, hadn't he?

"Who takes over if the president of the United States should be unable to fulfill his duties?"

"Alexander Haig," I blurted out. The lady laughed, and moved on to ask what the requirements were to be a presidential candidate. I had studied that in a political science class—seven years before, in Virginia.

"Well," I said, "you must be, uh, U.S.-born."

"That's good. Anything else?"

"Uh, you can't be mentally ill!"

The woman opened her mouth, her eyes bulging. I wondered whether she would ask me about football, hamburgers, Chevrolets. I survived a few more questions before she said, "Oh, get out of here. . . . You're really funny, you know that?

"By the way," she added—"congratulations."

At the courtroom ceremony a week later, I stood among three hundred other soon-to-be Americans. The judge managed to move me with a well-rehearsed speech about the American tradition of accepting immigrants, and about the democratic principles of the Founding Fathers.

Next to me stood a toupéed Filipino in a sky blue blazer over patterned bell-bottom golf pants, an American flag in his hand, another pinned to his lapel. He repeated the judge's lines word for word during the swearing-in ceremony, loudly pledging allegiance to his new country. He then turned to me with a big smile, and perhaps because he noticed the dampness in my eyes, extended his arms to hug me.

I patted his shoulder, and turned away.

How was I to explain to the jubilant man that my tears had not been tears of joy at becoming an American? How could I tell him that they had come when the judge talked about bearing arms for the United States? I did not want to explain the images of American marines pointing rifles at Vietnamese villagers in black pajamas.

On the first day of the lunar New Year, Tết 1983, armed with a brand-new passport (the eagle seal embossed over my picture, skewing my nose and left eye), I set off on a Boeing 747 for a tropical island where I was to meet America's newest huddled masses yearning to breathe free.

EIGHT

Nothing Is More Precious Than Independence and Liberty

My father stepped into his new cell. A man lifted himself out from under a blanket and sat up in bed, silently returning his startled look. My father glanced to the right and saw another bed. His isolation had ended.

As the guard closed the door to the cell, my father pushed his bag under the empty bed and sat down. He faced his cellmate. The men smiled. Finally my father asked, "Have you been here long?"

"Two days," the man replied in a Quảng Trị accent.

The man, Xuân, was born in a village next to my father's, in the district of Triệu Phong.

"Where were you held before?"

"Up north, in Yên Bái," Xuân said.

"When were you arrested?"

"Two years ago."

"In Quảng Trị?" my father asked.

"Yes. I was with the police force."

"Do you know which camp this is?"

"Thanh Liệt."

"Are these the cells near the courtyard with the longan tree?"

"Yes," Xuân said. "You've been here before, then?"

"Yes. Were you in isolation as well?"

"Yes, for four months. Then they took me to Yên Bái," Xuân said, becoming animated for the first time. "I couldn't take the isolation. In my third month here I drank some oil. Obviously, I didn't die. Then I ran away one day. I wanted them to shoot me."

"They didn't."

"No. They chased and caught me."

My father raised his hand. Both men listened to the footsteps outside their door. After a while Xuân resumed. "Have you been in prison a long time?"

"Yes," my father said, standing up to approach the door. He lowered his voice. "A long time. Since Tết of 1968."

"Were you in isolation?"

"Yes."

"How long?"

My father turned toward Xuân. "September 1968 until to-night."

Xuân's face paled. "How'd you survive?"

"You deal with it the best you can," said my father, returning to his bed. Kicking off his sandals, he swung his legs up and leaned against the wall. "We should sleep. Maybe we'll have labor duty tomorrow." The conversation had gone on long enough for a first meeting. He did not show his relief at having a cellmate to talk to. He feared it was a ploy, a setup by the Việt Cộng to keep him under observation. It was still an improvement, he thought, ignoring his disappointment: he was not being released.

The next day the one-eyed guard, Sủ, took Xuân and my father to the kitchen area and gave each a bowl of noodles for breakfast. "Better diet. It must mean they're planning to release us," Xuân observed back in the cell.

"They probably want to make sure we don't look too poorly."

"Have you heard they're about to sign a peace treaty in Paris?"

Sự came back to the cell before my father could answer. There was a measure of distrust in Xuân's eyes as Sự took my father away, following a series of twisting alleys to reach a brick building. The guard left him with two cadres. Tứ and Lộc appeared.

"This isn't a reeducation session. We'll simply talk a little," said the elder of the cadres before launching into a lecture on periods of warfare, division, and reunification in Vietnamese history. My father presumed the meeting would lead to a discussion of the peace agreement, but the cadres avoided his questions. "It will be signed in a spirit of national reconciliation," said one. "It'll end the fighting, but the details aren't clear."

My father and his companions waited, but for the next weeks no news came. More prisoners were brought in, each receiving a medical checkup. Occasionally the diet was augmented by some fruit, which increased their hopes of being released, but my father was unable to shake off his suspicion that the Việt Cộng merely wanted to boost their image.

⌖ At noon three days after Hà Nội Radio announced the peace talks in Paris had stalled and North Việt Nam's leader Lê Đức Thọ had returned to Hà Nội, the bombs pounded down again. My father and Xuân crawled under their beds. All through the next week American planes roared and glistened in the bright winter sky, dropping bombs that shook the entire area. The raids came every few hours in the afternoon and three or four times during the night. On the third day of bombing Sự took Xuân and my father to a large room across the courtyard. "From now on, don't wait for orders," Sự said. "The doors are not locked. Just run into the bunker." The bunker was in fact a simple hole in the ground, its opening covered with a plank. With sirens warning the men of approaching planes, antiaircraft missiles would boom up into the sky. Soldiers rushed around the compound, blowing their whistles, yelling orders. Branches fell from the longan tree; pieces of concrete dropped on the men, and their beds were covered with chips of dried whitewash. During the lulls my father and Xuân cleared the debris, but within hours the blasts would begin again. Waiting for the explosion, they whispered their speculations to each other at night.

"Hà Nội. They must be hitting Hà Nội," Xuân suggested.

"When will this war end?"

Xuân quoted Hồ Chí Minh: "Five, ten years, maybe longer."

Later on the day Sự had showed them the bunker, after an early dinner, the guard ordered the men to pack up. Some fifteen or sixteen inmates shivered near the prison gate. Xuân, Lộc, Tứ, my father, and a dozen others were bound and led away in a double file along side streets out of town and on back roads through darkened, lifeless villages. At a holding camp they were crowded into a long hut with other prisoners wearing the brown uniforms of common criminals. Tứ, Lộc, and my father clustered together.

"How are you two holding up?" my father asked.

"I've been bothered by hemorrhoids," Tứ answered.

"Any medicines?"

"Only when there's heavy bleeding. Vitamin K."

"What about you, Lộc?"

"Nothing serious, but I never have any energy. The worst is the nervous breakdowns."

"Does anybody know where Weaver is?" Lộc asked.

"No. Wasn't he taken to Thái Nguyên with you?"

"No. I was alone."

"Where could he be? Hà Nội Hilton?"

My father turned to Tứ. "What did you do to kill time all these years?"

"Oh, I repented my heinous crimes against the People. I've worked laboriously at reeducating myself so that, with the Party's generosity, I can return quickly to my family."

Lộc and my father restrained the impulse to laugh.

 The trip continued on foot, with the prisoners quartered at holding camps overnight. After a couple of days Lộc, Tứ, and my father were piled into a military truck and taken to a prison in the mountainous region in the north. After a week a soldier announced yet another move. My father assumed the war had intensified and that the prisoners were about to be taken into China. Instead they were driven south to a large camp where they were allowed to gather in groups or roam the compound freely, and play table tennis. The food improved. Genial guards spoke of the beginning of a new era in which the inmates were to forget past suffering and rancor, and to live with their "Northern brothers" in a spirit of "national reconciliation."

Tết 1973 arrived in this optimistic atmosphere. Along with white rice, the prisoners were given rare treats of poultry, goat meat, high-grade cigarettes, and plum wine. A volleyball net was put up in the courtyard. A few days later a young guard brought newspapers. The inmates gathered around, scanning the news items. The peace treaty had been signed.

"Right here!" shouted a young man. "Article eight. Listen. Exchange of prisoners—within sixty days for military captives, ninety days for civilians. Starts January 28, 1973."

The guard walked away, promising that questions about the treaty would be answered soon.

"Doesn't sound good," said a young prisoner named Văn. "Their soldiers will remain in the South. They'll continue the war, sabotage the whole thing."

"Signing the treaty is one thing," my father replied. "Respecting it is another question. The Việt Cộng—"

"Well, we'll have to wait and see. Let's get back," Lộc suggested.

In the next days my father and the other prisoners continued with their daily duties, and played Ping-Pong or volleyball as though nothing had changed. They were also permitted to play card games and Chinese chess.

"They must be preparing to welcome some big-shot cadres from the government," Văn told my father as the two bathed and washed their clothes in a brook. "I'm sure they've got plans for us."

"Why do you say that?"

"They'll make us work as spies in the South."

"No one will do it."

"Some people have relatives in the North. They'll be blackmailed. The Việt Cộng will threaten to keep you, delay your release."

"Some may agree to it now, but they won't once they're home."

"The Việt Cộng will tell people you agreed. They'll sow distrust. Have you noticed the cadres talking to some of the inmates in private?"

The early evening turned chilly. The two men gathered their clothes and hurried back to the camp, picking up dead branches on the way to explain their long absence. The possibility of freedom warmed the captives, but a wood fire was still needed each night.

A few days later three government officials turned up carrying briefcases, their uniforms indicating high rank. They asked about the prisoners' health conditions and offered them detailed documents about the treaty, but did not discuss them.

Tứ allowed a Việt Cộng photographer and a film cameraman

to include him in a shot with Southern special forces soldiers captured during spy missions in the North. "The Việt Cộng will surely distribute the photos," he explained that evening. "They can't deny that I'm held here."

My father and Lộc nevertheless avoided the photographers, who hunted them for over a week. Once a photographer hid in a corner to snap a picture of my father leaving his cell. My father was certain the photos were for international consumption, showing relaxed prisoners competing in sports and chess tournaments—instead of doing forced labor or suffering rough conditions in jungle areas.

At lunchtime one day he was summoned to the administration area to meet the two government officials. He was surprised to find them finishing an elaborate meal and some plum wine. They talked about his visit to Hà Nội when he was being returned to Thanh Liệt. An inmate named Mặc was brought into the room and quickly taken out again. Before my father could react, a photographer appeared and snapped a few shots. His captors could now show pictures of him having a meal with Communist officials, sitting under a red flag. By the time he returned to the compound Mặc had spread the damaging news among the prisoners.

It took a few days to regain the confidence of his fellow captives; then my father lost them. A guard ordered the prisoners to the administration building in groups of five. The inmates in the first group came back to announce they were being released the next day.

"To where?" asked my father.

"Quảng Trị. We'll be exchanged at the Thạch Hãn River."

"Don't worry. Your turn will come soon, too," someone said.

"Write a letter to your family. We'll put it in the tube of toothpaste they just gave us."

My father wrote a few lines on a piece of paper and handed

it to one of the prisoners. "I'll never forget you," he said. "I didn't say much, in case the guards find the letter. I hope you can reach my family and tell them about life here."

Some prisoners gave Tứ, Lộc, and my father their toothpaste and washcloths. Mặc gave my father a knife. "I misjudged you. When I saw you with the two officials I didn't remember you'd only been up there for a few minutes, so you couldn't have shared their meal. I didn't think about it then."

"Don't worry. I'll see you again under other circumstances."

The prisoners ate their evening meal in silence. No one slept. Tứ, Lộc, and my father went to the gate in the morning but were prevented from accompanying the prisoners to the trucks that would take them to freedom. My father stayed at the gate. The trucks disappeared behind clouds of red dust.

The three men were moved to another part of the camp two days later in order to prevent contact with Northern convicts. The sports and chess games ended.

Early the next morning all prisoners were ordered into the meeting hall. A flag was raised while the national anthem was played over the loudspeaker. It was announced that the signing of the treaty was a victory. The government had declared a general amnesty. For an hour a voice read out names and crimes. Prisoners convicted of robbery, gambling, embezzlement, corruption, rape— all were being freed. Lộc, Tứ, and my father did not hear their own names. My father asked one of the officers when he would be released. "I'm asking myself the same question," said the man.

My father kept his hopes up as he read reports about prisoners being released from other camps. The agreed date for the release of military detainees came and went—but the date set for political prisoners was a month later. A cadre casually counseled him, "Take care of the young banana trees in the courtyard. The bananas can give you added nourishment." It would be a long time before the trees would bear fruit.

As the weeks turned into months, he reasoned that the

exchange of prisoners had been delayed by unexpected complications. Then the *People's Daily* reported that the program had been a success. All prisoners had been released.

The next day Lộc and my father decided on an extreme step: they stopped eating. The strength gained during the previous months of exercise quickly drained out of them. They would take just a few glasses of water each day. The Việt Cộng waited three days before having a doctor see them. He gave the men canned milk and a few cigarettes, and an assurance that the government was still exchanging prisoners. Reluctantly, the two men ended their fast.

The year 1974 ended without significant changes. A guard brought his daily meals; otherwise my father had no contact with any human beings. He started to save pieces of paper, on which he wrote short stories set in South Việt Nam, and a historical novel he had started composing in 1972.

In March of 1975 Lộc, Tứ, and my father were moved to a cleaner, more secure compound. A loudspeaker outside their cells announced devastating news. In the South, town after town was falling into Communist hands: Huế, Quãng Ngãi, Bình Định, then cities farther and farther south.

Ten days after the fall of Sài Gòn, my father and his two friends were ordered to pack their bags. The years of captivity are about to end, he thought. The war was over. But he would only be released into a Communist society. It would still be a prison.

The road he thought would take him south went in the opposite direction.

"I can't believe we're back in Lào Cai," Tứ said.

"Weren't we in the other building last time?" Lộc asked.

"Does it matter? It was temporary then. This time, who knows?"

"Maybe there'll be a general amnesty."

The prisoners' hopes faded with the passing months. My

father's stories were discovered. The prison authorities considered the offense so serious that they sent the manuscripts to the Ministry of the Interior. Undoubtedly the government would conclude from these writings that he had not been sufficiently reeducated, and that he still nurtured bourgeois thoughts. Such a judgment would automatically prolong his sentence.

For two months he went to sleep and began each day terrified. He shivered whenever a guard approached his cell, but camp guards never mentioned his offense. Eventually he let go of his fear, but he had no explanation for his luck.

✿ "I know," said Sinh. "He's just skin and bones. He's got the eyes of a dead man."

Sinh was a convict who ferried meals to the political prisoners confined to their cells. Lộc had pleaded with him for help: my father had diarrhea and could not leave his bed. For weeks he received no attention. Việt Cộng health care had little concern for the gravity of the illness; only the political standing of the sick person mattered. A political prisoner would be the last to receive care.

"They're leaving me to die," my father whispered to Lộc. "There's no longer a prisoner exchange. That's it for me." The Việt Cộng no longer faced international pressure on the treatment of prisoners now that it had emerged victorious over the South. The prison nurse gave my father some pills and, when his condition did not improve, herbal medicine. Whether Sinh had persuaded the nurse to tend him was never certain, but my father was grateful to him. Until then Sinh had been disliked by many.

Sinh was among the Vietnamese who were sent to work in Thailand some years before. On his return from that capitalist neighbor he was detained. Since they were not required to labor in the jungle, Tứ, Lộc, and my father were able to observe Sinh daily, and had quickly detected his arrogance and cruelty toward the inmates. Though he was held in isolation in the disciplinary ward, he was allowed to move about freely in the political section, and even had keys to the cells. When the three men eventually discovered that Sinh had leprosy, they forced themselves to continue to eat the food he brought each day, but it tasted bitter.

Slowly, however, they developed a certain sympathy for him. When a young woman in the disciplinary ward rejected him, he began to sing sad songs at night. The songs at last became wails accompanied by loud banging on a metal container. In the quiet nights Sinh's voice was like that of a wounded animal. "*Kêu trời, trời không thấu. Kêu đất, đất khong hay. Kêu ông giám thị; ông giám thị ngũ say.* I call out to Heaven; Heaven won't listen. I call out to Earth; Earth won't reply. I call out to the warden; he's asleep and pays no attention."

My father heard in Sinh's voice the desperation of a man aware he would die, and of a nasty disease. Death had become a perverse obsession with Sinh; it also hung over my father's own sickly spirit. If left untreated, his illness could result in his own demise, most likely before that of Sinh.

But while washing one morning some weeks later my father said to Lộc, "Think I've conquered the diarrhea." He was strong enough now to walk about in the courtyard near his cell. That same morning, Sinh announced he was being released. The wailing had worked: the authorities had given in.

My father later learned that another political prisoner simply packed his belongings one morning and requested to be freed because he considered himself "sufficiently reeducated." When the authorities denied his request, he went back to his labor duties. But the next morning, and thereafter, he'd bring out his bags and make the request again. Some thought him naive and eccentric. Four months later they were stunned to learn that the cadres had released him.

After being held for years without trial or sentencing, some prisoners would be told they had been classified as state laborers. They had to work in particular jobs at specified locations and were not allowed to go home or to move. They were known by the designation "Pardoned-But-Not-Freed."

Several female prisoners who had been nuns were told they could be released, but only if they would get married. Other prisoners received official sentences of "supervision for an undetermined length of time," which meant they could travel miles to the southern part of the country, stay out for weeks or months, but then had to report back to prison. In every village or town they visited they had to declare their presence and status to the local security authority, and would be reported if they showed no intention of returning to prison.

∽. Toward the end of 1975 a reign of vengeance had begun in the South, and the camp received a new influx of political prisoners. Although there was no bloodbath, the number of prisoners was multiplied by the thousands. Former soldiers and officers, along with members of the Sài Gòn government, were herded into labor camps throughout the country, with the higher-ranking ones taken to the North.

"If they bring people from the South up here, that can only mean they won't be taking us South," Lộc speculated.

"But if we're lumped in with the new inmates, we'll be here forever!" Tứ replied.

My father said, "We won't be allowed to mix with the new ones."

He was right; the prisoners were segregated. Only through chance meetings did he learn from the newcomers that thousands of Southerners had left the country.

"I hope my family escaped overseas," he said to Lộc.

"Mine too. Maybe that's why we haven't heard from them."

After the fall of the South the men had been allowed to write to their families.

"But who knows whether the letters were ever sent?"

"You know, if our families escaped, we'll never get out."

My father sighed.

This far north, winter was glacial. Tết 1976 came without fanfare, and some weeks later my father was moved, with Lộc and Tứ, into a compound housing about eighty men, all Southern special forces officers captured in their missions north of the seventeenth parallel. Some had been already been imprisoned for fifteen years.

Lộc was assigned to a construction detail, but my father and Tứ were too weak for heavy work. Peeling potatoes was my father's task. It became a zen exercise that enhanced his extraordinary concentration. It also left his mind free to brood. He still had had no news from his family. In the meantime a series of "general amnesties" had been announced, without his name ever being included on the list of those to be freed.

One morning the three men were moved to a set of bamboo houses on the side of a hill overlooking the prison camp. They had now been redesignated "state laborers," which in effect meant that their detention could now stretch on without end. They had fallen into that peculiar category of prisoner called "Pardoned-But-Not-Freed."

On a late afternoon walk with Lộc and my father along a small path on the hill, Tứ remarked, "We have no identification. We could walk out there, but we'd just get arrested. They're not responsible for us. In theory, we're not even prisoners; we're unpaid laborers. Even if there is international pressure, the Việt Cộng can simply claim they don't have us in detention."

"I know," my father said. "We volunteered to stay."

"But who's going to mention our names?"

The men slowed their pace in the diminishing light of the early evening. Its dampness reminded my father of the night he was taken from Huế. Ten years had passed, arduous years that, in retrospect, seemed to have gone by incredibly quickly. Though

Lộc and Tứ had been his close companions in suffering for a decade, he could not tell them how devastated he felt about the loss of the years that should have been his most productive.

A month after his transfer to the new compound, he was assigned to draw plans and maps for the construction of schools and other buildings—even though they had actually already been constructed. Obsessed with proper party procedures, the Việt Cộng often carried out tasks simply because they were part of a process. He appreciated the work nonetheless. It kept him occupied and allowed occasional trips into nearby villages.

Etched on the villagers' faces and bent frames were the years of warfare, poverty, and hardship. Some had journeyed to the South after unification, taking precious sacks of rice and pieces of cloth as gifts to relatives. They came back furious and disillusioned with the years of Communist propaganda. "We believed in the war. We thought we were fighting to liberate the South from poverty and American exploitation," one woman lamented. "I couldn't believe all the things they had in Sài Gòn. Mind you, we didn't have the money to buy them. I wish it had been the South that had liberated us."

⁓ Suddenly, unexpectedly, a letter came from my mother, shocking and thrilling my father, and intensifying his thirst for news about his family. She told him about Diệu-Hà's departure in 1974, and my own escape in 1975—but she feared mentioning the U.S. "They've moved," she wrote, "to stay with their brother and sister-in-law. Diệu-Quỳnh helps her mother sell odds and ends on the streets."

The next letter tore him apart. "We feel there's no reason to keep the news from you," my mother wrote. "Your father passed away in June of 1971 from cancer."

He dropped the letter. It was now seven years since his father's death. Years of waiting: he in prison, waiting to be freed, to return to his parents and family. His father in Huế, waiting for his return, dying without knowing whether his only son was still alive.

He turned to his maps, drawing horizontal and vertical lines, but images of his childhood and memories of his father came alive in his mind. Turbulent times during the war against the French had sent father and son in different directions. All his adult life he had been posted at assignments far from Huế, returning only on rare occasions. He had promised to come home more often. Tết 1968 was to be the first in a series of regular visits to his parents.

Abandoning the maps, he let his tears flow. For the first time in his life, the first time in all the years of isolation, he felt he was being punished by a higher being. He had lost his father. His mother had already been frail when he was taken away. If freedom ever came, it would come too late.

He fell severely ill, but his captors dismissed the illness and transferred him to a new camp called Hồng Thắng, "Red Victory." Though called a "manufacturing area," it was enclosed in barbed wire and differed little from the prison on the next hill. Two hundred men crowded into a couple of ancient barracks at Hồng Thắng, the women in a third building behind a bamboo fence. Both areas were surrounded by heaps of trash. The workers formed a fragmented group and had no motivation to maintain the compound grounds. There were Southern commandos captured so long ago that they had come to accept prison life as normal, members of suspect ethnic communities, and Việt Cộng troops sent to Hồng Thắng after their tour of duty in the South because they'd complained about government treatment of veterans. The women had been prostitutes or smugglers, or had failed to perform the tasks demanded of them by their neighborhood organizations. They were in Hồng Thắng for three-year terms, with a government promise that if they could be sufficiently reeducated in that period they would be "officially" allowed to remain in Hồng Thắng as workers.

Hồng Thắng had a small lumber operation; the workers also grew tea, manioc, pineapple, and vegetables. My father and Tứ cleaned vegetables ten hours a day in the kitchen; Lộc, younger and stronger, worked in the fields.

Trouble started without warning. One day a young cadre named Duy switched my father to a more physically taxing job, without giving any explanation. He now had to chop up bamboo branches and slice them into strips used to weave mats and baskets. Then Duy accused him of spreading lies about the government and the party in order to sow discontent among the workers. My father protested, and refused to sign a confession Duy had written.

"So you want to be obstinate," Duy said. "I'll make sure you get transferred to prison."

My father left Duy's office frightened at the prospect of life in a criminal prison compound, where the convicts were notorious for abusing new arrivals. He thought he might escape violence, but he would be assigned especially onerous labor duties. The extra clothes and provisions he had recently received from my mother would be taken away. It was now the spring of 1979. The cold mornings grew colder with the piercing winds that blew from the Chinese hills just north of the border.

He waited, unaware that Duy and the other cadres were faced with a more pressing problem. Hà Nội had invaded Cambodia in December 1978 to drive out the ruthless Khmer Rouge. Now Việt Nam was at war with China, which was allied with the Khmer Rouge. Deadly battles had taken place in the border area a few miles from Hồng Thắng, and Chinese troops had taken over a nearby prison camp and freed its inmates.

At three o'clock in the morning, sixty Hồng Thắng workers were yanked out of bed and ordered to the gate with their belongings. Pushed into two army transport trucks, the men squeezed themselves into impossibly contorted positions. Rattling their way again in the darkness, Tứ, Lộc, and my father wrestled with the same questions. Where would they end up this time? Why had just this group been chosen? Was their status again that of political prisoners?

The trucks dropped them at a holding camp the next night. When they woke up in the morning they were taken in small boats across a river. They then struggled their way through dry fields and up a few hills to Tân Lập, a prison camp. The barbed wire, the admission procedures, and the cell assignment confirmed their suspicions. They were once more prisoners under strict rules.

"This is a reeducation camp," said the prison commander at the first gathering of the newcomers. "You must obey all rules and observe all set times for labor duties and meals. You're not to keep cash, watches, lighters. . . . There'll be daily and weekly roll calls. We will check your work and evaluate your progress." The cadre talked for twenty minutes, leaving out the allusions to the party's generosity, amnesty, early release, returning to one's family. Despite his past cynicism, my father missed hearing those words.

The Việt Cộng dispatched him to help make roof tiles. At sunrise each day he would make his way up the hill just outside the camp with a dozen other men to collect and bring back soggy, clayey earth. They piled it into a massive heap in the yard of the compound, then poured gallons of water over it. Finally they waded into it, marching around in their bare feet like animals until the clay became a mud pond. My father's knees gave out repeatedly, sending him into the mud. At the end of the day he would help pour the mud into thin boxes to be baked into tiles. Returning to his hut, he would lie on the ground, his arms, chest, shoulders, and face covered with thick layers of dried mud.

For the next months the confrontation with China was an excuse to maintain strict security, and the prisoners' occasional protests failed to bring about any change in their grueling conditions. The only gain was permission to listen to the radio or to read a rare newspaper carrying a few lines of censored news, pages of boring and boastful reports about above-quota outputs at a myriad of factories. Rare candid reports of food shortages and hunger in the South were accompanied by articles announcing logical solutions. Late in 1979 my father learned that the measures discussed in the papers were proposed merely to placate the people. The solutions could not be implemented, and the quality of life continued to worsen.

"Nothing is more precious than independence and liberty," my father thought. It was Hồ Chí Minh's most famous saying, his justification for the war against foreigners. Four years after the guns had gone quiet, Vietnamese life, both in the North and the South, was one of hardship. And for my father there was neither independence nor freedom.

La Fin d'un Cauchemar

Sometime in early 1979 a woman in Hà Nội named Nguyễn-Khoa Diệu-Hồng, head of the National Women's Association of the Socialist Republic of Việt Nam, received a letter in the mail. She knew the sender as a man married to her niece, but she had never met him, and she did not want anything to do with him. He was classified as an enemy of the socialist state. She did not open the letter, but instead of throwing it away she put it in an envelope and sent it on to a relative in Paris.

Nguyễn-Khoa Diệu-Hồng was my mother's aunt, converted to communism and residing in the North since the 1930s. The letter she sent to Paris wound its way back to Việt Nam, to my mother's mailbox in Hồ Chí Minh City. She opened it to learn that my father was still alive, imprisoned in a remote region of North Việt Nam called Vĩnh Phú. "I have no idea where it is, and I don't know how I'll do it, but I will find my way there," my mother said.

"Good morning, cadre," she said.

My father looked a decade older than his fifty-five years. His hair had thinned and all gone white. His cheeks were hollow valleys beneath sunken eyes, his skin yellow and dry and flaky. His entire frame was so wasted that it looked as though the slightest bit of wind could carry him away like an old piece of paper.

From the time she received my father's letter, my mother had been writing to my father. Now, almost twelve years after their separation, she had made a tortuous journey to visit him. When she finally saw him she did not recognize him at first, thinking he was a Việt Cộng cadre.

Neither did my father recognize her. Her hair was cut short in no particular style, and she was dressed simply in a khaki shirt, its golden dried-grass color faded, and a pair of shapeless black slacks. She was limping, and in the dim light of the prison's shack used to receive visitors, her thinness and paleness shocked my father. Her soft-spoken, weary manner filled him with tenderness.

"It's taken me days to get here," she said. "Did they tell you I was here?"

"I wanted to come out last night, but the guards wouldn't let me. What happened to your leg?"

"I rode a bicycle over here from the train station. I fell and sprained my ankle. It'll be all right," she assured him, hiding how much it was hurting her.

They continued to talk, my mother keeping an eye on the fire she had built to cook my father a lunch of rice and the fish she had bought near the entrance to the camp.

"Didn't you get my letter? It's so far away, I didn't want you to make the journey."

"It's been so long," my mother said. The two of them then fell into silence. They were lost.

"The train from Sài Gòn to Hà Nội took three days and two nights. It stopped everywhere."

"Did you stop in Huế—did you visit my mother?"

"I couldn't, with all the luggage. I didn't have permission."

She had fought for two months to get a permit to visit my father, and then waited just as long to get train tickets on the black market. Hordes of people going to Hà Nội with Southern goods took up all the space on the train.

"There was no light on the train—none at all. The light bulbs had all been stolen. The compartments hadn't been cleaned in I don't know how long. The train would stop in deserted areas so that people could unload their merchandise and not have to pay duties. A lot were smugglers trying to avoid the public security police."

"How did you carry all the stuff?" my father asked. My mother had brought three bags of food, clothing, and medicine.

"I paid people. I couldn't sleep on the train because everything would be stolen. Thieves everywhere. Even in the hotel in Hà Nội I stayed awake. They come into your room to steal things while you sleep. There was no electricity. I shared a room with a couple of women who were also visiting relatives in the camp."

"Why don't you rest a bit now? I'm not all that hungry. Did you sleep last night?"

"Some, yes," she answered, again not telling my father that her eyes had hardly closed because of the pain from her ankle, and the mosquitoes, and the anticipation. She turned the conversation back to her journey.

"I got on the train from Hà Nội to Vĩnh Phú, but it stopped in Ấm Thượng and wouldn't go any farther. You know that river near there? It took hours to get a boat across. Tiny little sampan— and the man couldn't row, and the bags were so heavy. I thought we were going to sink."

"Yes, that river can be a bit rough in this season."

"Well, never mind; I'm here now."

She had arrived the afternoon before; a prisoner helped carry her bags up to the visitors' shack. While she registered with the

camp authorities, the prisoner sent word to my father. Not allowed
to meet her immediately, he too had stayed up most of the night.

My father gave no sign of his feelings about Diệu-Hà's and
my being in the United States. He listened as my mother told
him the details of his father's death. His mother was now too
weak to get out of bed most days.

"Đà Nẵng was unbearable after liberation," my mother said.
"I thought you'd be released then. A lot of people quit teaching
in the end; you couldn't live on a teacher's salary anymore. You
wouldn't believe how many people were actually Việt Cộng
agents."

As she fried the fish she spoke in a low voice about her life
in the South—her noodle stand, her botched attempt to leave on
a boat, her fear and suffering without her husband, her separation
from her children. "I don't know how I survived it all." My father
wondered at how the years had changed her. She had trained
herself to be always vigilant, fearful of the eyes and ears of the
government and the party.

While they ate their first meal together in over ten years,
my father asked about his children's progress in school in the
United States, about Diệu-Quỳnh's condition, about relatives and
friends, and about the world outside. There was one subject he
avoided: he did not talk about his release. He had no way of
knowing how much longer his captivity would last. Just a few
weeks before, the camp authorities had decided that he was
misleading his fellow prisoners about the government and the
party, and he had been placed under disciplinary watch. To
complicate matters, my father had refused to sign a report that
he was encouraging an attitude of resistance toward the party
instead of regretting his past mistakes.

Finished with the meal, my parents sat together on a bamboo
platform for the rest of the day. The years of separation had not
estranged them. It was not hard for them to talk to each other;
they just did not know what subject to touch on next, and the

thought that their reunion would last but a few hours was constantly in the backs of their minds. Then my mother would again have to face the boat, the bicycle, and the train to make her lonely journey south, leaving my father to his long days of isolation.

"Perhaps things will change soon," he said. He didn't truly believe things would change, or that he would be released.

"I've heard of anti-Hà Nội movements abroad, but there's nothing like a government in exile. The BBC would have reported any fighting or infiltration from anticommunist resistance groups," my mother told him.

"You can listen to the BBC?"

"It's illegal, but people do. You get put in jail if you get caught, of course, but people talk on the streets about the news they hear on the BBC or the Voice of America. Other than that we don't get any more news than you get in prison."

My father kept alert for Việt Cộng soldiers listening outside the shack. A few times when he heard noises, the sounds turned out to be made by prisoners, who darted inside to hand my mother letters to take to their families in the South.

"The food and medicine you brought will last me a long time," my father said. "I know it costs a lot to visit. You shouldn't do it anymore."

"We'll see—I hope I won't have to make the journey again."

"I hope so too. Maybe there will be an amnesty."

Darkness arrived, and they hadn't said enough to each other.

"Don't you have to go back?" she asked.

"I'll stay here until they come to get me," he replied.

No one came, to my father's surprise, and they spent the night exchanging more news. He handed my mother a notebook.

"Please give it to Diệu-Quỳnh. It's a diary; I made it myself."

My mother put the notebook in her small bag and left early in the morning. She had to report about her visit to the camp officials, and get them to sign her travel documents for the authorities in Hồ Chí Minh City. From the steps to the visitors' shack my father watched her limp away. He felt a sudden fear that this might be the last time he would see her.

Just before she disappeared behind the hill, my mother looked back. Her husband stood in the door of the shack with his usual self-possessed demeanor, hiding the pain in his heart. Standing in silence, his arms, hands, everything about him seemed foreign and superfluous. Nothing of his physical being could express his aching regret about his separation from his family, about his gratitude for her visit, for her loyal friendship. Beneath his poised and composed manner he felt the same wrenching pain he had known in Huế nearly twelve years earlier.

∾ "Tell Chị Đãi I'll come tomorrow and bring her whatever else she needs," my aunt Hồng-Khuê called to her husband. It was a week after my mother had returned from her visit to my father. Uncle Anh-Anh wheeled his Honda motorcycle through the gate. At that evening hour, the streets of Hồ Chí Minh City were full of people. Communism had not exorcised the entrepreneurial spirit of the town, and now black markets flourished out of control. My uncle had to take great care with the motorcycle to avoid the swarm of shoppers and traders doing business by the roadside.

He parked the motorcycle in a lot by the sidewalk, paid the attendant, and holding a bag in his right arm, walked through the gate of the Sùng Chính hospital. He crossed the courtyard and climbed up the steps to the third floor. Walking down the corridors, he noticed the place did not smell like a hospital. People crouched in the halls while kids roamed around selling oranges and peanuts from baskets they held against their hips. This is a market, my uncle thought as he turned to find the door to the intensive care unit.

There were no medical staff around. The dozens of rusted iron beds in the room were all occupied, the patients looking like dead bodies in the dim light of dusk. The neon lamps flickered when the flow of electricity into the building waned. Uncle Anh-Anh walked to the end of the room and stood between two beds, deciding where to put down his bag.

On his right, Diệu-Quỳnh was in a coma, breathing through plastic tubes that had yellowed and turned opaque with age and overuse. A serum bag hung from a bamboo stick tied to a pipe that was screwed into the side of the bed. On the bed to my uncle's left my mother was sleeping. Her bandaged foot protruded from under the thin cotton blanket patterned with yellow roses, its brown trim tattered and hanging in bits over the dirty black and white floor tiles. My mother's foot had become infected and swollen badly. She had a fever and had to be hospitalized the moment she came home from the train station.

Diệu-Quỳnh had fallen ill a few days after my mother went north. She was first thought to have just a cold. When she grew worse, my uncle took her to a series of hospitals and doctors. Some refused her service because our family did not have the correct revolutionary background; some could not diagnose her illness; others dismissed it simply as the flu, which would pass. Every visit was a bureaucratic horror, and no one gave her any medicine. When she was finally admitted at Sùng Chính, the use of whatever medical equipment or supplies she would need had to be paid for. Socialism only worked when you had money and were politically correct. Uncle Anh-Anh borrowed money everywhere to pay for syringes and needles and pills, and paid off the state doctors and nurses, but Diệu-Quỳnh's condition did not improve. A doctor and a friend of the family at last diagnosed her as having severe kidney failure. Her bed-wetting many years before was the first sign of kidney trouble, not a symptom of her mental illness. But by this time her urinary tract had burst, sending urine into her bloodstream. She went into a coma as my mother was hospitalized.

Diệu-Quỳnh regained consciousness a few times, uttering a few words in answer to my mother's questions before falling back

into a coma. She said that she loved Diệu-Hà the most among
her three siblings. She mentioned the name of a French teacher
who had not returned her love some fifteen years before. The
only other time any of us had heard her mention him was in Đà
Lạt, during a cold night when she burst into tears all of a sudden
and locked her face in a pillow. "He doesn't love me," she had
said. My mother dismissed the episode as teenage moodiness,
though later we realized that it marked the onset of Diệu-Quỳnh's
emotional illness. Fifteen years later, lying next to her daughter
in the hospital bed, my mother heard the French name again and
suddenly understood the times when Diệu-Quỳnh, in a state
between dreaming and waking, had muttered disjointed phrases
in French.

A week later, all hope lost, my mother limped out of the
hospital and took Diệu-Quỳnh home to die. My sister's face was
a strange mottled mixture of purple and paleness, her eyes didn't
completely close, and the sparks that occasionally accompanied
her reasonless giggles were gone forever.

Diệu-Quỳnh was cremated, the service a simple affair with
only a few relatives attending. My mother, now alone, did not
want to keep fighting. The grief of losing her daughter tore at
her, making it hard for her to breathe. She wondered whether
Diệu-Quỳnh would still be alive if she had not gone north to see
her husband. She wondered about all the things she did and did
not do for her gentle, ill-fated daughter. She wondered, cried and
sighed, and mourned, and all alone, she thought she no longer
wanted to live. But like all Vietnamese mothers, she found the
courage to nourish her spirit until she could face, and overcome
yet again, the troubles of her life.

Thanh Hóa has always been among the toughest parts of Việt
Nam. For centuries it had bred fierce sons and daughters who
grew up accepting their fate: the most devastating storms, the
hottest sun, the worst drought. It was to a remote area deep

inside the province of Thanh Hóa that my father's captors transferred him in 1979.

The conflict with China had simmered down, so there was no reason for the Việt Cộng to move him south. The move did nothing to allay his fears that he would live out the rest of his days as a prisoner. Tứ and Lộc were also transferred, and the three returned to their status as laborers. From early morning to late afternoon Lộc walked a few water buffaloes to an open field to let them eat grass and bathe in a pond. My father and Tứ, along with other old, weak men, gathered branches and dried hay and wove them into thick sheets used as roof covers.

A letter arrived in Thanh Hóa in October with two pictures of my sister's body just before her cremation. The fall afternoon was fading. My father took the letter and photographs to his room. He lit a low flame on the kerosene lamp in a corner.

Always at the periphery, Diệu-Quỳnh had lived quietly in her own world. She had had few friends and as a small girl did not have the rich happy laughter, engage in the vibrant games, or do the funny things of children her age. When she first became ill, my father was in the United States; during her worst suffering he had been in prison.

He lay on the bed, trying to control himself enough to read my mother's description of Diệu-Quỳnh's last days. He imagined the desperation she must have felt. When he could no longer read, he held up the photos. The tears came slowly; then he had to put the pictures away. He turned away from the light and pulled the pillow under his cheek. He felt wounded and wronged. He held his stomach and gathered his knees to his chest, and just as quickly he had to sit up to take a breath. In the next moment he threw himself down again on the bed. There was nothing he could do to stay calm. Darkness suffocated him. Sobbing, stopping, sobbing again, he could not think rationally. He felt bursts of anger flow through him, at how unfair life had been to Diệu-Quỳnh, and to him. After a while he could only lie unresisting as pain stabbed at his stomach, a pain neither sharp nor dull, stabbing again and again until he fell unconscious.

When he woke up it came to him that he had a reason to seek permission to go to Sài Gòn. "Do it—do it! Ask them," said another inmate encouragingly. "You need to be with your wife in this moment of grief. Go. And don't come back!"

The camp authorities denied his request. "Your daughter died already. What would you go back for?"

My father walked back to his room, to the darkness of life in captivity.

◦◦ "Another Tết away from home," my father said. It was now early 1980.

Tứ nodded. The months since the news of Diệu-Quỳnh's death had gone by slowly, growing colder as my father grew weaker. He learned that Võ Thành Minh, the founder of the Boy Scouts, had died. A woman from Huế who had come to visit her husband gave him the news: "He was kept in the mountains, and died up there. That's all we know." The news brought home to the prisoners their own fragility. Even Lộc, ten years younger than my father, now had the eyes of an old man, sunken above the protruding cheekbones. He too was emaciated. All three men still faced daily labor duties.

Twenty-two workers, including Lộc, were allowed out on furlough to visit their families for Tết. The names were announced on the first day of Tết, and the twenty-two men were immediately driven away. Many of them had already packed their bags in the hope that they would be among the lucky ones. My father had not bothered to pack. He barely had a chance to say farewell to Lộc.

Two months later Lộc had not returned. "I don't blame him," Tứ said.

"No. Who would come back here?"

The fear of being overheard had taught Tứ and my father to communicate with few words. Both understood that if Lộc didn't return from his furlough, they would have no chance of being allowed out themselves.

But then came the news that Tứ would be freed. My father was bathing in the spring when he heard. He went straight to see Tứ.

"Well. I'm happy—"

"I'm sorry," Tứ said.

"What can I say? When do you leave?"

"In a day or two. I'm going to Đà Nẵng. My family's there."

"*La fin d'un cauchemar,*" said my father in French.

"No, not really," Tứ answered. "My nightmare isn't over yet. Many people know me in Đà Nẵng. The local government is bound to be strict. They'll keep a critical eye on me. I'll stay there for a few months, then I'll go to Sài Gòn. I hope to see you there, soon. Take good care."

"I will. If you can, send me a letter."

Tứ nodded. For the rest of that evening he had many visitors. My father retreated to his bed. The sound of people celebrating drifted in from the outside, their voices already becoming unfamiliar. In the darkness of his own room he worked at accepting that he would be detained for the rest of his life.

Two months after Tứ left, my father was called to the camp's meeting room. Six people were allowed to go south on furlough; six others were released for good. My father was among the second group. He stood stupefied, unbelieving. "*Anh, đáng ra anh không được thả. Người như anh không bao giờ cải tạo được,*" the camp commander finally grumbled. "You—you should never be freed. People like you are impossible to reeducate."

The next morning my father completed the paperwork and went directly to the train station, where he bought a ticket for Huế. The trip took a day and a half. He wandered out of the station, a frail man in faded brown pants and a threadbare white shirt stretched over a skeletal frame. He held his few bundled belongings in one arm. He was fifty-six years old.

When he turned up the street toward town, a peach-colored building came into view. He slowed his steps. The paint had faded unevenly, and trim around the windows and balconies was brown with dust that must have taken years to accumulate. The green shutters, also faded, were closed. The grounds were abandoned and neglected, the bushes grown so full that they blocked the view of the River of Perfume. Nonetheless, in the softening afternoon light, the old government guest house managed to retain its charm.

On this afternoon in July of 1980, Hué had the smell of summer. The royal poincianas were in bloom, their red flowers vibrant against the sky. Petals were scattered on the sidewalks, fallen along with delicate tamarind leaves to turn the street into an impressionistic canvas. The colors overwhelmed him. He remembered the summers of his youth, the high school close by where he had once been a student, and a teacher, and where he had first met my mother. As he gazed at the streets, the river on his left, the houses on his right, the tears came, tears that mourned the twelve years of his life he had lost.

Switching his bundle to the other arm, he glanced back at the guest house one last time. His moist eyes recognized in the faded paint the color of home, and of freedom.

TEN

Among the Huddled Masses

Fifty miles south of Singapore, four hours by boat, Galang is so tiny that it fails to appear on most maps of the South China Sea. Until 1979 it meant little to anyone except a few families of hardy Indonesian fishermen. By that year thousands of Vietnamese had escaped by boat from their oppressive homeland and landed on the northern archipelagos of Indonesia. In response, the Indonesian government and the U.N. High Commissioner for Refugees established a camp on Galang, a refugee processing center that was inaugurated in 1980. The camp served largely as a crude boarding school for those housed in its decrepit army barracks, known around the world as "boat people."

In the next four years Galang took in over a hundred thousand refugees who built temporary lives on the sun-drenched island while they waited for the chance to re-settle in Western countries. Many would languish there for years; others ended up in Canada, Australia, or France. About half were approved for immigration to the United States. Under the equatorial heat, classrooms echoed with beginners' English phrases and lessons on American culture. In addition, refugees in vocational programs learned rudimentary skills thought to be helpful in assembly line jobs.

Under contract with the U.S. Department of State, the Experiment in International Living and the Save the Children Fund jointly administered the training program. The Indonesian government required that local teachers be hired, so refugees fleeing Việt Nam and Cambodia heard about life in America from people who had never been there; English lessons were taught by those to whom English was a second language. American educators were brought in to write the curriculum, and to train and supervise the Indonesian staff. I was part of the American team.

"Careful—the police have been watching you. Everything you do," said Firmus, one of the teachers. "They've been watching you since you came here."

In the office we shared, a lone incandescent bulb shed a faint light over Firmus's face. I could not tell whether or not his smile carried a measure of sympathy. I thanked him, thinking, I've been here three months. Why didn't you tell me earlier?

I left Firmus and walked out into the evening. The next morning another teacher told me that Firmus was under orders to watch me.

I was the sole Vietnamese on a staff of twenty-five Americans living and working on an isolated island in the Riau archipelago of Indonesia with some two hundred local teachers. Their students were among the ten thousand refugees living in the bare rooms of the barracks, which backed up to the foot of mountains ringing two valleys of sand and dry soil. The majority of the refugees were Vietnamese "boat people"; the rest were Cambodians transferred from overcrowded camps in Thailand.

A tangled combination of Indonesian authorities controlled the island: Interior Ministry bureaucrats, police, army, customs, and immigration officers, and workers for the Red Crescent. This odd mélange watched me because they thought I might tell the refugees things they shouldn't know, or I might help them fight

abuses. Indonesian teachers watched me because they were curious, and because the police ordered them to. The refugees watched
me because I looked like them and spoke their language but did
not live their lives. And the Americans—the Americans watched
me because they could not figure me out.

Whether all the scrutiny made a difference, I never found
out. There wasn't much the teachers could learn from me other
than an aggressive attitude, a Western lack of patience and grace.
On my first night on Galang an Indonesian soldier pulled a gun
on me, assuming I was a refugee out past the eleven o'clock
curfew. Ultimately I was intimidated enough by the security forces
in the camp to curtail my activities. During my fourth month I
failed to start a protest among the refugees against the corruption
that kept food from being distributed to them. I failed too, I
thought, at my job, which was to help explain to the refugees
what it meant to live in America. They wanted to hear encouraging
stories about immigrants who had succeeded, whereas I told them
stories of discrimination and cultural clashes, about a mechanical
life dominated by work and freeways and a sense of isolation.
Before leaving the camp for a new home somewhere in the
Midwest a doctor told me, "You've been extremely helpful, but
you talk about so many truths. You're a double-edged sword. A
surgical knife that removes the rotten flesh, but leaves behind a
deeper wound."

I was indeed forced to confront many truths in Galang. I
was watching myself as well, a man transformed from a Vietnamese
to an American, to a Vietnamese again, carrying the pain of seeing
all these people from my homeland living in such misery. When
I had set off for the job in Indonesia I thought I had a good idea
of the difficulties of life in a refugee camp, but my mental image
did not match the intensity of what I came to witness.

There were always so many refugees crowding near my dorm
room that I finally had to be moved. Others would not leave my
office window, where they came to observe the strange manners

I had adopted in America. Refugees employed as our aides often stood stupefied near my desk, innocently questioning my behavior.

"Brother Đức, you barely wrote anything on that piece of paper! Look at you, throwing it away!"

"Do you write down every appointment in that diary book? What's wrong with your memory?"

"Why don't you just write it out? You type up everything, don't you?"

"All you do is work, Brother Đức. It's so hot your body fat can melt. Why don't you just relax? Go take a nap!"

"That's the fourth piece of brown paper you've used up in an hour. It's weird how you have to put everything in charts and boxes. They like diagrams in America, huh?"

The comments often made me laugh. I believed that I retained in my most profound self a Vietnamese way of thinking, but outwardly I no longer acted Vietnamese. After a while the refugees' words added up to convince me how much I had changed.

～ The training programs in Galang were mandatory, with few exceptions. The American staff, professionals with impressive academic credentials, emphasized the educational aspects. A few built extraordinary friendships with the refugees, but most stayed within their roles as educators. The language and teaching skills the Americans brought to Galang had their uses, but it often seemed my colleagues and I rushed about from sunrise to late at night merely creating work to justify our positions. After "classroom observations," we conducted "feedback" sessions with the teachers in the evenings. Special workshops or video or slide shows followed daily training sessions. In between were retreats and conferences. We convinced ourselves that we were being helpful, pleased with our "methods," "designs," and "models," and "student-centered lesson plans." Perhaps we did give the refugees some basis to start life in the United States, at least at the bottom rung of society. But in Galang the refugees lived a cheerless existence; however exciting the lessons were, they simply had no relevance to their daily reality.

Galang was called "life at the stop sign." After the hardships under the repressive regime, Vietnamese refugees suffered the horrors of the boat trip out of the country. Large numbers perished at sea. Women were repeatedly raped; others were attacked, robbed, and left to die by Thai pirates. Survivors were picked up adrift on the South China Sea, dehydrated, hungry, exhausted, traumatized. They would wait in Galang for long months for a chance at a new life. The Khmer Rouge years always showed on the faces of Cambodians, whether in their dazed eyes or in the smiles that said the eyes had seen too much. In the end the faces of the refugees, even the youngest ones, bore an expression of stoic resignation and acceptance which could only be acknowledged but never fully understood.

The refugees went from their wooden barracks to the river for water, and stood in line for half the day for their meals as well as countless interviews with Indonesian or U.N. officers. There was a myriad of forms to fill out and more questions to answer from American, French, or Canadian immigration officers whose emotions or sympathy, if any, were always kept hidden. Relatives in the West would have to offer sponsorship; documents and proof had to be produced. The refugees could not leave Galang until all paperwork had been processed. When they had been officially accepted as legitimate political refugees, they could enter the mandatory training programs.

In that mess of humanity I was to help teach about riding buses, renting apartments, getting welfare; the importance of eye contact during job interviews and showing up for work on time; family planning and racial discrimination. None of it made any sense to the refugees.

I fulfilled my duties as best I could, organizing the training programs and class schedules and devising lesson plans in cooperation with my colleagues. But there were always refugees who came to seek my help with translating official documents, or understanding the bureaucratic hurdles they needed to overcome, or mailing letters to the world outside.

Letters to refugees in the camp did not always reach them. Indonesian officials often searched through the envelopes, confiscating checks and cash that relatives in the United States or elsewhere had sent to those in Galang. My mailbox, part of a diplomatic pouch which escaped Indonesian scrutiny, soon became the address for hundreds of refugees. Monday and Thursday mornings the courtyard in front of my office turned into a sea of desperate faces. Scores of refugees sat hoping that I'd call out their names, that a letter, a bit of news, some money had arrived for them. I received dozens of letters from people I didn't know, seeking assurances that a relative had not died at sea, or pleading for my help in getting a brother, a cousin, or a friend out of the camp. The Indonesians threatened to throw me out of the country, but the letters kept coming.

On my trips to a nearby town or to Singapore I could always find a shirt, shoes, medicine, or a dictionary to bring back to the refugees, who were grateful for anything. Sometimes I was able to help clear up misunderstandings that were keeping refugee families from resettling in the United States. I could clarify to authorities that someone had not shown up at work because he had been secretly held and beaten up by other refugees who claimed he had betrayed them while in Communist reeducation camps in Việt Nam. I could explain that a woman had been missing classes because her husband had left her, and she was pregnant; program administrators had been ready to keep her in the camp for three extra months to go through the training courses again.

For these and other refugees I was a man with extraordinary power. Unwittingly I was placed in the role of "savior of the people." I went to bed anxious that I had not done enough. In the morning I would be faced with refugees who came bearing gifts that I knew cost them dearly, even though they were of little monetary value to me. Not to accept would be offensive, and so I ended up with a monkey, a collection of rattan bracelets, ashtrays and flowers made out of beer cans, and a chess set meticulously carved out of scrap rubber. Others offered hand-knit scarves, or insisted on mending my torn shirts.

Among the Americans, a few became great advocates for the refugees. Many more removed themselves from their hardships. They simply went to the training sessions, became close to one or two Indonesians, but left the refugees largely on their own. When the workday was over they retreated to their dorms, stayed within a small circle of friends, and avoided discussing the difficulties the refugees underwent.

Not far from the dorms were the refugee barracks, but some staff members never ventured into them, never listened to the refugees. Others expressed a patronizing kind of sympathy, seeing the refugees as helpless, pitiful figures rather than individuals with feelings and their own histories.

I was unable to distance myself in this way. But then, each day in Galang brought a parade of people who showed how easy it was to slip across the line between sanity and insanity.

There was Every-Man-Communist, a long-haired man with an ugly beard who always wore a blanket over his shoulders, despite the extreme heat and humidity. He would frequently escape from the hospital to walk around the camp, muttering or yelling out "Every man Communist! Every man Communist!" No one knew his real name. There were rumors that he had once been violent. Finally he was pumped so full of morphine that he lost his mind. For some refugees it eventually didn't matter whether we were unable or unwilling to help. There wasn't much anyone could do for Every-Man-Communist.

There was a woman, rumored to have been raped at sea by pirates, who kept complaining about losing her purse. She could carry on a normal conversation for a quarter of an hour, then suddenly become hysterical over her stolen or misplaced purse. I tried giving her odd jobs in our office, but she lasted only a few days. There was talk later that she had been caught several times making love to Indonesian soldiers in bushes around the camp. The stories were passed around; no one had proof, but no one suppressed them.

The body of a refugee washed up on the beach one day. The police said the death was a suicide, but those who saw the body swore there was a ghastly cut on the side of the man's head. Checking out rumors and making inquiries led nowhere. What good would it do? The man was dead. And so no investigation was carried out. The man whose body washed up on the shores of Galang was buried with no further thought.

There was also the "rapist."

"Đức! Đức!" shouted my supervisor through the screen of my window. "D'you know what's going on out there?"

"It's Sunday, Carrie," I shouted back. "I'm in the shower! Go away! Leave a note, I might read it tomorrow."

"You'd better come out here!"

I didn't like Carrie's tone of voice.

I joined her on the porch of my dorm room. "What's the matter? What's your problem?" I asked, buttoning my shirt.

"At the camp office! Look what they're doing!"

I followed Carrie out of the dorm compound. A mass of refugees had gathered in the courtyard in front of the camp's administrative office. They made no sound. The silence of the hundreds of people was terrifying.

As the people moved about, their collective anger was almost visible, like a terrible flame. A gaunt man in his thirties stood on top of a table on the paved porch of the office. His white shirt was tattered and bloodied, his shorts also torn, revealing rangy legs full of bruises. His hands were tied behind his back.

I snaked my way through the crowd. The man looked

straight at the throng of people, managing a defiant expression despite the fact that his face was a bruised, pulpy mess. His sagging cheeks were purple, his lips swollen, white and grotesque. Someone had tried to shave his head, but the job seemed to have been done with a pair of dull scissors, leaving patches of long blood-matted hair next to bare spots. I stared at the man in shock. He looked like a sewer rat caught in a downpour.

Hanging from the man's neck was a cardboard sign on which someone had written, in big uneven letters, RAPIST.

By the time I reached the table the crowd had surged forward to follow my movements, not knowing how I would react.

"Please go home," I said. In the silence, the sound of my voice caught everyone by surprise. No one moved, and I repeated, almost pleading, "Go, go. Get away from here."

The faces around me registered a kind of disbelief. It took a moment for them to understand my words; then the refugees turned defiant. They were not about to go away.

I knew that if anyone in the crowd threw a stone at the man, if anyone began an attack, he would be beaten to death within minutes.

The crowd stared at him in the charged silence until I spoke again. This time I screamed. "Go away! Go back to your barracks! What are you standing here for? Go away!"

People moved a few feet away from me, stunned by my anger. I charged furiously into the crush in front of me, swinging my arms and again yelling "Go! Go away!"

A few people were beginning to turn away, pushing others. I walked toward the men at the entrance to the camp office. "Who did this?" I demanded. "How could you?"

One of them held me back. "Brother Đức, don't get involved! Let us handle this."

"Get that man off the table," I shouted.

I felt a hand on my shoulder. "Đức, watch it." It was Mark

Bishop, a colleague. Mark and I both saw the Indonesian army officer at the same time. He had a hand on his gun holster, a grin on his face.

"Rapist," the officer said with a sinister laugh.

"I don't care," I said. There was no stopping me. "Take him down! What kind of people are you?"

I expected the man to pull out his gun. Feeling the crowd surge closer, I turned and shouted louder than before, "Get out of here!"

The mob dispersed. I turned back toward the Indonesian army man as he signaled to his aides to remove the accused man from the table. Eyes lowered, he was whisked inside.

I turned to walk away. Mark followed me across the court-yard into the street that led to my dorm. Refugees grouped along the sides of the road watched me silently. What went through their minds was a mystery to me. They had shown no pity toward the man, nor did they seem repelled by the ugliness of the event. As I walked away I felt wounded and ashamed. I started crying in the middle of the crowd; by the time I reached my room I was sobbing helplessly.

A young girl was said to have been raped. A girl of seventeen, who had already been raped by Thai pirates. The girl had lost all her family, and on arriving at the camp was put up at the hospital. It was rumored that while there she had been abused by an Indonesian doctor. Then came the rapist. People in the camp couldn't do anything about the Indonesian doctor, but they were ready to beat a refugee to a pulp for allegedly raping the young woman. Later I would hear that the man had been forcing women to sleep with Indonesian army men. Vietnamese men who were members of the camp's disciplinary force had decided to punish him.

Under the control of so many different agencies, Galang had no clear legal jurisdiction. The accused rapist ended up in the hands of U.N. officials, who at first hid him in a room behind their office and later sent him off the island in secret. Indonesian soldiers often beat up other refugees accused of crimes.

The incident depressed me for weeks. I was despondent also because colleagues often asked my opinion about it. Did they expect me to find it less repugnant simply because I was Vietnamese? I spoke Vietnamese, but what could I have found out that would have explained what happened? What could I have told them that would have made the episode more acceptable? I had come to Galang hoping to help my people. Instead I became confused, and I confused them.

I understood that the desperation of life under communism and then in a refugee camp had forced many to abandon normal standards of behavior. Yet it never ceased to astonish me that others managed to keep their sense of humor, their goodwill, and their dignity. The years of war had taught the Vietnamese to accept suffering and loss as part of their destiny. Despite the tedium of the months of waiting in the camp, there were Saturdays when lovers continued to love, to meet and walk together down moonlit paths. There were Sundays when people got dressed up as best they could and climbed the hills where the Catholic church and Buddhist temple stood. In the afternoon they would sit at tables in makeshift cafés and smoke, or go to the beach to play soccer. There was the midautumn evening when parents made small lanterns and allowed their children to parade with them until late at night. It didn't seem strange that the lanterns were shaped like B-52 bombers. And when Tét arrived it rained and rained, keeping everyone indoors. Instead of elaborate meals and complicated ceremonies, the refugees merely gathered and told stories and shared the traditional watermelon seeds. Life at the stop sign was hard and frustrating, but it was still life. Ancient rituals and traditions were observed as best one could in the circumstances.

I tried to stay away from the Tét celebrations, but a refugee came to my room to look for me. I went to his barracks and got a bit drunk with him and his brothers. At midnight I joined them in beating pots and pans. There were no firecrackers. Clangs echoed through the rain to announce the hour. The noise gave me a horrendous headache.

From the refugee barracks I went to the camp office to offer New Year's greetings on the public address system on behalf of all Vietnamese overseas. "Please know that I share with you the pain and sadness of being away from home at Tết.

"The pain must weigh heavy on your heart, for it is your first Tết away from home. They say time heals all wounds, but from now on, you are going farther and farther away from home. I hope you will find the kind of success in your new life which can help dull the pain of exile."

Mark Bishop came to my room to apologize for not being with me when the New Year arrived. He'd been with some refugees when they heard my message. "I don't know what you said, but boy, they just sobbed." He laughed. "You're good at making people cry."

Mark and I drank the bottle of cognac he'd brought, and then it was our turn to cry. He knew my tears that night were drunken tears, but also tears of mourning, for I had told him I wanted to go home, and couldn't. I wanted to have my parents safe, and couldn't.

"Maybe this year, Đức," Mark muttered under his cognac breath. "This year—they'll be out this year. Trust me, I know. This very year. Your parents will come out of Việt Nam, and they'll come to live with you in San Francisco, and everything will be all right. I'm telling you, it's gonna be this year."

Mark was almost singing by this time, but he managed to sound convincing. Or perhaps I was too drunk not to believe him. "Yeah, Mark," I said. "You're right. It'll be this year. This very miserable year!"

By Tết, I had been in Galang for eleven months of my one-year contract. I had decided to stay for just another six months, since I had been accepted for a job with the Vietnamese Service of the British Broadcasting Corporation, to begin in October of 1984. That would give me two months after my work in Galang was done to travel northward by rail, up the Malay Peninsula to Thailand. From there I would make my way through Burma and India up to Nepal, then fly directly to London.

A telegram from Sài Gòn put an end to my travel plans.

It was signed MẠCHA "Momdad." Putting two words together to make one saved my parents money. The message read, "EXIT-VISAS APPROVED. PREPAREFOR ARRIVAL."

For four years my brother and I had filed dozens of papers to apply for their departure from Việt Nam: affidavits of support, proof of citizenship, bank statements, proof of relationship, and on and on. Copies to the Immigration and Naturalization Service. Copies to the American embassy and related agencies in Bangkok. Copies to my parents. Obtaining an entry visa from the United States was not easy, but it eventually came. My father's studies in Michigan, his government service, and his status as a former political prisoner earned him the highest priority.

The same factors gave him the lowest priority for exit in the eyes of Vietnamese authorities. My mother, as resourceful as ever, bribed one Việt Cộng official after another. The Ministry of the Interior finally approved an exit visa.

When the telegram came, Mark rushed to get out the cognac. In the middle of a staff meeting he stood up to announce the news. My colleagues and I passed the bottle around, and we drank to my parents' visas.

All my plans were now up in the air. I was to have parents again. Life was not going to be the same.

ELEVEN

Land of Freedom

I returned from Indonesia in February 1984. The outlines of San Francisco's buildings were blurred by the fine drizzle that sprayed the city from dawn to dusk. The days were gray and cold, the nights colder still. In an upstairs room at a friend's house in Berkeley I stared at the blanket of fog, listened to the droning rain, and hid from the American world of wealth and waste. A year in Galang had robbed me of the ability to accept the superfluous amenities of Western societies: television sets, stereos, cars, unlimited fuel and electricity, an abundance of food and wine. Life in Galang, as emotionally demanding and complex as it was, contained not much more than four walls, a bowl of rice and dried fish each day, and perhaps a stubborn hope for a chance, a life and a future in the West.

Occasionally I went to work as a court interpreter, supplementing the money I'd saved while in Indonesia. With friends I kept up incessant talk about refugees and Galang. Otherwise I waited, for the memory of the refugee camp to fade away, for the time to move to London, and for my parents.

In March they sent a telegram announcing that the paperwork was complete. Since I had no regular job, my days felt endless as I waited for them. Before fading into sleep at night I relished the thought that I was about to get back my mother and father. Each night I felt the excitement of a boy impatient for the gifts tomorrow's birthday would bring. My parents appeared in my mind as a happy, healthy couple. But as daylight returned, I would wake up knowing I had had a nightmare full of uncertainties. In my sleep, as in the waking hours that followed, I worried about their physical and mental condition, and feared the distance that time and circumstances had imposed.

At twenty-five, after living on my own for eight years, I was about to have parents again. They would no doubt assess all I had done in my years alone and judge all I was to do from now on. I was sure they would be disappointed. In my years in America I had moved away from my brother and sister and frequently disrupted my education. I had not obtained a degree conferring professional stature. The job in Indonesia would be considered a distracting adventure. As for the offer I had lately accepted, I knew my parents held the BBC in high esteem, but surely they would regard my leaving for London just as they began life in a foreign country as desertion. What dutiful son could think of his own advancement under the circumstances?

I had earlier failed to set myself on the path of becoming the gentleman-scholar that was the aristocratic ideal of my family. Now I was prepared to abandon my Confucian duty to ease the later years of my elders. It was with such doubts and shame that I went to the San Francisco airport to meet my parents. I had been quite excited about their arrival. Now I was worried. I didn't know what we'd say to each other; after so much time, we could hardly chat about the weather, or the latest movie. I worried that they would not recognize me. I was only nine when my father was captured. What excuses could I offer for the way I'd turned out through my years in America? As for my father, after twelve years in prison, would he not have all kinds of psychological problems? How was his physical health?

The words flashed on the television screen: their flight had landed. I tried to smooth my hair, my tie, and my fears. With nervous gestures, I conned my way into the customs area. An airline official followed me up the ramp to the plane. The door opened. I spotted the gray-haired couple in the fifth row. "Ma!" I shouted. "Cha!"

Others heard me, but not my parents. Slowly they worked their way out of their seats. They took another eternity to reach the door. I grabbed my father's arm, lost my ability to speak, and led him down the ramp. As we reached the waiting area, I felt his arm on my back. Then he spoke: "Listen, how's Jesse Jackson doing with his campaign?"

Sixteen years apart is a long time, a formidable gap in any relationship. But my father had a wonderful way of bridging the gap, dispelling any fears, and going on with life as though twelve years in prison was a few days.

My mother spoke to an immigration officer of her happiness at arriving in "the land of freedom." Slapping me playfully on the cheeks, she asked, "Have you abandoned your studies altogether now?"

I managed a grin. I kept my eyes dry, but my throat was choked all the same. I drove my parents from the airport to their new home on Interstate 280. The freeway seemed paved with balls of cotton.

The rain had stopped by June. I had rented a garden apartment at the southern edge of the city, furnishing it with a small Japanese sofa, a dining table and some chairs, a bookcase, and a grand piano a friend had left with me. I sensed that my parents liked the simplicity of their new home, though they were surprised that I had not accumulated more after all these years. They never commented on the flat, and I had little chance to talk to them. The first days together were filled with endless visits from relatives and my parents' former colleagues and students. I answered the door, pulled up chairs, and poured tea from morning to night. Out of respect I left my parents to talk in private with relatives and old friends, but my nonchalance barely masked the burning fear that I might overhear stories of the atrocities my father had suffered. Every visitor asked him about the years in prison. In the months before they arrived I had thought much about the hardships my parents had experienced, but I was still unprepared to deal with detailed knowledge of their great adversities.

My father was sixty years old. At an age when others contemplate retirement, he was faced with finding work and starting a new life in a foreign country. His English was rusty. He had not held a proper job, or been free of extreme government control, in sixteen years. Yet he was astonishingly healthy and sane, and was looking forward to starting over. The years of prison had left no visible mark on him. My mother was less sure of herself than I remembered her being, but she refrained from expressing her fears.

They both seemed unaffected by jet lag. After a couple of weeks the visits became less frequent, and we turned to practical matters. I gave my friend Tom, an investment banker, a résumé I had prepared for my father.

"There's a gap here, Đức. Sixteen years."

"I know," I said. "What am I going to do? Put it in there, about him being in prison?"

"Why not?" Tom laughed. He looked the résumé over again. "It'll look strange, sixteen years missing, but I'll try. Can he count?"

"Yes," I answered. "Up to sixteen. Twelve years in jail, four more to get here."

"Jesus, Đức, you're cruel. How's his English?"

"Okay, I guess. A bit rusty maybe. I don't know that he's used it for a while. . . ."

"I'll try to find him something in my office, maybe to help our brokers, but he can probably run this city."

"Sure, Tom," I said. "Whatever. He just wants something to do."

Early one morning in his third week in San Francisco, my father appeared in a gray suit, a subdued blue tie with a red diamond pattern, and a pair of oxblood shoes.

"Cha, where are you going?" I raised my head from the arm of the sofa.

"To the job interview."

"The appointment isn't till next week," I said.

"Oh, this is different. I must have forgotten to tell you."

"You didn't tell me. What time is the appointment? I'll be ready in a minute."

"You don't have to drive me. I'll take the bus."

"How do you know which bus to take? It's complicated. What's the job, anyway?"

"Translating. Nothing much. I'll take the M line to the Powell Street station. Halliday Plaza is right there."

I'd never heard of the plaza. "How did you find out about it?"

"In the phone book," he said. "I should get going."

My father walked out the front door, confident, purposeful.

"I hope I'll be like him when I'm sixty," I said to my mother.

"*Con biết tính cha,*" my mother replied. "You know your father. Always so disciplined. He's rigid. Or maybe he's making up for all those years." She paused, then said, "How many more years do we have left, I wonder?"

"Mạ, please," I said.

"Let's have some tea. When you're gone to London, who's going to make tea for me?"

I said nothing. The silence echoed all of a sudden.

San Francisco summers can be beastly cold. It turns from sunny to gray at two or three o'clock in the afternoon, and the wind that ushers in the fog descends swiftly.

On such an afternoon in July 1984 I drove through Golden Gate Park with my parents. We had been talking about the city, and I mentioned how much the fog and the tall old pine trees reminded me of Đà Lạt, and how great it would be to visit the town of my childhood again.

"Oh, it wouldn't be the same. The Việt Cộng wouldn't allow you back, anyway."

"Mạ, we've been through this already," I said. "I'm just talking . . . a visit. I just want to see it again."

"I know. When the Việt Cộng got to Đà Lạt, they cut down all the trees at your school, did you know?"

"What does my memory have to do with the Việt Cộng? I just miss Đà Lạt. It was my favorite town, that's all."

It was my father's turn. "You've never lived with them—"

"I know, I know. . . . I've never lived with them. But that's not my fault, is it?"

"You don't know. They're wicked!"

"Why do you always have to bring them up? In any conversation? I'm talking about Đà Lạt."

"Look," my father began, measuring his words. "We were—"

"*Thôi, anh,*" said my mother. "Let's drop it."

It was too late. "I can't stand it!" I shouted, slamming my foot on the brakes.

Switching off the ignition, I swung out of the car, crossed the street, and stomped onto the grass. I sent a pine cone flying into the bushes. Suddenly all the rage went out of me. I felt the cold wind on my cheeks. It quickly chilled my spine. Or perhaps it was the recognition that I had lost my temper with my parents.

I turned back. I did not know what to say as I climbed into the car and drove on. I did not know how to apologize for my outburst, which my parents surely considered distasteful. They maintained an embarrassing silence on the way home.

The scene served notice that after a mere month together there was a grievous rupture between parents and son. Anything they said wound up being about how terrible the Việt Cộng were. And as long as I failed to agree with them whenever they criticized the Việt Cộng, it was their duty to continue to criticize. I had not lived with the Việt Cộng, and I couldn't know how bad it had really been. Until I relented, what was the point in saying anything else? My parents refrained from mentioning what my father had gone through in prison camps. We both knew that there was absolutely no argument against that.

We tiptoed around each other for days. I came to accept that for my parents, Việt Nam had been destroyed by cruel men blinded by Communist propaganda. For me, however, Việt Nam still existed: it was the place that held my cultural roots, my childhood. It was my homeland.

My father continued to look for a job during the day. At night he would sit at the small desk and write down the poems he had committed to memory while in prison. At those times I came to recognize the ravages of the years on him, his frame smaller than I had remembered, thinner as he bent over the desk. Reading his poems, I slowly overcame my fear of learning about his life in prison, and what things were like in Việt Nam after his release.

∞ My mother found a job first. A month after her arrival she became a social worker, helping young inner-city mothers in a government nutrition program. The pride on her face each day as she recounted what had happened at work was sweet to see. My father mostly listened in silence, until he himself found a job as a social worker a few weeks later.

Home at night, both continued to prove they could adapt

to their new life. My mother cooked; my father washed the dishes. I too prepared evening meals, for I wanted to show myself to be a good son.

Dinner over, my mother and I would look at old photographs, and talk of relatives and family friends at home and in the United States. My father retreated to his desk, methodically preparing a memoir of his years in isolation. Conversations about the process of writing would lead to criticism of Communist control and censorship of writers. After a while I gave up trying to convince him that I agreed with him, but the constant criticism annoyed me. There was no choice but to retreat to more neutral ground. My father and I talked of historical issues or of literature of more ancient times. In our conversations my father looked for signs that I had, after all, some understanding of Eastern thought, if only to compensate for behavior that remained far from the ideal conduct of an Asian man. Still, my ideas of Eastern cultures could be hopelessly inadequate, and I could hear in my father's sighs his regret that he had been robbed of the chance to guide my education.

I also began to hear unspoken regrets that he had lost the chance to devote himself to literature. On weekends, when I caught him gazing out the window, I assumed he was missing the pine trees surrounding the house he had built in Đà Lạt. He had taught classical literature in his youth, and dreamed of retiring among rosebushes and pine trees, researching and writing about Vietnamese, Chinese, and French literature. That quiet life was now a faded dream.

Because of such losses, my parents came to appreciate American society. Whereas I stubbornly lamented the impersonal, work-dominated, materialistic way of life, the impossibility of continued close friendships, the hypocritical government, the racial discrimination. My parents were always willing to overlook America's faults. Having lived under the Việt Cộng, they felt tremendous relief to be in a country whose government left them alone. "You don't know what it's like not to be able to say anything you like, travel anywhere, move from one place to another anytime you want," my father repeated. His criticism of the Communists was relentless, yet his words remained measured. He never sounded bitter.

My parents were happiest when Đỉnh and Diệu-Hà visited. Diệu-Hà was married and still living in Ohio, but talked of moving to California. Đỉnh came with Becky and Donnie from Buffalo. On their first visit my father greeted Đỉnh at the front door, draped an arm over his shoulder, and guided him to the back door. It was midafternoon. They huddled in the courtyard. We left them to fill in the eighteen years they had been separated. I was ready to serve dinner when they came back inside.

During these visits the house echoed with laughter as we took turns teasing each other. There was the past to remember, the days in Đà Lạt we had in common, the tricks we played on each other, books we read, incidents still in our memories. Certain events would recall Diệu-Quỳnh's solitary youth, her sorrow and illness, and her death. We each held the image of Diệu-Quỳnh in our minds at such moments, but we let them pass in silence, then moved on to other topics. The war, the years of separation, our parents' struggle also seemed to have been erased from our minds.

My parents sometimes sat back, wordless, to look at their children. Diệu-Hà, Đỉnh, and I carried on the conversation, sometimes in English. My parents understood us, for they laughed with us, but they did not participate. When you are happy, you don't need to talk.

☙ For many months I let my family praise my opportunity with the BBC, and what it would mean for my career. Accepting their assurances that they would be fine without me, I left for London in October, four months after my parents joined me in America.

The BBC turned out to be a wonderful place to work, and it was there that I met my future wife. London is a fantastic city. I called my parents every week, and came back to visit three times in the two years I was away. The last time, as I set off again to the airport, I glimpsed the tears my father fought from his eyes. I had never seen him cry before. He had not cried the winter evening in 1968 in Huế, when my mother brought me to the guest house to see him before the Việt Cộng took him away. Perhaps he truly believed then that he would be gone just for a few days. As it turned out, we were apart for sixteen years; he lost me a child. Now in his sixties, he did not have me as an adult son. The phone calls I made from London were not enough. Six months later I returned to San Francisco.

I had no job, but my mother had other ideas. "We've always considered it our responsibility to take care of you, to make sure you get a proper education. We didn't have the chance all these years. It's not too late now; we can still work. Why don't you let us help? Go back, further your education."

I took her advice about school, but I also got a job at KALW-FM, a public radio station in San Francisco, and began writing as a free-lance journalist. I moved to a nearby apartment when my girlfriend joined me from London in 1988. Even then I was not completely free of my parents. The phone would ring, and it would be them calling: "Are you eating your dinner?" or "Are you still awake?" or "How is work?" Whenever I visited there would be more questions. "Why don't you wear your jacket?" "Have you read this book?" "Have you talked to your sister?" "What about your cough medicine?"

The questions were relentless, even as I remembered that they were my parents' way of expressing their love. They cared about everything that happened to me, but other than the topic of my education they seldom directly expressed their concerns.

And so it was that when my girlfriend and I mentioned that we wanted to get married, my father smiled and my mother merely commented, "Oh, that's good."

In typical Asian fashion, praises were left unsaid; spoken praise is thought to cheapen any accomplishment. Besides, my family's undeclared but undisputed motto had always been that "one could do better," and no encouragement was necessary— achievement was acknowledged by the absence of disapproval.

When my mother merely said, "Oh, that's good," I knew my parents were happy with my decision to get married. There had been no pressure on me to get married, but to my parents, my decision meant I was ready to abandon my "nomadic" lifestyle. "Oh, that's good." I heard in those three simple words my parents' clear conclusion that a miracle had happened: I wanted to "settle down."

I was happy that they could be at the wedding, for they had witnessed neither Đỉnh's or Diệu-Hà's marriage ceremonies. Ours took place in June of 1989 at a nondenominational church, and was conducted by a friend. No part of the wedding resembled the traditional Vietnamese ceremony; I simply approached the altar with some flowers for my parents. The ritual of asking for their permission would have normally involved ceremonies in which I would bow to them and to images of my grandparents and ancestors. We would light candles and incense and then leave the house in a complicated observance. After the marriage ceremony at a temple, I would have had to bring my wife back to my parents' house for even more bowing and ceremonies, and for a talk in which my parents would formally give me advice on building a good marriage.

☙ Two and a half months after the wedding I disappointed my parents' hope that I would settle down. Worse, I followed through on an idea that had frightened them for months. I decided to go back to Việt Nam.

I had been planning the trip since the beginning of 1989. National Public Radio had accepted my proposal to document a return trip after fourteen years, and to report on Việt Cộng soldiers who were facing tough times as civilians in postwar Việt Nam.

"They'll arrest you!" cried my mother.

"Your mother's right." My father tried to sound reasonable, but his displeasure and anxiety crept into his voice. "How can you possibly think they'd let you in?"

"Well, if they won't let me in, they can't arrest me," I said.

"I can't believe you're joking about this!"

"But Mạ," I said, "look at how many people have gone back. Nothing's happened to anyone!"

"But, how do you know they won't harm you?" asked my father. "Don't you realize that the Việt Cộng lie all the time? They're cruel; they'll trick you. They won't let you meet anyone who will contradict them. And if you do, they'll arrest you! And—"

"I know all that. I won't be stupid. And I won't be alone. They wouldn't dare do anything."

"They can arrange an accident. If they put you in prison, who's there to help you? There's no American embassy."

"Why would they put me in prison? I'm getting an official visa. As a journalist!"

"That's the worst thing you can do," declared my father. "Others go there, maybe to do business, they'll accept that. . . . But you—nosing around . . . with your BBC connections . . ."

The argument went on. My mother sighed. "I wish I'd known this; I would have stayed back there."

"I can't believe you said that," I said.

"I would have stayed."

"But you can't stand the Việt Cộng," I protested.

"I came here to be with you. We lost the country—"

"There you go again. . . . We didn't lose the country. It's still there. It's—"

"I wish you wouldn't go. That's all. Go only when the Việt Cộng aren't there anymore!"

"When is that going to happen? They're there forever. The war is over; the Việt Cộng came to power!"

"They've changed the place!" exclaimed my father.

"I don't care. Việt Cộng or not, what does it matter?"

My mother raised her voice. "How dare you say that? All the years, all the destruction. Your father—"

"It's where I was born! I want to go home!"

For weeks my parents and I fought. I could not persuade them; they could not dissuade me. We stopped listening to each other. Đinh and Diệu-Hà attempted to change my mind, but on the other hand they wanted to assure themselves that it was safe for me to go. They were never convinced. Oddly, it was my father who found a compromise in our opposing positions.

"Well," he said one evening after we had exhausted ourselves arguing, "it's probably good you go. Go as a journalist—go and see. It'll change your mind, open your eyes. When you come back you can tell the story of how bad it is."

By August I had completed the paperwork, obtaining visa clearance through the Vietnamese embassy at the United Nations in New York. On the eve of my departure, National Public Radio sent producer Peter Breslow and sound engineer Arthur Laurent to join me. We had dinner at my parents' apartment.

My father said to Peter, "I believe he should do a general radio documentary, as an outside observer." He was still thinking of my safety.

Peter feigned a naive air. "D'you think so?"

"Yes," said my father. "He shouldn't reveal anything about himself or his family."

My father didn't know that Peter and I had already agreed to record and report every part of my trip. I would take him to visit relatives and friends, to document my taking the gifts my mother had prepared for Aunt Diệu-Mai in Sài Gòn. I was also to return to the site of my father's capture almost twenty-two years before, and to fulfill a duty to the sister I had left behind.

Fat Man's Come Home

H Ồ C H Í M I N H C I T Y

"*Ô, vô đây, vô đây!*" "Oh, come in, come in!"

Aunt Diệu-Mai hadn't changed much, her hair still smooth and long, her eyes sad yet sparkling. She grabbed my arms and sobbed as we hugged. Her dog barked at us: Peter Breslow, Arthur Laurent, the Foreign Ministry guide, and me. We came unannounced, setting up our recording equipment at the entrance to the little alley leading to her house.

She had had to give up her villa, and now lived in a dark apartment in this narrow way. I was concerned about her health; she had had a stroke.

"I'm better now," she said. "How come you're so fat?"

"American food." I laughed.

"Everyone here is so poor, have you noticed?"

"Yes." I didn't know what else to say. "Mạ and Cha sent a letter."

"I'll read it later. Have some tea first. Who are these people?"

I explained my assignment. I'd arrived home the day before, on my thirty-first birthday. Anxious about my reunion with Aunt Diệu-Mai after fourteen years, I couldn't sleep that first night. From San Francisco I had written to arrange for her to meet me at my hotel. I feared the curiosity of the police and her neighbors, especially as I would be accompanied by Americans with microphones, tape machines, and other suspicious recording equipment. Once in Hồ Chí Minh City (or Sài Gòn, as it was still known), I became impatient. "Let's just go over there," I said to my guide. I wanted to save Aunt Diệu-Mai the trip to the hotel since I knew she had trouble walking. Peter also preferred capturing on tape our spontaneous reunion.

The ceiling fan at my aunt's didn't do much to cool us; there was barely enough power to make it spin. Sài Gòn was always hot. "You want a hand fan?" Aunt Diệu-Mai asked me. She shuffled away.

"It was hotter than this back in April '75," I yelled after her.

"We should have left then, too," my aunt said when she came back, a purple paper fan in her hand. Like hundreds of thousands of others, her husband, my uncle Hải, had been put in jail—officially a reeducation camp—shortly after the Communists came. He died in captivity in 1983. I asked about Diệu-Quỳnh's illnesses.

"She just gave up, I think," Aunt Diệu-Mai replied. "Now what about your parents? Are they okay?"

"They're both working," I said.

"Your mom wrote and said you've abandoned her. She doesn't get to see you. Why don't you let them live with you? How come you're not supporting them?"

"But I'm so poor!"

"Poor as the people here?"

It hit home. I couldn't decide whether Aunt Diệu-Mai was joking. "You unfilial son!"

"I'll wait until you get there—then we can all live together."

"If I had to wait for you, Cu Bé, to house me, and to feed me"—she laughed—"I'd die of hunger, or old age." Her using my childhood nickname told me I was home again.

Among my mother's many siblings—my grandfather had had four wives—Aunt Diệu-Mai was the only one still in Việt Nam. She had no children. Soon she might be on her way to America. My uncle Thịnh-Anh in Maryland had completed the paperwork to sponsor her.

"Your uncles all live in such cold places! Maryland, Virginia—I'd rather live with your parents in California."

"You should," I replied.

"And who will cook for me? You? Vietnamese food?"

"If you'll teach me," I said. "Huế beef noodle."

"Don't be smart!" She laughed, then said, "Who knows when I'll be able to leave?" She patted my cheeks. "I'm glad you're home. Of all the people who left, you're the only one to come back. Come to dinner tomorrow! Bring your American friends."

I wondered who would cook. Aunt Diệu-Mai was nearly seventy years old.

ॐ At two in the afternoon, my cousins were asleep on the floor when I knocked. Seven people, all living in one room. The cousins had also been primary school classmates. Their mother had worked at my mother's school. I apologized for my unannounced arrival. "I was afraid you might be at work," I said.

They smiled. No one had a job. They warned that the shoes I left outside the door might get stolen.

"They're cheap," I said. "Just a few dollars." I then looked at the shoes lying haphazardly in the hallway. My white canvas sneakers looked obscenely opulent next to the seven pairs of ragged flip-flops.

Crouched in a corner of the room where he smoked a cigarette, my cousin Bảo avoided my eyes. He directed a remark to his mother. "Cu Bé's so fat, don't you think, Mạ?"

I felt obese. My white shirt was soaked in sweat.

"Can you get Vietnamese food in California?" his mother asked.

From across the room, Bảo's sister Lý stared at me. She had been my sister's classmate. "Is Diệu-Hà still beautiful? She must be."

I smiled in the way a Vietnamese smiles to avoid having to answer a question. I had suddenly realized that Bảo and his siblings all had extremely dark skin. I glanced at my hand, seeing as if for the first time how pale it was.

"Cu Bé, you have any pictures of your house in America?"

"Oh, I just have a rented flat," I answered.

"Big?"

"No, no, a plain two-bedroom apartment."

"For you and your wife? Why can't your parents live with you?"

My aunt asked to see pictures of my wife. I picked my shoulder bag off the floor and began to rummage through it, looking for the photos. As I did so I pulled out my professional tools. Microphones, cassette recorder, camera—all looked like monstrous objects from outer space, and expensive. The T-shirts I had thought would be good gifts now seemed inadequate. I stuffed everything back in the bag. "I must have forgotten the photos at the hotel," I said.

Looking up, I caught my cousins averting their eyes. The wonderful reunion I had anticipated seemed to have stabbed them with glimpses of a rich world they could never know.

❧ Again I could not sleep in my stuffy hotel room that night, so I wandered out into the street. Gaunt men, young and old, buzzed like flies around the block of hotels near the river, fighting to sell a pedicab tour of Sài Gòn at half past midnight. "*Đi vòng vòng chỏi mà—cho mát*," one driver suggested. "Let's go round and round, for fun—get some breeze."

We went a few blocks along the river, then doubled back on the wide boulevards forming Sài Gòn's downtown. The Continental Hotel had a new coat of paint; its veranda, once a café made famous by Graham Greene and later hordes of foreign correspondents covering the Việt Nam War, was now enclosed in a garish glass structure. The old National Assembly building was again a theater, and across from it the square was no longer covered with grass. The ugly concrete statue of a South Vietnamese marine brandishing a rifle was torn down just after the Communists arrived; in its place now sat a few sorry benches around a cement fountain with no water. Over on General Uprising Street, once Freedom Street, a row of hotels competed for attention on the only block in the city which had regular, uninterrupted electricity. The whole area had somehow recaptured the gaudiness of days gone by when noisy bars and kiosks selling bootleg tapes of Bob Dylan and the Beatles had catered to American soldiers, and those who came to profit from the war. On my first night back I was shocked to see smartly dressed bands of youths as well as entire families circling the area on motorcycles, riding aimlessly as though gasoline were something that had to be used up by the end of the night.

My midnight pedicab turned into a small road. The naked poverty of the neighborhood struck me abruptly. Shadows dragged tattered burlap sacks back and forth across dim streets. Frail, half-dressed boys sang and chewed old bread, pissing on the walls or in the gutters all the while. Rows and rows of people were trying to sleep on straw mats on the pavement, surrounded by skeletal dogs too weak to fight over the contents of rubbish heaps. The turning wheels of the pedicab echoed deep in my bones, and in the darkness the scene took on a nightmarish and sinister character.

🙣 "Is there anything you won't do for a story, Đức?" I hated Peter's sarcastic tone. Half naked, trousers rolled up to my knees, I was about to slip through a narrow hole into a maze of underground tunnels the Việt Cộng had built during the war. The Foreign Ministry had organized this trip to the village of Củ Chi, half an hour from Sài Gòn, where I met Út Nghiệp, a former Việt Cộng soldier whose ideal of life was shaped by war. He had joined the National Liberation Front in 1961, when he was fourteen. He and men like him fought for ten, fifteen years in the war, as their fathers had done against foreign invaders. During the war Nghiệp would live underground for two weeks at a time.

"He's so fat," said a villager, "how's he gonna get through?"

Down below I could neither breathe nor see. Bats flew out of walls of packed earth. I was petrified of getting lost. Gasping, I crouched along inch by inch, fearing Nghiệp might abandon me. I hated the thought that I had trusted a former enemy to guide me through these tunnels.

Waves of late morning breeze softened the heat in Củ Chi when we emerged. Our amiable guide Tiến suggested a coconut drink at the thatched-roof local "café." The barefooted owner was a peasant wearing a simple shirt over a pair of loose black pants. Her hair was knotted into a small bundle in back, revealing the wrinkles on her face. Her irregular teeth were dyed black; her hands were rough and calloused.

Nodding toward Peter, she said, "Tell him I used to have a house over there." Her arm made an arc. "The Americans burned it down. My husband died too. Americans killed him."

Tiến and the driver were nervous, smiling the way Asians do when they are embarrassed. I was exact in my translation. Arthur looked away.

Peter asked me to say something back. Anything.

"Ah, it's okay," the old woman laughed. "Why doesn't he just marry my daughter? Take her to America!"

Our van baking in the early afternoon heat, we headed back to the mad mess called Sài Gòn.

∼ It was cloudy the afternoon Peter, Arthur, and I arrived at the pagoda on the outskirts of Sài Gòn. My father's sister Xuân-Liễu and her husband, my uncle Vịnh, came with us. Dozens of kids followed us from the main street into the alley leading to the courtyard in front of the pagoda. For some inexplicable reason they wouldn't stop screaming as they surrounded us on the path to the main temple. All eyes were on us. Arthur, not as tall or as thin as the muscular Peter, looked painfully pale. A bright red bag swung from his shoulder along with coils of black wires. His microphones were hooked to a metal pole and encased in a plastic zeppelin the size of a watermelon. My own baggy trousers and canvas shoes were hideously bright and white.

In the principal chamber a man was sitting before an enormous statue of the Buddha. Chanting a monotonous prayer, he dragged out his words, accompanying himself on a wooden bell the size of a skull. I knelt down and prayed as two monks looked on. They had been watching over Diệu-Quỳnh's ashes for the last ten years. When the physical and mental illnesses had finally taken their toll, only my mother was still in Sài Gòn. I had now come for my sister's ashes.

It was pouring, Sài Gòn's usual afternoon shower. The man at the altar continued to chant, undisturbed. I was taken around the veranda to a room full of urns. I wandered between the shelves, stopping at the urns bearing names I recognized. The one containing Diệu-Quỳnh's ashes was made of ceramic, with blue flowers. A black-and-white photo of Diệu-Quỳnh was glued to the outside. I recognized my mother's handwriting on the piece of paper that gave her name and dates: 1950–1979.

For a time I stood before the urn. Soon I was to be on my way again. Like me, my aunt, my cousins, friends, and other relatives still in Việt Nam might all leave one day to create new lives in a place of exile. We'd live there for ten, twelve, fifteen years, perhaps the rest of our lives. But some of us had to come back for the things we had left behind: our childhood home— the place, as the Vietnamese say, where our umbilical cords were cut. We would come back changed, but we would come back, for a loved one, and her ashes.

ĐÀ NẴNG

I could no longer recognize the street that led from the Đà Nẵng airport into town. I was impatient for landmarks I could pick out, buildings, shops, cafés I remembered. My exile was ending, and I strained to spot a familiar face on the streets. I wanted to be home.

Ngã Năm was the bustling crossroads where five streets met. At three in the afternoon the streets were full. People kept their distance, but their gaze was fixed on us as I took the first steps toward my old school, toward my past.

"I was a student here," I said to the pair of eyes behind the school's iron gates. "I've been away and have just come back— would it be possible to come in?"

The door cracked open slightly. Puny as she was, the woman's questions alarmed me. "Have you notified all the appropriate agencies? Do you have permission? Any papers?"

"I was just walking past. . . . There's my classroom." Like the rest of the school, it was painted the same ocher color with white trim. The woman looked at it without speaking, then turned back toward us. Pointing to the zeppelin over our heads, she asked, "What's that?"

"Uh, just some microphones . . . We're recording for radio. . . ."

She lowered her voice. "You'd better talk to the principal."

The principal's office was in the same room as when I was a student. The portrait of Hồ Chí Minh on the wall was the most visible change.

"You'll have some tea, won't you?" the principal began.

I wanted to explain our sudden presence, but I knew the gaunt and severe man who sat across the small coffee table from us must speak first. Though his shirt was untucked and his feet were encased in plastic sandals, he held himself with dignity, never once smiling.

"Your name is Đức?" the man intoned.

I became a student again. "Yes, my dear Mr. Principal."

"When did you come back?"

"A week ago, my dear Mr. Principal."

"A guest of the Foreign Ministry, I presume?"

"That's correct, my dear Mr. Principal."

"Do they know you're here?"

"Uh, no, my dear Mr. Principal."

"Ah."

I wasn't about to give up. "I hope it's not a problem, my dear Mr. Principal. I have longed to see the school again so very much." I was honest.

"There is no problem," the man said. "No one would ever object—a former student returning to visit an old school? That is sweet. A delightful thing to do. Normally the ministry would phone us first. But there is no problem."

The principal then maintained a long silence. I began to apologize again, but he ignored me. The woman who had met us at the gate brought in a teapot with some cups on a tray. The principal reached for the pot, moving it to one side.

"When were you a student here?"

"In 1974 and '75," I said. The principal arranged the cups as though ready to pour the tea, but in the end merely moved them around on the tray. I stole a glance out the window, catching a quick look at my old classroom across the rectangular courtyard.

"And these men are colleagues of yours?"

"Yes, Mr. Principal."

"Have they been to Việt Nam before?"

"No, Mr. Principal."

"You will translate, please? I do not know English, you see."

I said I would.

"I am happy they have come. Do they like our country?"

"He's asking whether you like our country," I translated. "Say you're grateful."

"We're grateful to be here," Peter said, and I translated.

"We're very poor, you know," the principal said.

"He says we're a poor country."

Peter was quick: "Tell him I admire how hard-working the Vietnamese seem to be." I translated.

"Oh, he's noticed," the principal said. "That is good. But we're still poor. Wars. Many wars. It makes, you work hard."

"Did you tell him I didn't fight in the Việt Nam War?" Peter said to me.

"He says the Việt Nam War was destructive," I said to our host.

"But we don't blame the American people." The principal nodded toward Peter. Tea was poured.

"Can we go to your classroom? Let's get this show on the road," Peter muttered.

"Wait. He says they don't blame you guys. I mean, the American people."

"For what?" asked Peter.

The principal looked at me. I said, "My colleague says it's all in the past."

"Let's have some tea," the principal said after a moment. We took our cups, sipping slowly. The principal was silent again.

I nodded at Peter and began my speech about visiting my one-time classroom. "My dear Mr. Principal, in America I work as a radio journalist. When I decided to come back, Peter here suggested—"

"And who were your teachers?" the principal interrupted.

I hesitated. Could I mention their names without jeopardizing them? Perhaps I would expose a former teacher who had adopted another identity after the Communists took over. And could anyone be blamed for having a student who lacked the wisdom to stay and welcome the Việt Cộng and the liberation of the South? Would I be in trouble if whoever I named turned out to be a person with a record of crimes against the people? Finally I mentioned a Vietnamese literature teacher who had been well known for his nationalist sympathies.

"Have you been to see him?"

"No, Mr. Principal. I just arrived."

"And you intend to, of course?"

The interview went on, and I continued to dance around each question. Arthur patiently sat in the corner with his instruments, sweat glistening on his forehead. Peter and the principal tolerated my not-so-perfect translation of both the spoken and the unspoken words. It was the gatekeeper who rescued us, appearing at the doorway and giving the principal a nod. The principal said, "Go to your classroom—they're expecting you now. I'll phone the ministry and public security."

"Thank you, my dear Mr. Principal," I said.

"Class!" the teacher called out as I appeared. Everyone stood up. "We have guests," he announced, waving his arm to invite Peter and Arthur in. The teacher insisted I climb up on the platform beneath the blackboard to address the students. There were about forty of them, arms folded in front of their chests in a gesture of respect. In my rush to see the school, I hadn't anticipated this situation. Standing three feet off the floor under a portrait of Hồ Chí Minh, I faced the students and began: "It's a great feeling, after almost fifteen years . . ."

Arthur, shoved by Peter onto the platform, extended the zeppelin over my head. I felt ridiculous. The teacher did not signal the students to sit down; they stood waiting for me to speak.

"I was once a student here," I said, then immediately my mind went blank. The students all looked so young, the boys in their white shirts and blue trousers, the girls in the traditional white costume, an *aó dài* worn over pants. Their expectant faces suddenly blurred, and I seemed to see in their place my schoolmate Khủong-An in the bench in back and Thúy-Loan in the middle and dozens of other faces of my youth. I saw myself at sixteen.

"I don't know what to say!" I blurted to Peter in English. His laughter suddenly boomed out in the quiet of the classroom. It had an immediate effect on the students; their roars made my face red. "Well done!" the gatekeeper said with her eyes. Abandoning my attempt at a speech, I thanked the students. Their laughter had died down, and now the expectant silence returned. The class was still standing. Fumbling for a subject to ask them about, I said, "What are you studying here?" No one spoke. After a long hushed moment, everyone roared again.

Kindly trying to save me, the teacher spoke a few lines about how wonderful it was that an alumnus had returned. But though his words were eloquent, after my comical performance everything he said only made the students laugh more. The teacher clapped his hands for order; the class clapped in response. Arthur aimed the microphones at the students. I turned to shake hands with the teacher. "Exile is a sweet thing to end," wrote the South African writer Rian Malan. So is a botched speech in a schoolroom that once harbored your youth.

🙞 The crew recorded the clanging sound of the school handyman banging on an old iron wheel that once belonged on an army truck. It was five o'clock, and school was letting out. The students immediately surrounded me as they emerged from the building. We took some photographs, then after a while I moved away from the young faces.

The street seemed narrower as I crossed it, and in front of what had been my family's house the royal poincianas had grown, their leaves forming a soft canopy. I glanced back toward the school. The library was still there, its gray concrete walls dusty, the doors still painted blue. The bench in front of it was gone— the place where almost fifteen years before I had said goodbye to Khuởng-An.

I felt anxious as I stepped through the gate to my former home. The small quaint house was now an ugly mess. Additions had been tacked on every which way to accommodate the many families I could tell resided there, and barbed wire ran across the front yard to separate the plot of land on which the old kindergarten building stood. Where once children had run shrieking with joy amid tot-size furniture and colorful swings and slides, now there was no sign of life. The doors and windows were all closed. The bamboo in the front yard was gone; haphazard concrete-block walls had taken its place. I wished I could look through the front windows into the living room. The sound of Diệu-Hà's piano playing drifted back into my mind. Even with all the changes that had taken place, it seemed impossible that fifteen years had passed since the time when strains of Chopin would flow into my room at six in the morning and wake me up.

I glanced over to another part of the house. The green paint had faded on the louvered doors framing the small balcony. I imagined the frail, timid form of my sister Diệu-Quỳnh. She used to stand on that balcony in the afternoon, leaning against the railing with a vacant smile on her face. Sometimes she would not be completely dressed, and someone would have to nudge her back into her room.

As I gazed at the house, a man stepped out and stopped me from approaching.

∾ "When did you come back?" Đoàn Duy Tân asked me between fits of laughter. "Damn, you're so fat!"

Tân fired off a hundred more questions as I tried to mumble answers. "Radio reporter . . . Fine, my parents are fine . . . In California . . . Yeah, married . . . No, no kids." Cigarettes were offered, then lit up. "I'm here for a few weeks."

I had last seen Tân when we were sixteen. He had lived around the block from me and attended the same school. Now he had a wife and two children, and a job teaching English to adult students.

"Do you remember that last Christmas, in 1974?" he asked. "We danced all night."

"Yes . . . You still have one of my albums," I reminded him. "Yeah. *Who's Next.*"

Tân had given up the Who long ago, and Neil Young and the Beatles. The Communists banned rock music after they took over in 1975. Life had changed a lot since I left.

"Between 1975 and '80 it was really hard. We didn't have enough clothes, food, anything. . . . But at that time everyone was alike. We were all poor, so no one was disappointed.

"At the university in Huế we never had enough to eat, and you couldn't visit girls in their rooms. They would hang up pieces of fabric they had washed out, which they'd keep using over and over as tampons!"

Tân and some other friends had dropped out of school after the Communist takeover and sold coal for a few years. In the mornings they would pedal a three-wheeled contraption to the outskirts of town and transport the coal back, selling it on the black market. "One load would buy dinner for four or five of us guys," he explained. "But at least we were free from the prying eyes in town. It was hard work, but you could get away and the authorities would leave you alone."

"What about Khuông-An?" I asked.

"Oh, he came with us for a while. Then we all started together at the university in Huế. He moved south a few years ago. Got married to a woman from a moneyed family in Qui-Nhơn. He's doing all right."

"And Thúy-Loan?"

"They broke up in Huế. You know who she ended up with for a while? Thu-Hảo's brother Cẩm! They were just like Khuông-An and Thúy-Loan had been in those years, holding hands, kissing on the streets. The Communists couldn't believe it. They got in trouble, though; they both became alcoholics. She straightened out later. I'll take you to see her. She's married now and pregnant. . . . And Thu-Hảo, have you seen her?"

"No . . . she's in Texas, I just found out a year or so ago. She's married."

"You didn't get in touch with her? She was in Huế with us, at the university."

I dropped the subject. What would I find out about my old girlfriend? That she had had a new boyfriend? That she had suffered the years of hunger?

After all this time I was uncomfortable hearing about what my friends had been through after the fall of the South. In a few weeks I would pick up my bags and return to my comfortable life in America. Tân had to worry that he would be questioned by the security police after my visit. "I don't know what will happen," he said. "I might get into trouble. . . . A lot of people still do for talking to foreigners. But it was worse a few years ago." At that time he would have been immediately jailed for talking to me, Peter, or Arthur. During the last two years the national government had relaxed its control over people's private lives considerably. But "renovation"—the official term for a pro-

gram of reforms—centered on economic policies rather than political ones. And local authorities were still nervous about outsid-
ers, however. Provincial party cadres were old revolutionaries, and
they could be politically as rigid as the doctrinaire national leaders.
I was comforted when Tân said he knew all the secret police and
public security officers; many had taken his English classes.

In the darkness later that evening I perched behind Tân on
his tiny motorcycle. An English teacher could do well, tutoring
people hoping for jobs in the tourist industry, or to those intending
to leave the country, whether by boat or by being sponsored by
relatives already in the West. Tân also had family members in the
United States who regularly sent him money, thus helping him
buy the Honda. We rode through a maze of alleys, swerving left
and right to avoid kids, dogs, chickens, and open sewage on the
way to see another friend, Võ Thế Hoà. Peter's and Arthur's
presence would have been uncomfortable, so they went back to
the hotel.

Hoà had been a rowdy kid in school, but instead of the old
prankster I now found an embittered war veteran. The year before
he had returned to live with his family in Đà Nẵng after eight
years of fighting in Cambodia. There was no talk of the good old
days.

"All I get is propaganda from the government," he said. A
former captain, he had joined the army in 1976 and attended
officers' training school for four years. "I learned to use a gun,
but no one hires me for that now," he told me. After his discharge
from the army he bribed officials to state that he was 60 percent
physically disabled as a result of his years in Cambodia. He was
entitled to compensation of sixty-six thousand đồng, or about
$15. "I had to wait six months to get it, and that's after spending
twenty-five thousand đồng to buy beers for the officials," he
recounted.

A few days before I saw him, Hoà had accepted a job as a
clerk in a communications office. He was to earn forty thousand

Vietnamese đồng a month, about $10. "That'll buy eight beers,"
he said.

"You're stupid to take such a pitiful salary!" Tân said. He
could earn infinitely more spending his days wheeling and dealing
on the black market.

"I wouldn't know where to start," Hoà replied, "and besides,
I haven't got the money."

Tân turned to me. "It's impossible to live honestly in this
country."

I had been at Hoà's house for less than half an hour when
we were interrupted by two uniformed public security officers.
As Hoà asked them to sit down, one of them declared, "We just
dropped by to say hello."

Reaching into my shoulder bag, I pulled out an unopened
pack of British cigarettes and laid it on the table in front of the
officers. From my shirt pocket I took another pack, already
opened, and invited both to smoke. Tân congratulated me casually—and openly. "You haven't been back long, but you've picked
up some good habits."

British cigarettes were valuable in Việt Nam. They made
awkward situations less so, opened doors, got you things. Leaving
the pack on the table for the officers to take, I put the other one
back in my pocket and left with Tân, feeling abused.

"Hoà will be all right," Tân assured me as we sped along
the emptied streets on the way back to my hotel.

"But how dare they enter Hoà's house in such a blatant
way?" I shouted back over the rush of wind.

In the 1970s, I learned from Tân, Hoà's parents had harbored
an underground Communist agent who was now a high-ranking
official in Hà Nội. For this service the house had since been
declared a "historic site." Moreover, Hoà's brother had once been
Hồ Chí Minh's private secretary. A poster-sized photograph of
him standing next to Hồ hung on the living room wall.

⮿ It was six o'clock in the morning. I wanted to ignore the knocks on my hotel door, but they were insistent, urgent. I crawled out of bed. It was Hoà.

"Are you okay?" I asked.

"Yeah, yeah. That was nothing, last night. I know those guys."

I sat down on the bed, leaving the armchair for Hoà. "I just wanted to see you before you left," he said. I wasn't leaving for a few days.

Sinking into the chair, he asked me to turn off the air conditioner. Within minutes he started to complain again about his treatment as a veteran. He did not talk about school days, other than mentioning that I looked just as I had when I left. I couldn't find a trace of his old self. His skin looked jaundiced and the whites of his eyes were yellowish. His bones jutted out in angular prominences under his clothes. Though he kept saying how bad conditions were, he could not bring himself to ask for help. I reached into my bag to find my wallet and sat with it on my bed for a long while. I couldn't think of a delicate way to hand him the dollar bills I had inside.

"I shouldn't be here," my old friend finally said.

That was true; I wasn't supposed to have guests in the room. "Here, go get some breakfast downstairs. I'll put on some clothes and join you later," I said. I handed him fifty dollars.

I didn't find Hoà among the crowd in the restaurant next to the hotel when I came down at 7 A.M. to meet Tân. The day was starting, and already the faces all looked like those of the sad souls in a bar at closing time. Tân called out to me from the back. He had brought another old friend, Phạm Văn Vĩnh, to see me. Vĩnh grinned at me, his smile as boyish as ever. The gap between his front teeth made him look like a teenager. "You haven't changed much," I said.

He smiled again. I wanted to hug him but didn't. Back in

school Vĩnh was the diminutive kid everyone wanted to protect. He didn't say anything to me. The waitress came and went. Talk to me—tell me what has happened, I wanted to say. Has it been bad for you?

He had been in and out of jail three times, trying to escape from Việt Nam by boat. "The third time around I just couldn't bear to look at my mother anymore."

I put my slice of bread down on the plate. The piece of egg slid off.

"She looked horrible each time she came to visit me in prison," he continued.

Each attempted escape had cost Vĩnh and his family a lot of money. Getting out of prison required still more, and each time the authorities harassed him more. He finally had to drop out of teachers' training school.

"What do you do now?"

"Oh, I buy and sell things."

Things: coffee, medical equipment, old cars, spare parts, whatever. Vĩnh was vague about his dealings. Along with his mother, who ran a coffee shop in the front yard, he was supporting six brothers and sisters. His father, a collaborator with the Việt Cộng during the war, was now a disillusioned man who sat in his room all day.

A man joined us at the table, a customs officer who helped Vĩnh get shipments of "things" up and down the length of the country. After a while I realized he was calling my school friend by another name. Vĩnh apparently had a set of different identities.

"It's impossible to live honestly in this country, I'm telling you," Tân said to me again after the man left.

"Sixty, seventy percent of my earnings get eaten up by corruption," Vĩnh explained. In order to deal on the black market he had to take officials out drinking most nights. "I always come home drunk, crying in front of my brothers and sisters."

❧ One afternoon while I was in Đà Nẵng I abandoned my assignment and wandered alone, soaking in the atmosphere of my old town. Darkness was collecting when I found myself near Uncle Phạm's house. What my mother had told me about his refusal to help her find another teaching job after "liberation" came back to me. I was reluctant to visit him. What would I say? In a café next to his house I sipped coffee as though it were my last cup. The loud music didn't help me clear my thoughts. I had traveled an enormous distance to be back home; why should I not see someone I once knew, a relative whose gentle manner I had always liked? Could fifteen years heal a rift that had occurred when I wasn't even in the country?

Uncle Phạm recognized me immediately as I walked in front of his house. "Hey, Cu Bé," he called out. "You're back!"

Yes, indeed, I was home. For a moment my apprehension and hesitation swelled. But his smile, the gentleness in his eyes, the happiness on his face—all were genuine, and I cried when we hugged.

We didn't talk about the time before I left Đà Nẵng in 1975. I didn't ask about the kindergarten, about his role in the People's Committee, about his Việt Cộng hat. I didn't apologize for having left the country. We talked of my flight home, about banal aspects of life in America, and in between we looked at each other and smiled. I understood how deeply disillusioned he had been by the Communists and all that had happened since the takeover; he allowed the embarrassment to show in his eyes, and I offered my sympathy in silence.

The next night we shared a sumptuous meal, or so it seemed—a loving and heartwarming meal. Tears came to my eyes again when I said goodnight. Uncle Phạm's wife surprised me the next day, coming with her sister, an old friend of mine, to visit me at Tân's house, and to bring me some guavas, which I had said I missed in the States, along with a lacquer box for my mother and another one for my wife, whom they had never met.

On my last afternoon in Đà Nẵng, Tân gathered some of our old group to meet me at a sidewalk café. "Fat man's come home," he said. "What do you think of your old home, fat man?"

I had expected the question, but I had no answer. I smiled.

"I'm still dealing with putting food on the table every night," Vĩnh said. The four of us, Vĩnh, Tân, another classmate named Trí, and I, squatted on tiny wooden stools. Around us there was an incessant stream of bicycles and scooters, every one of them, it seemed, blaring its horn. There were no longer any military jeeps on the streets, but I didn't remember Đà Nẵng being this noisy, even during the war. Life here was on the streets; everyone was hustling, fixing bikes, selling loose cigarettes or a few oranges.

For a while my friends and I sat in silence. I toyed with my glass of iced coffee. The heat was unbearable, and the silence was equally difficult. When we finally spoke, it wasn't about the good times we'd shared. My friends all talked about leaving Việt Nam to become refugees in America.

Another friend had just arrived: Lê Văn Tiến-Dũng had ridden a scooter to the café and was now struggling to stand it up on the sidewalk. We stopped talking, but no one offered to help him. He had lost a leg fighting in Cambodia. When he reached the table he asked me, "Did you get a Ph.D. yet?" If I had stayed in Việt Nam, school would have been out of the question; my father had worked for the "puppet government" of the South. For someone like me the options would have been few: driving a pedicab, or maybe working at a construction site.

"Why did you join the army?" I asked Tiến-Dũng.

"At that time you did what the government told you to," he replied.

"I thought all soldiers sent to Cambodia were volunteers."

"That's what they said. But it doesn't matter now." Tiến-Dũng was a tailor, supporting a wife and a two-year-old son.

A woman appeared on a bicycle. I almost didn't recognize Cẩm-Túy. In high school she was fun-loving, vibrant. Her large eyes had once shone brilliantly. In those days she made everybody laugh, but her smile now just made me sad, the way it embodied stoic acceptance as well as profound embarrassment. "I can't stay," she said, handing me a letter to take to the States. An overseas stamp would cost her a fourth of her monthly teacher's salary. "It's just a letter to ask a friend for some help," Cẩm-Túy said. "My little daughter isn't well."

I got out photographs of classmates now living in California to show.

"Look how fat everyone is!" someone said.

The glossy surface of the photographs intensified the opulence in the pictures. My friends turned their eyes to the houses and cars in these emulsion versions of a dream world. I couldn't explain that life in America is controlled by mortgages, bills, and credit card payments. Their lives were controlled by the state and the security police. Being with me at the outdoor café put them at risk.

"Many of our friends fled for the States, promising to send us gifts, to help us survive," Tân said. "They promised and promised, but they forgot it all. Not even a letter—they never wrote us, never wrote—"

"I left without your address. . . . I had no address for any of you." My own reason for not writing sounded like an excuse. "Is there anything you want me to tell the guys in California?" I asked.

"Please tell them to come back to Việt Nam, to spend their summer vacations here," Tân said. "We'd be very happy to see them—not to ask for gifts or money . . ." His voice trailed off, then he became stern: "Give anything you like now, but don't promise to do anything for the ones who still live here."

"I'll be back next year," I promised. "I'll write."

"Yeah, write us," Vĩnh said. We fell into silence again.

I went to the counter inside to pay, surprised that my friends allowed me to do so. All week they had been paying for our

244 •• *Where the Ashes Are*

meals and coffee. When I came back Tân said, "Now you can go back to the States and tell our friends you came home and bought us coffee."

The remark bothered me. Yes, I had gone home, I could say to friends in America, and I had treated our impoverished friends. Six glasses of iced coffee, one each for four friends and two for me, since I was no longer able to deal with the humidity of the old town or simply because I could afford to.

H U Ế

Sông Hương, the River of Perfume, had not lost its beauty, but the picturesque trees on its banks had mostly disappeared and one could smell the destitution on either side. Though I felt uncertain at being back in Huế, the green water of the river no longer divided the city into two domains of enmity. I hadn't forgotten the cannons hurling death across the River of Perfume, but the rockets were silenced now. Coming back to the riverbank was to confront the memory of those terrible early days of the Year of the Monkey once more, but homecoming is always like that.

Peter, Arthur, and I took a boat upriver. Sliding slowly along, only after some time did we reach a stretch of the river where the houses thinned out along the banks and the foliage grew dense. "There it is," I said to Peter.

Among the greenery, high above the riverbank, stood the government guest house. It looked a bit desolate, despite the bright light of the midday sun.

Nearly twenty-two years had gone by; the horror of the war, of the Việt Cộng, and of the gunfire that started along with the New Year's firecrackers had left me. The procession that accompanied my grandfather's body past here on a cold, rainy day in 1971 had also faded from my mind. I remembered more clearly seeing my father take his first steps into the long years of isolation. But on that boat going up the River of Perfume, what I remembered best was the grandeur of the guest house—its arched corridors that went on forever, and its imposing rooms with their lofty tall ceilings. I remembered the elephant tusks that rose beneath the ornate staircase and the broad, spacious roof terrace that led to still more terraces. I remembered the few moments of my childhood spent there, before Tết, when I was a little boy lucky to have such an empty palace in which to roam, a fortunate boy whose father could give him such a castle. I knew this was why I had come home.

✎ Huế has always been a severe town, suffering from harsh weather and poverty. It bred fierce leaders as well as mandarins, scholars, and renowned poets. Its people were proud of its history as the capital of the first unified Việt Nam under the Nguyễn dynasty at the beginning of the nineteenth century. For nearly a hundred years it was the political and cultural center of the country. I stood on the Trường Tiền looking out at either side of the river, wondering whether I had changed, or was it the town? The main boulevards had lost their ancient tamarind and royal poinciana trees. The famous girls' school where my mother had once been a pupil and later, along with my father, a teacher, had been merged with a boys' school. Gone were the shy girls in their flowing *aó dài;* now the students wore workers' garb—short thin shirts and black pants. The party preferred such clothing for its practicality, whereas the people said its skimpy design was due to the shortage of fabric.

Built on the narrow stretch between the Trường Sơn Mountains and the sea, Huế was short of everything: cultivable land, rice, food. Now it seemed short of its old charm also. Still, people retained their ideas of propriety. Whenever I left my hotel room someone would remind me to have my shirt pressed. The moment I spoke my accent revealed me to be a son of Huế, and if, with the changed circumstances the people of Huế couldn't afford to press their own shirts, I at least must carry on. Communist egalitarianism had not taken root in the city. I noticed that whenever people pieced together my family's background the forms they used in addressing me would become more formal and deferential. Some were appalled that I would walk instead of hiring a pedicab. I also ate at street stalls: "Go to a proper restaurant," they implored. Not that Huế had any left.

Our white van was the only motorized vehicle bigger than a motorbike on the road near the province of Quảng Trị, my father's birthplace, over an hour's drive from Huế. We had received permission to go up to the Hồ Chí Minh Trail to meet Việt Cộng veterans. Leaving Huế early in the morning, Peter, Arthur and I piled into the back with our equipment. Tiến, our ever-present Foreign Ministry guide on these official working trips, sat up front with the driver, Minh, a dark man in his twenties whose mustache made him look South American. A disorderly hodgepodge of carts, motorbikes, and bicycles—as well as pedestrians, pigs, dogs, and chickens—vied for space on the narrow highway.

Minh kept hitting the horn lightly, keeping a regular beat that Peter asked Arthur to record. Peter always had his ears attuned to the sounds of the story we were to produce. The road was no more than a collection of potholes, and our van was further shaken by Minh's constant swerving around the other vehicles. My ears hurt, my bones ached, my stomach was twisted. We stayed on Highway 1, the main road running the length of the country, for a long while. Tiến and the driver smoked endlessly. All three of us in the back felt dizzy. The countryside was green and lush. Rice paddies surrounded thatched-roof houses, and little boys were perched atop huge slimy water buffaloes.

"Look at all those cemeteries," I said to Peter, who was sitting next to me. "A lot of people were killed here in 1972, and again in 1975, when the Việt Cộng moved south." I glanced at

Tiến, who didn't seem to be paying attention. The area had seen some of the fiercest fighting during the war, particularly in 1972, when the highway was covered with bodies, abandoned vehicles, and motorcycles as people rushed south in panic. Now tombstones dotted the land on both sides of the highway, the sandy graves sad, neglected scars on the greenery. The monuments all bore the same inscription: REMEMBERED WITH GRATITUDE FOR THEIR SERVICES TO THE FATHERLAND. There were no monuments for those who had fought for the South.

An hour away from Quảng Trị we arrived at Đông Hà, where we were to spend the night. I had never been to a town as desolate as this. Everything was covered in a film of reddish brown dust; even the people and their lives seemed covered with dust. "Yeah, go to Đông Hà, you'll see real poverty," Tân had told me. During the war I had associated the name Đông Hà with a village that either had just been bombed, or was about to be. The years of war had devastated the place. "I'm not lying to you," Tân said. "Say you run over a kid there; you give the family a dollar—one dollar—they'll come out and bow down at your feet. It'll be the kid's dumb fate to step in front of your car, his destiny to die. They'll tell you that, and thank you for your dollar."

Minh turned the van into the open area that served as a market, a cloud of dust behind us. A rusted American tank stood on a mound of red earth ringed by irregular pieces of brick, a crude memorial to the war that had destroyed the town. As I gazed out the window, Tiến played guide: "Our troops captured that tank in 1972. And behind there, that's an old French fort."

Up the hill from the tank, there was indeed an outpost I had not noticed. The walls were made of bricks whose haphazard shape hinted at its age, and the round holes that served as windows and the crenellated square tower recalled similar forts I had seen in Europe. It looked out of place, and so did the tank, both tributes to the absurdity of the foreigners, who had tried to control this region of Việt Nam. I wondered whether the people of Đông Hà saw the irony of these two reminders of war standing prominently at the town's entrance while they themselves had nothing.

The village comprised an open-air market in the dirt, one paved road, and bombed-out houses that had not been repaired in the fifteen or twenty years since they were shelled. The only thing that looked more incongruous than the French fort and American tank was our hotel, an abominable angular structure. It must have taken a warped collective imagination to think that anyone would want to visit Đông Hà. The whole hotel, from walls to windows to bedding, was covered with dust. None of the rooms was usable, and it did not appear that any could ever be. We ended up sleeping in temporary cubicles, in each of which a naked light bulb dangling from the tin roof shed amber light on a twin-size bed and a chair. The odor kept me away from the toilet, and the dark shower stalls had no plumbing. I registered for a bath the next morning; the water had to be boiled first.

By midmorning my clothes and I reeked of sweat, making me feel utterly inadequate when I faced Colonel Lê Văn Hoan. There was no doubt he was one of the men haunting my dreams for years past, even though I'd never met him until this day.

There had always been men in my dreams—faceless, nameless men in uniforms, looking for me. I was always running away from them, on foot, on a bike. But I'd keep falling, I'd tumble. I couldn't get away. I would wake up, drift back to sleep, and they would be there again. Long after I left home, the dreams persisted in Virginia and Indonesia and California. Now I had returned home, and here in Đông Hà I had found one of the places where the men in my dreams lived. These were Việt Cộng soldiers, the invisible enemies in the mountains, the fighters who sent mortar fire into our town, our street. They were the agents of terror, dropping grenades in the marketplace. They were the men who captured my father during the Tết offensive in 1968. When the war ended, they were the victors. When I left my country, the soldiers entered my dreams.

Twenty years before, Lê Văn Hoan had formed the region's first guerrilla unit, recruiting peasants to take up arms against the South and the Americans. His stories of suffering and of stoicism during wartime intimidated me. His movements, words, and expressions, which seemed to have been permanently conditioned by his years in the military, belied his civilian clothes, a gray polo shirt worn not tucked in over a pair of immaculate black pants.

"We are a poor country. We've gone through too many wars, and now we have young men coming home from Cambodia," he began when we talked.

I had an eerie sense that everything had been arranged—that the former colonel had known of my arrival in Đông Hà, and that the luncheon at the restaurant where we met was a setup. I wondered whether there had been a memorandum sent down from on high directing that everyone I encountered say the same thing.

"What did we ever do to the world—why does our nation have to be punished with all the fighting and the killing? No one wants war in this country," Hoan continued. "The war is in the past. I don't hold the American people responsible; I don't blame the Americans—I don't hate them, or hold rancor against them. It's the White House—Johnson, Nixon, Kissinger—those are the men who will have to answer the ultimate questions."

I knew Hoan was feeding me the party line, yet I sensed that he genuinely believed what he was saying. I dropped the subject, not wishing to expose my own views—fearing I would appear to be too quick to agree with him. Inexplicably I found myself keeping my distance while at the same time desperately wanting to be open to a former enemy.

In my meetings with officials and veterans, many had asked about my family, our hometown, and the circumstances of our

leaving the country. I always offered that I had left before "liberation," letting them interpret how long before, though no one
showed any hostility on learning that in fact I left as the Communists came. It was harder to answer questions about my father,
but I'd been able to avoid revealing that he had been imprisoned
for twelve years in Communist dungeons. Just before I left the
restaurant, I lost control.

"Were you around in 1968, at Tết?" I asked Hoan.

"Oh, yes."

"In this area?"

"Yes." He hesitated after that answer.

"Was the fighting really bad?"

"We served as a link in a supply line. Some of our own men
went farther south—"

"Did you?"

"No—I was in charge of the region here."

"When the troops withdrew, did they come back through
here?"

"Some did, yes."

He did not show whether he disliked my questions or losing
control over the conversation. I edged closer. "Did you know the
prisoners who were taken through here?"

"Not really. The troops stayed with them. I knew there were
some around here, on their way farther north. Most of them were
closer to the Hồ Chí Minh Trail."

"My father came through here; you might have heard of
him—"

"There were many, and I didn't—"

"He was the South's civilian governor of this region . . . He
came through here. Captured in Huế . . . ?"

"No, I don't know. Where is he now?"

"He left the country. He was released in 1980."

"Well, he's alive," he said. "That's all that matters."

"Yes," I answered. He was right; but for me, the twelve

years in prison also mattered. Sixteen years without my father mattered.

"*Dân mình khổ nhiều*," he said. "*Chiến tranh*. Our people suffered. War."

I agreed with that answer, but I also disagreed.

Everything about the Bến Hải River seemed sad. For twenty-one years it had been the boundary between the two parts of Việt Nam, and it seemed that all the sadness of a people separated by war, by habits and customs, by different viewpoints and aspirations was imprinted in the scenery around it. The fields stretching to the horizon were gray and lifeless; the grass stalks growing along its banks drooped; the small boats moored in its unmoving water seemed paralyzed. But though I'd hoped that viewing this historical site simply as a river rather than a dividing line might make me happy I found my visit disquieting. Of all the people I knew, friends and relatives, no one except my father had seen this river. I felt oddly privileged to have been able to come to its banks. But as we drove away, I submerged myself in silence, thinking about the crossing made long ago by my father on his way into exile and imprisonment.

From the Bến Hải River we traced our way back to the highway, traveling farther uphill until we reached the Hồ Chí Minh Trail. "This entire region is the trail," Tiến said. "Soldiers and people moved weapons and equipment south through any areas that weren't bombed. There wasn't really one single trail."

A pile of rusted scrap metal on the side of the road was the only sign that this was once a battlefield. The pine trees that had been planted since the war seemed out of place in this tropical landscape. A thunderstorm was approaching. It was here that I saw another face from my dreams. Lieutenant Colonel Hồ Minh Thanh once commanded the troops who fought in this region. We had picked him up on the way, and as he sat next to me in the van I was fascinated by how fierce he looked. His face, like

Hoan's, beamed with pride. He still wore his uniform, and the battles of twenty years before were still fresh in his mind: "I secretly crossed over eleven barbed-wire fences," he told us, relating one incident. "I stumbled into a trench just as someone in a lookout tower trained his floodlight on me. An American crossed my path. He looked terrified as he dove onto the ground. I shot him."

I asked about his feelings, repeating my questions or coming up with different versions but Colonel Thanh would not reveal his emotions. "But what went through your mind when you shot the man?" I finally asked, straightforward as no Vietnamese would be.

"You know, it's not the individual American soldiers. It's not the American people. I only blame those in the White House," he replied. I abandoned the effort. I knew it would serve no purpose to bring up my father.

Colonel Thanh placed a hand on my shoulder as he led me up a hill, all the while recounting other battles for me. We reached the top, where there was yet another monument honoring the dead. The storm moved closer, the clouds above us lowering. The colonel raised his voice as the wind picked up. In my dreams no one had a face, or a name—or even a voice. Here, out in the fields under the darkening sky, I heard Colonel Thanh and knew I was hearing the men in my nightmares. They will probably appear again in my dreams, I thought, but next time I won't run away. I'll have names to call them; there will be faces I can remember, and former enemies I can talk to.

HÀ NỘI

In elementary school I learned about Hà Nội as a place called Thăng Long, the Ascending Dragon. Long, long ago, boys who grew up here became warriors, fighting invaders from the north. The war years made Hà Nội even more distant; it was, after all, the enemy's capital for all the years I was at home. Now I was in Hà Nội for the first time. Every faded facade seemed to hide a wealth of legends. Everything had decayed. After Sài Gòn and Đà Nẵng, Hà Nội was like a silent movie in slow motion. There were few motorcycles, just noiseless bicycles, hundreds on every street. The placid inhabitants took drowsy steps on the wide boulevards and tiny alleys. The streets were still named after the goods that used to be sold on them in the 1930s and 1940s: Pottery Street, Cotton Street, Silk Street. The shops now sold electronic parts and disco jackets, but they still exuded a quiet charm. I kept coming back to those streets every night, the darkness in them somehow less anguishing than that of Sài Gòn, even comforting. A sense of dignity survived among the weary people of Hà Nội, and on those dark streets I thought I had stepped back into another century, into a time when life was quieter, when people had little and lived simply but were real.

I wandered about looking for the Hà Nội of fifty or sixty years ago, the Hà Nội described in books I had read as a student. I wanted to see elegant people dancing the tango. I imagined men and women exchanging secret messages in hidden alleys, organizing clandestine resistance groups against the French, or revolutionary cells to spread the words of Marx, Lenin, and Hồ Chí Minh. But that was all in the past. Việt Nam was now at peace for the first time in half a century.

In the late afternoon sun the old buildings on Hà Nội's main boulevard took on an amber tone. From the balcony of my hotel room I looked across to the National Bank Building. On the roof was a large portrait of Hồ Chí Minh, and underneath it, his famous quotation: NOTHING IS MORE PRECIOUS THAN INDEPENDENCE AND LIBERTY.

I looked at the people on the streets and wondered whether they would agree. Fifty years of war, and what had been gained? Everyone I talked to seemed discontent, even in this ancient city that had always known austerity. There were goods in the markets, but people couldn't afford them. Unlike people in the South, Northerners didn't have relatives in Australia, France, Canada, or the United States sending them money to buy food and some few bits of material comfort. The handful of restaurants were frequented by Western tourists and Thai or Japanese businessmen. Even the alley soup stands were deserted. Cultural exhibits and events had been closed down because of lack of attendance. The Museum of War was almost empty.

Hà Nội's central lake, attractive and unassuming, is called the Lake of the Restored Sword. Legend has it that a turtle once appeared here to offer King Lê Lợi a sword. The king used it to fight off northern invaders, returning victorious to give the sword back to the turtle and the lake. I made the mistake later of visiting the temple at the lake. Though the lake itself was enchanting, the turtle on display in the temple deflated the magic of the legend. Like many big animals, it looked sad, and stupid. The fear it must have felt when it was killed was frozen in its huge eyes.

☙ The An Dương factory, just outside Hà Nội, originated as a self-help solution to the problem of the government's inability to provide for those who had served in the war. About a hundred veterans, most of them disabled, were proud to be working there, making nails and rubber facings for Ping-Pong paddles. The small factory had just two buildings, both old and dilapidated. The chalk paint on the walls had faded enough to reveal rough cement bricks whose deeply etched lines matched those on the faces of the former soldiers. Often walking only with difficulty, they squeeze themselves into contortions to operate their rusted, noisy equipment.

The government had given these men and women a small amount of start-up money to launch the factory, and they seemed to have made a go of it. One of the workers, Nguyễn Kim Linh, joined the army in 1965. In 1973 he lost part of an arm to artillery fire. We talked in the sun, and as I held a microphone to his face, I had to keep my eyes from wandering down to where his arm ended in a stump. For a while I couldn't concentrate on his words; I kept thinking that, with his hollow eyes and pointed chin, which was accentuated by a thin goatee, he would have made a perfect stand-in for the young Hồ Chí Minh. "We are at a disadvantage physically," Linh told me. "The compensation we received from the state was not enough, and our country is still very poor. We can only help ourselves. We can't ask anyone else to shoulder the burden. We accepted the worst during wartime—what can't we endure in peacetime?"

Other veterans at the factory repeated his sentiments. No one said a harsh word about the United States. Their lack of hostility toward their former enemy seemed to be part of the Vietnamese character. Like most Vietnamese, the workers at An Dương hoped the Americans would return, but with investment dollars instead of guns. The factory represented a modest beginning, but it had attracted the attention of American veterans. For a cynical moment I thought the Foreign Ministry had alerted those who ran the factory about my visit, asking that I be given a warm reception since I was the first overseas Vietnamese, and a Southerner, to visit An Dương. Yet I could feel the genuine warmth they displayed during my afternoon there. It was never mentioned explicitly, but I knew that the men and women at the factory also had hopes that I would tell their stories back in the United States and create some further attention for their project. As the visit ended, I knew I would try to help.

Veteran after veteran came to shake Peter's and Arthur's hands before we left. The man who had shown me around the factory said he hoped I would return. He looked directly in my eyes for a moment in a way the Vietnamese normally would never do, then hugged me. Tears came to my eyes. Everything in my life up to this point dictated that I should feel hatred and distrust toward the Việt Cộng. Nine years after they had released my father from their isolation cells; fourteen years after they had taken the South and thereby torn my mother's life apart; fourteen years since my own exile from my native country, I found myself hugged by a former Việt Cộng soldier. When he released me from his embrace and we smiled at each other, I saw that he too had tears on his face.

Oddly, Hà Nội felt like home. I knew there was a prison somewhere in this city where my father had suffered long months in dark and damp cells, and I knew it was from this city that the orders went out during my youth to fill the skies of the South with exploding rockets and the nights with incomparable fear. Yet for all that, Hà Nội's ancient history, its half-lit narrow streets and decaying French balconies, its mystical and legendary lakes, and finally its people and its charm had seduced me.

🍂 My days in Việt Nam were ending. My parents' prediction had not come true: I had not been arrested, had had no obstacles put in my way, had been free to travel throughout the country, even to meet writers and artists critical of the government. Things had changed; my friends and relatives, like all the people of Việt Nam, had suffered. I was already harboring ideas about coming back for another visit, perhaps to stay longer next time. I'll fit back in, I said to myself. There would be no trouble.

A filmmaker we had met a few days before had arranged for us to see his film about soldiers who had been abandoned in the battlefield. During the screening of the mediocre black-and-white movie, the Foreign Ministry guide reached up from the row behind me to slip an envelope into my hand. "Read it later, and don't tell anybody about it," Tiến whispered.

"What is it?"

"Shhh," he said, putting his hand on my shoulder.

I fidgeted with the letter, unable to concentrate on the film. As we were leaving the small theater Tiến again put a hand on my shoulder. Feigning laughter, he teased, "Brother Đức, you're

gonna sleep well tonight." I smiled back, trying to look unconcerned, but also letting him know I wanted to slug him.

Inside the envelope was an invitation to see the chief of
security police in Hà Nội at eight o'clock the next morning.
Something has to go wrong now, I thought, two days before I'm
to leave.

At dinner later in a hotel I discussed the letter with Peter,
Arthur, Murray Hiebert, a correspondent for the *Far Eastern Economic Review,* and a French journalist.

"Of course, here you are, telling everybody about the invitation," Murray commented.

"Of course," I retorted. "Wouldn't you?"

"They're normally curious about Vietnamese-Americans,
that's all," the Frenchman assured me. "I wouldn't worry."

"Hey, man, what if you don't come back by two in the
afternoon?" Peter asked.

"That's not funny. But then, everyone else in this country
has been through prison, or reeducation camp. I suppose I'll have
to put in my time too."

"Oh, come on!" said Murray. "It'll be interesting to see what
it's all about."

"Yeah, meet me here at two tomorrow. I'll give you the
scoop."

"Hey, don't we get it first? Come on, man, you're doing
stories for NPR!" Peter said in mock protest.

Later that night, while we dragged ourselves up the stairs
to our fifth-floor rooms, Peter put on his radio news-reader voice.
"A Vietnamese-American journalist was found dead today in his
prison cell in Hà Nội, Việt Nam. . . ."

It didn't sound good, but I laughed all the same. "Goodnight,
Peter. 'Night, Arthur."

"See you tomorrow, Đức," Arthur replied.

"Sleep well, man," said Peter.

I didn't, of course. I stood on my balcony for a long while, and thought of writing a postcard to my wife, but didn't know what to say.

❧ The chief came out to the lobby of the headquarters of the security police as soon as I arrived. Tiến introduced me to the man, then walked out. "I'll wait for you outside," he said.

"Wait!" I called after him.

Tiến was already outside, but he turned to stick his head through the door and raised a hand. He had a smile on his face I didn't trust.

"Just come out when you're done," he said. "We'll be here!"

A thin, balding man, the chief of the security police was wearing a simple white shirt and gray trousers. He didn't look the least bit menacing, so much so that at first I thought he was an assistant. As with many other meetings, I had to wait.

"You'll have some tea, won't you?" he asked. I hated the display of hospitality. It was always sincere, but it often announced endless inconsequential talk, or interview sessions I could not escape. Indeed, the security chief grilled me about life in the United States, and especially about the Vietnamese-American community. In my irritation I gave inadequate answers, which only prolonged the interrogation. Half an hour passed before he brought up the reason for my presence in his office, introducing it as though it were almost incidental.

"The authorities in Hồ Chí Minh City contacted me yesterday," he began.

I searched my memory for some crime against the state I might have inadvertently committed during my stay in the South. Was it my conversation with Nguyễn Khải, the war veteran turned dissident writer? Perhaps my visit with the painter whose work dealt with environmental destruction? It could be anything.

"I hope it's nothing serious. I'm sorry you've been bothered," I said, surprised that I had remained calm, and able to talk.

"No, no. They are, uh, just curious—no problem—about a vase, a ceramic pot, rather delicate—"

"I know," I interrupted.

"Yes, a vase you left in your hotel room—no problem—uh, just a, uh, matter of curiosity—"

"Yes, I know; I know what you're talking about," I repeated.

"Well, I suspect you do," he replied.

"I'd forgotten it. . . . My relatives were going to—"

"Ah, exactly . . . On the one hand, we are concerned about giving back to you whatever you may have forgotten here—we know it's not easy to come all this way from America—"

"I don't need it, actually."

"Ah, exactly. We assume you have taken the contents of the vase with you. . . ."

"Uh, yes, I have it—"

"You do? I see. And you do intend to take it out of the country, I assume?"

"Yes, you know how important—"

"But now, in Hồ Chí Minh City they're not sure about the content, and they were thinking of conducting some tests . . . and that would take a week—at least a week, and we know you're planning to leave tomorrow—"

Indeed, my ticket was booked for the next day. My mind struggled with my impatience at being detained for at least a week, being alone in Hà Nội. . . . Abruptly, from my stomach a new fear arose: what if it wasn't just a week; what if this was an excuse to detain me indefinitely? Perhaps for years?

"Yes, I am leaving tomorrow, I cannot be delayed—"

"Well, this matter must be cleared up first. I mean, I can probably call Hồ Chí Minh City, explain things—"

"Please do," I said.

"But then, you'll have to explain things to me first," he requested.

The chief of Hà Nội's security police leaned back in his chair and crossed his legs. I began to tell him the story. He nodded throughout, showing great sympathy.

I had brought the urn containing Diệu-Qùynh's ashes back to my hotel room in Sài Gòn and had transferred the ashes into a small lacquer box, which I wrapped to look like a gift. "I couldn't take the ceramic urn with me. It was too big," I said to the security chief. "I didn't think it would be a problem to leave the urn behind in my hotel room."

When I had finished, the chief simply said, "There's no problem. We'll get you on the plane tomorrow—but do fill out an application to leave the country with the ashes."

I filled out the form, and left the police station.

The next morning the customs officer searched through my bags thoroughly and asked numerous questions about the recording equipment, finally satisfied that I was taking no antiquities out of the country. Neither he nor his colleagues noticed the jacket draped over my arm, hiding the lacquer box I clutched in my hand. I held the box close to my chest as I stepped away from the terminal and onto the plane. Thus it was that I left my homeland for the second time.

I had fulfilled a dream: I had come home. And I would come back again; this would be just my first trip. It felt triumphant to prove I could come home, and to take Diệu-Qùynh's ashes to my family in San Francisco.

Where the Ashes Are

Every few weeks there will come a moment when I deeply miss home.

San Francisco lies beyond my front door, but I will shut it out and think of the tree-covered streets of Đà Nẵng, the sound of a summer shower on its unpaved sidewalks, the smell of freshly wet soil, or of charcoal and chicken broth near a noodle stand. I miss the voices of men and women at the riverside markets in Huế, the freshness of the mornings in Đà Lạt when the sun breaks through the fog, and the winding paths up and down the hills near my childhood house. I even miss the heat, the insane traffic, and the crowded shops in downtown Sài Gòn.

And then there's Hà Nội, never a part of my childhood, but a city that now occupies a beloved space in my memory, or rather my heart: an exquisite city, tempered, irresistible, full of timid young girls on ancient bicycles and old men sitting immobile, passing time on lakeside cement benches, wool hats on their heads, scarves around their necks, an expression of quiet dignity on their faces.

Hà Nội: a magical city where wide boulevards turn into narrow streets, one light bulb to each block; a city of red roofs and walled temples, of villas behind rusty gates, of trees as old as life; a city that has endured many wars and can't help but reflect the stoic and accepting ways of its people; a city that has become timeless with the centuries of history which imbue its spirit.

It's been nearly twenty years since I sailed away from it, but Việt Nam is still the place I call home. I miss it, and think always of returning.

In those moments when I shut out San Francisco and think of home, memories of war and a difficult past fade away. The pain is then replaced by the remembrance of family and friends, of rediscovered time and space, of a simpler way of life. Unlike Western countries with all their stress and troubles, Việt Nam is a place where there is always time for friends and for friendship, for human contacts that deepen effortlessly and remain nurtured.

I know that my notions of my homeland are romanticized. But I am also aware of the difficulties I would face if I were to return to live and work in Việt Nam. And yet, how could I not yearn for the open and gracious ways of the Vietnamese, from city folks to villagers, who smile and share with me everything from food to time and wisdom? How could I not be drawn to a people whose foremost quality is their ability to sustain unceasing hardship and loss, all the while retaining hope and faith and dignity? How could I not be drawn to a people whose dark-humored cynicism can also easily blossom into radiant innocence? How could I not be drawn to a people who can so easily laugh in the midst of their own misery? I miss it all so deeply, and I want it all back, yet I know that going home and staying there is nearly impossible.

Having traveled and worked in a dozen different countries, I can adjust to most any living conditions. But I have also come to see Việt Nam as a nation run by men and women whose rigidity and inefficiency will always annoy my impatient nature. I have yet to think of anything I could do for a living in Việt Nam which would be both socially helpful—for that would be expected of a returning son—and at the same time personally satisfying.

Nearly two decades away from my home have changed me. Living in the United States has shaped my adult characteristics: I am independent and fiercely individualistic. I have learned to value achievements the way Americans do—that is, to work toward them almost in disregard at times of tradition and age-old wisdom. How would I function in Việt Nam, where there is so much resistance to change, and where progress is always slow?

If I were to return to Việt Nam I would certainly miss the opportunities I have in America. I would surely miss movies and theaters and the stimulating intellectual life of this country. And I would surely miss the physical beauty and free spirit of San Francisco. The sights that greet me—colorful neighborhoods, splendid Victorian buildings—each time I turn a corner or come over a hill always remind me of how lucky I am to live in such a place. I have wonderful friends in San Francisco (if only I had more time to see them). I take advantage of San Francisco's fabulous restaurants and cafés and bookstores, and I am proud of my association with San Francisco's respected KALW. It would not be easy to leave, but I know I can always come back to it.

There is still a much more formidable obstacle to going home. There is my family. Our years of separation have ended. Đinh and Diệu-Hà have moved to California, living within forty minutes of my parents. My brother and sister are both firmly established in their careers. They retain their curiosity about Việt Nam and say they'll visit sometime, in a way that probably means neither of them will ever make the trip. Even if they did, it would be for no more than a monthlong visit.

My parents too are curious about what is now happening in Việt Nam, but they see no possibility of going back. "I'll wait until communism is destroyed," Mạ says. "I'm tired of your talk about going to Việt Nam to live. *Khùng sao mà đòi về đó ỏ?* Aren't you crazy to want to go back there to live?"

"*Thôi, con ỏi,*" my father counsels. "Drop it, son. You'd feel stifled. You couldn't do anything there that would help. Think of the things you can do here. Besides, the whole family is here now."

My father is, as always, right. My trip home let me accomplish something that was for a long time impossible. And I have brought Diệu-Quỳnh's ashes to San Francisco. The whole family is here. Where the ashes are, one should make that home.

In reality, the notion has worked only for my parents and for Đinh and Diệu-Hà. I still yearn for Việt Nam, and I am not convinced that my life in San Francisco is permanent.

I have now lived more years abroad than at home. That realization only intensifies my desire to go back. It intensifies the frustration and the sadness of feeling I am in a quagmire: Asian values dictate loyalty to one's parents, but also to one's homeland; living according to the American ideal means pursuing one's dreams with vigor. Meanwhile, my parents are growing older, weaker. Though they don't, they can rightfully expect their children to take care of them. Often when Đinh, Diệu-Hà, and I visit them I can feel the tension. My father prefers not to talk about their health. My mother worries about a proper funeral. "You kids never talk about it," she says.

"But, Mạ, you know we will take care of things," I try to assure her. "I would rather we talk about how we can help you in the years to come."

"Who knows? How do I know how many years I have left?"

"You should stop eating all that fattening food," Đinh says.

My mother sighs. So does my father. Đinh and Diệu-Hà and I look at each other. None of us quite knows how to reassure my mother. On the drive home I think of her and worry. Then I think of returning to Việt Nam, and feel guilty.

I have often thought of raising children in Việt Nam, and my wife agrees: it is important to us that when we have children, they have the chance to speak Vietnamese. Even more, I want them to absorb what I think are the central traits of the Vietnamese people: profound respect for elders, unfailing belief in family and community, a strong sense of discipline, and esteem for education. These are the Confucian values I have been taught since my childhood. I hope that my children will cherish such values.

Perhaps I will come to accept life in America. In the end, it is imperfect, and it will always remain so, for to me it is not home. But it will be the place where my parents have found a home, and the place where my parents were given back to me.

As for Việt Nam—perhaps I should be content that it may one day be the home of my children. It may be they who, in the future, will welcome me back there. And they will know, they will know, to bring my ashes home.

.